EXTRATERRESTRIAL ARCHAEOLOGY

The **New Science Series**:
- THE FREE ENERGY DEVICE HANDBOOK
- THE FANTASTIC INVENTIONS OF NIKOLA TESLA
- THE ANTI-GRAVITY HANDBOOK
- ANTI-GRAVITY & THE WORLD GRID
- ANTI-GRAVITY & THE UNIFIED FIELD
- VIMANA AIRCRAFT OF ANCIENT INDIA & ATLANTIS
- THE COSMIC CONSPIRACY
- TAPPING THE ZERO POINT ENERGY
- THE HARMONIC CONQUEST OF SPACE
- THE ENERGY GRID
- THE BRIDGE TO INFINITY

The **Lost Cities Series**:
- LOST CITIES OF ATLANTIS, ANCIENT EUROPE
  & THE MEDITERRANEAN
- LOST CITIES OF NORTH & CENTRAL AMERICA
- LOST CITIES & ANCIENT MYSTERIES OF SOUTH AMERICA
- LOST CITIES OF ANCIENT LEMURIA & THE PACIFIC
- LOST CITIES & ANCIENT MYSTERIES OF AFRICA & ARABIA
- LOST CITIES OF CHINA, CENTRAL ASIA & INDIA

The **Mystic Traveller Series**:
- IN SECRET TIBET by Theodore Illion (1937)
- DARKNESS OVER TIBET by Theodore Illion (1938)
- ATLANTIS IN SPAIN by Elena Whishaw (1929)
- IS SECRET MONGOLIA by Henning Haslund (1934)
- MEN AND GODS IN MONGOLIA by Henning Haslund (1935)
- DANGER MY ALLY by Mike Mitchell-Hedges (1957)
- RIDDLE OF THE PACIFIC by John MacMillan Brown (1924)
- MYSTERY CITIES by Thomas Gann (1925)
- IN QUEST OF LOST WORLDS by Byron de Prorok (1937)

EXTRATERRESTRIAL ARCHAEOLOGY

by
David Hatcher Childress

This book is dedicated to the scientists and engineers
who continue to forge ahead despite opposition from all sides.

Special thanks to Mark Carlotto, Fred Steckling, Zechariah Sitchin, Brian Crowley,
James Hurtak, Vince DiPietro, Don Wilson, George Leonard, Richard Corliss and the
Sourcebook Project, Patrick Moore, Harry Osoff, and many more!

EXTRATERRESTRIAL ARCHAEOLOGY
Revised Edition

by David Hatcher Childress

Printed in the United States of America

ISBN 0-932813-77-1

Published by
Adventures Unlimited Press
Kempton, Illinois 60946 USA
www.adventuresunlimited.co.nz
auphq@frontiernet.net

The Lost Science Series:
- EXTRATERRESTRIAL ARCHAEOLOGY
- THE CASE FOR THE FACE
- FLYING SAUCERS OVER LOS ANGELES
- THE FREE ENERGY DEVICE HANDBOOK
- THE ANTI-GRAVITY HANDBOOK
- ANTI-GRAVITY & THE WORLD GRID
- ANTI-GRAVITY & THE UNIFIED FIELD
- THE FANTASTIC INVENTIONS OF NIKOLA TESLA
- VIMANA AIRCRAFT OF ANCIENT INDIA & ATLANTIS
- UFOs AND ANTI-GRAVITY
- COSMIC MATRIX
- ETHER TECHNOLOGY
- LOST SCIENCE
- SECRETS OF COLD WAR TECHNOLOGY
- HAARP: THE ULTIMATE WEAPON
- THE HARMONIC CONQUEST OF SPACE
- THE ENERGY GRID
- THE BRIDGE TO INFINITY

TABLE OF CONTENTS

THE MOON

GENERAL PHYSIOGRAPHY

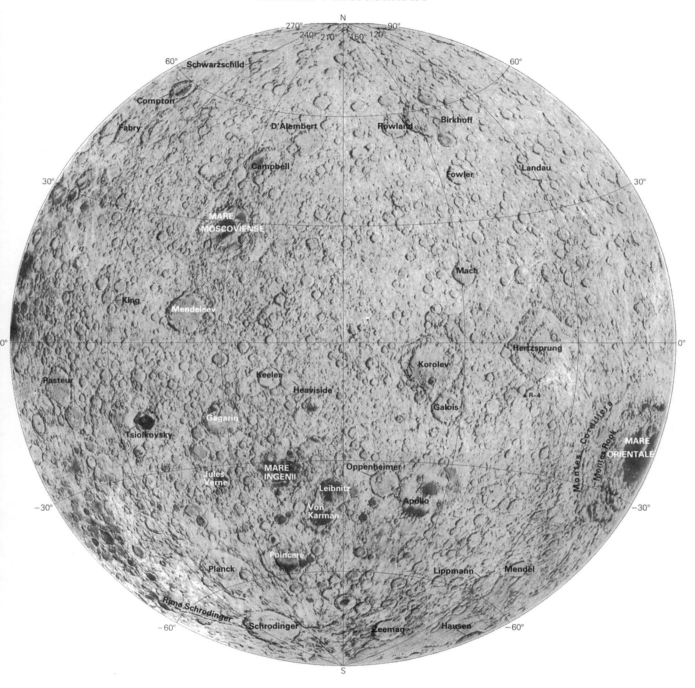

A lunar map by John Hevelius published in his work *Selenographia* published in 1647. North is at the top and east is to the right. The maria are presented as light areas and the uplands are shaded. Like many mappers of the Moon, Hevelius decided that there were cities on the satellite.

Chapter 1

Our Mysterious Moon

> The more you study the Moon, the more you will become aware that it is an orb of mystery—a great luminous cyclops that swings around the Earth as though it were keeping a celestial eye on human affairs..
> —Frank Edwards, *science writer*

Welcome to the amazing and wonderful world of Extra-terrestrial Archaeology! Why *Extra-terrestrial?* Because it of things not of this earth, but of other nearby orbs and planets. *Archaeology* because the book is about artifacts. Ancient artifacts. Artifacts so old, and so out-of-place that their very existence threatens every religious and scientific dogma cherished by modern man.

Is the world ready for pyramids, obelisks, platforms, huge walls, giant statues and glowing UFOs that have been photographed by NASA and Russian space-probes over the last thirty years? Would our governments have any reason to cover these discoveries up if they were authentic? Would they seek to avert attention, or would they send further space probes to these areas to investigate them? Perhaps both.

Before our space program sent probing mechanical eyes to the Moon, throughout the many decades and even centuries of the so-called telescopic age of lunar study, competent observers on Earth saw strange things on our satellite: unexplainable weird lights and glows sighted on the surface, inexplicable changes, and the sudden appearance of structures. Astronomers thought that the Moon was a lifeless, airless, windless, and for the most part erosionless world. In fact, a completely changeless orb. Yet unquestionably many changes did take place.

For instance, in 1843 Johann Schroeter recorded unexplainable changes in a six-mile crater named Linne. This German astronomer made hundreds of maps of the Moon over many years. Over a lifetime of observations, the crater Linne gradually disappeared. Today Linne is just a tiny bright spot with little depth or height, a small pit surrounded by whitish deposits. What happened? No one knows for sure.

It is interesting to note that NASA photographs taken by Apollo 15 reveal that Linne today is a tiny crater (1 1/2 miles across). The mystery of what astronomers observed has remained just that — a mystery.

Could this competent astronomer have been mistaken? Schroeter himself believed there was intelligent life on the Moon, and he attributed some of these changes to "the industrial activities of the Selenites."

Although Schroeter's contemporaries heartily attacked his hasty conclusion that the Moon was inhabited by intelligent beings, nevertheless, in Schroeter's day, unlike our times, many scientists did consider the Moon to be an inhabited world as is Earth.

The great British astronomer H. P. Wilkins, commenting on these unexplainable changes and Schroeter's beliefs, makes this striking observation:

We cannot subscribe to this idea because without air to breathe it is exceedingly difficult to contemplate the existence of Selenites let alone to speculate as to their possible activities, industrial or otherwise. It is equally difficult to explain these things on natural grounds.

But there remain some still greater puzzles. Some objects do not vary in their physical features so much as to the tints or hues of their interiors. There are craters which change color in a very peculiar manner. What looks like a green carpet can be seen spreading over their floors! (H. P. Wilkins, *Our Moon*, Frederick Muller, Ltd., 1954, p. 130)

Even more wild than Schroeter's speculations were those of his fellow countryman and astronomer Gruithuisen, who was convinced that great cracks on the Moon were actually canals or roads. Wilkins wryly notes: "It was just before the first railways were built, otherwise he would probably have said they were railways." (*Our Moon*, p. 57.)

Other bizarre reports were made by other competent astronomers. On the night of July 6, 1954, Frank Halstead, former curator at the Darling Observatory in Minnesota, along with his assistant and sixteen visitors, observed a straight black line in the crater Piccolomini, where none had been detected before. It was to disappear shortly thereafter, although not before other competent astronomers confirmed the discovery.

But before we delve too deeply into structes on the Moon, let us first take a look at some general mysteries of our companion satellite.

The Puzzle of the Moon's Origin:

Scientists have generally offered three major theories to account for the moon in orbit around our planet. All three are in serious trouble, but the least likely theory emerged from the Apollo missions as the favorite theory. One theory was that the moon might have been born alongside the earth out of the same cosmic cloud of gas dust about 4.6 billion years ago. Another theory was that the moon was the earth's child, ripped out of the Pacific basin, possibly. Evidence gathered by the Apollo program indicates though that the moon and the earth differ greatly in composition. Scientists now tend to lean toward the third theory — that the moon was "captured" by the earth's gravitational field and locked into orbit ages ago. Opponents of the theory point to the immensely difficult celestial mechanics involved in such a capture. All of the theories are in doubt, and none satisfactory. NASA scientist Dr. Robin Brett sums it up best: "It seems much easier to explain the nonexistence of the moon than its existence."

The Puzzle of the Moon's Age:

Incredibly, over 99 percent of the moon rocks brought back turned out upon analysis to be older than 90 percent of the oldest rocks that can be found on earth. The first rock that Neil Armstrong picked up after landing on the Sea of Tranquility turned out to be more than 3.6 billion years old. Other rocks turned out to be even older; 4.3, 4.5, 4.6, and one even alleged to be 5.3 billion years old! The oldest rocks found on earth are about 3.7 billion years old, and the area that the moon rocks came from was thought by scientists to be one of the youngest areas of the moon! Based on such evidence, some scientists have concluded that the moon was formed among the stars long before our sun was born.

The Puzzle of How Moon Soil Could Be Older Than Lunar Rocks:

The mystery of the age of the Moon is even more perplexing when rocks taken from the Sea of Tranquility were young compared to the soil on which they rested. Upon analysis, the soil proved to be at least a billion years older. This would appear impossible, since the soil was presumably the powdered remains of the rocks lying alongside it. Chemical analysis of the soil revealed that the lunar soil did not come from the rocks, but from somewhere else.

The Puzzle of Why the Moon "Rings" Like a Hollow Sphere When a Large Object Hits It:

During the Apollo Moon missions, ascent stages of lunar modules as well as the spent third stages of rockets crashed on the hard surface of the moon. Each time, these caused the moon, according to NASA, to "ring like a gong or a bell." On one of the Apollo 12 flights, reverberations lasted from nearly an hour to as much as four hours. NASA is reluctant to suggest that the moon may actually be hollow, but can otherwise not explain this strange fact.

The Puzzle of the Mystifying Maria of the Moon:

The dark areas of the moon are known as maria (seas, as this is what they looked like to early astronomers — dried-up seas). Some of these maria form the familiar "man-in-the-moon" and are, strangely, located almost entirely on one side of the moon. Astronauts found it extremely difficult to drill into the surface of these dark plain-like areas. Soil samples were loaded with rare metals and elements like titanium, zirconium, yttrium, and beryllium. This dumbfounded scientists because these elements require tremendous heat, approximately 4,500 degrees Fahrenheit, to melt and fuse with surrounding rock, as it had.

The Puzzle of the Rustproof Iron Found on the Moon:

Samples brought back to earth by both Soviet and American space probes contain pure iron particles. The Soviets announced that pure iron particles brought back by the remote controlled lunar probe Zond 20 have not oxidized even after several years on earth. Pure iron particles that do not rust are unheard of in the scientific world (although there is a solid iron pillar of unknown age in New Delhi, India, that has also never rusted, and no one knows why).

The Puzzle of the Moon's High Radioactivity:

Apparently, the upper 8 miles of the moon's crust are surprisingly radioactive. When Apollo 15 astronauts used thermal equipment, they got unusually high readings, which indicated that the heat flow near the Apennine Mountains was rather hot. In fact, one lunar expert confessed: "When we saw that we said, "My God, this place is about to melt! The core must be very hot.'" But that is the puzzle. The core is not hot at all, but cold (in fact, as was assumed, it is a hollow sphere). The amount of radioactive materials on the surface is not only "embarrassingly high" but, difficult to account for. Where did all this hot radioactive material (uranium, thorium, and potassium) come from? And if it came from the interior of the moon (unlikely), how did it get to the moon's surface?

The Puzzle of the Immense Clouds of Water Vapor on the Dry Moon:

The few lunar excursions indicated that the moon was a very dry world. One lunar expert said that it was "a million times as dry as the Gobi Desert." The early Apollo missions did not find even the slightest trace of water. But after Apollo 15, NASA experts were stunned when a cloud of water vapor more than 100 square miles in size was detected on the moon's surface. Red-faced scientists suggested that two tiny tanks, abandoned on the moon by U.S. astronauts, had somehow ruptured. But the tanks could not have produced a cloud of such magnitude. Nor would the astronauts' urine, which had been dumped into the lunar skies, be an answer. The water vapor appears to have come from the moon's interior, according to NASA. Mists, clouds and surface changes have allegedly been seen on the moon over the years by astronomers. For instance, six astronomers in the last century have claimed to have seen a mist which obscured details in the floor of the crater Plato. Clouds on the moon are extremely odd, because the moon's supposed small gravity (one sixth of the earth's, claim many conventional scientists and NASA) could not hold an atmosphere or have any clouds on it at all.

The Puzzle of the Glassy Surface on the Moon:

Lunar explorations have revealed that much of the moon's surface is covered with a glassy glaze, which indicates that the moon's surface has been scorched by an unknown source of intense heat. As one scientist put it, the moon is "paved with glass." The experts' analysis shows this did not result from massive meteor impactings. One explanation forwarded was that an intense solar flare, of awesome proportions, scorched the moon some 30,000 years or so ago. Scientists have remarked that the glassy glaze is not unlike that created by atomic weapons (the high radiation of the moon should also be considered in light of this theory).

The Puzzle of the Moon's Strange Magnetism:

Early lunar tests and studies indicated that the moon had little or no magnetic field. Then lunar rocks proved upon analysis to be strongly magnetized. This was shocking to scientists who had always assumed that the rocks had "some very strange magnetic properties...which were not expected." NASA can not explain where this magnetic field came from.

The Puzzle of the Mysterious "Mascons" Inside the Moon:

In 1968, tracking data of the lunar orbiters first indicated that massive concentrations (mascons) existed under the surface of the circular maria. NASA even reported that the gravitational pull caused by them was so pronounced that the spacecraft passing overhead dipped slightly and accelerated when flitting by the circular lunar plains, thus revealing the existence of these hidden structures, whatever they were. Scientists have calculated that they are enormous concentrations of dense, heavy matter centered like a bull's-eye under the circular maria. As one scientist put it, "No one seems to know quite what to do with them."

The Puzzle of the Lack of Dust on the Moon:

If the age of the Moon is to be measured in billions of years, then some scientists maintain that there should be a layer of dust on the Moon over 180 feet thick! British science writer Richard Milton points out in his best-selling book, *The Facts of Life,* [50] that cosmic dust particles and micrometeorites continually enter the Moon's (and Earth's) atmosphere from space and settle on the surface. Says Milton, "Hans Petterson of the Oceanographic Institute of Goteborg has measured the rate at which this dust arrives and has found that it is constant from year to year at roughly 14 million tons annually.

"The implications of this finding are pretty clear. We are dealing with a process which consists of an aggregation of random microevents; which is not known to be interfered with by any outside agency; and whose startling value in the present context is not relevant. It is not relevant because it is the absence of dust we are concerned with."

Milton points out that if the Earth is 4,500 million years old, then some 63 million billion tons of dust have settled on its surface. The Earth has a surface area in the region of 5.5×10^{15} square feet, and compacted dust can be assumed to have density in the region of 140 pounds per cubic foot. These figures indicate that enough meteoric dust would have entered the atmosphere to create a layer 180-feet thick.

Says Milton, "The dust problem applies not only to the Earth, but to the Moon as well, which uniformitarians also believe to be billions of years old. Before the first manned landing by Apollo 11 in 1969, it was feared by some lunar geologists that the dust layer on the Moon's surface — undisturbed by atmospheric movement or by oceans — might be so thick that the landing craft would simply disappear into a sea of dust. In the even, of course, Neil Armstrong took his 'giant leap' into merely an inch or two of dust — the sort of amount that would accumulate in thousands, rather than billions of years." [50]

§§§

Lights, clouds, apparent structures, and mysterious streaks have fueled speculation on the mysteries of the Moon for hundreds of years. The crater Plato, a large one on the "northern" top of the Moon, where domes, streaks and lights were often seen. Astronomer Jackson Carle wrote an article which appeared in issue number 14 (1955) of *Sky and Telescope*, (14:221-223) on what he called the "Three Riddles of Plato."

THE THREE RIDDLES OF PLATO
by Jackson Carle

During the past century Plato, "the Great Black Lake," nestling at the northeast tip of the lunar Alps near the edge of Mare Imbrium, probably has been the most intensively observed feature on the moon. And many who have studied this great walled plain are reluctant to accept the general belief that the moon is a dead world where nothing ever happens. For it appears that subtle details on Plato's dark floor undergo changes which many experienced selenographers say cannot be explained by the varying illumination and libration."

Plato is about 60 miles in diameter, with rim walls rising from 3,000 to 5,000 feet above the floor, and peaks up to 7,400 feet high.

If you first look at the Great Black Lake as the sun is rising there—about a day and a half after first quarter—you will be struck by the extraordinary ruggedness of the west rim as revealed by its shadow cast upon the floor. With the sun low on the horizon viewed from Plato, even minor elevations cast long shadows, giving an exaggerated idea of the heights of the summits on the rim.

From our telescopic vantage point we see the shadow of the western ramparts extending completely across the 60-mile floor in jagged outline, and most of the interior of the crater is hidden in velvety blackness which knows no morning twilight. Even as we watch, the shadows recede across the floor with surprising speed. Within an hour the eastern half of the plain lies revealed in sunlight except for one needle-like black shadow still extending completely across Plato. Watch this shadow carefully as it quickly draws westward before the rising sun. Does its outline change? Does it grow broader or narrower? Does the shadow at any time present a hooked tip?

This shadow is cast by a solid, immovable mountain, and can change only from the increasing elevation of the sun and the nature of the surface across which the shadow falls. Herein lies one of the three riddles of Plato we shall discuss.

The Second Riddle of Plato:
Patches of green and other colors on the crater floor

The testimony as to the conformation of the crater floor is surprisingly contradictory. In 1892-93 William H. Pickering studied Plato carefully at Harvard Observatory's station at Arequipa, Peru. His results, published in Vol. 32 of the Harvard Annals, report the floor of Plato as "extremely convex," much more so than the regular spherical curve of the moon. He also remarks upon irregularities and slopes in the floor.

The Mount Wilson picture... is one of the best photographs ever taken of Plato. In addition to five interior craterlets, the variegated pattern of light and dark splotches may be seen. The wedge-shaped light area at the upper right of the floor is the "sector." Under magnification, the original negative shows a series of parallel light and dark areas running from the upper rim across the floor. These look like rolling ridges with intervening hollows, extending from the south rim northward to the central part of the interior. On a number of occasions, I have seen a similar appearance, and so have other amateurs, among them David P. Barcroft and T. E. Howe. The latter's map of Plato, in the February, 1952, issue of The Strolling Astronomer, shows a ridge in the floor just south of the center. The ridge is one of two floor features mentioned in Barcroft's comments.

Twice I have noted dark oval patches soon after sunrise, which quickly disappeared; at other times, with similar illumination, no patches were seen.

On April 3, 1952, H. P. Wilkins and Patrick Moore observed Plato with the 33-inch Meudon refractor. The former reported that "the floor or plateau appeared remarkably uniform and level," but he does show some details in the accompanying drawing made that night. Similarly, in his book, *A Guide to the Moon*, Moore describes Plato from his view that night as "probably the most level spot on the Moon."

In Dr. Wilkins' drawing the shadow of the west wall extends about a fifth of the way across the floor. The long shadow of the southerly peak juts farther east, and is hooked to the south. Does this shadow appear hooked because of some strange conformation of the rim, or from falling upon an uneven surface? I have looked unsuccessfully for this hook at a number of sunrises, but this failure may mean that the appearance requires certain combinations of libration and sun direction. Is Plato's interior level, convex, rolling, or irregular? Or perhaps, does it change? I don't know.

With good seeing, we may glimpse some of the tiny and difficult craterlets strewn over the darkish floor. In the apparently changing visibility and relative sizes of these elusive features over a period of years lies a second riddle posed by the Great Black Lake.

Since an intensive study of Plato was first organized by the British selenographer W. R. Birt and his co-workers in 1869, some 80 craterlets and spots have been charted. These have never all been seen by one observer or within a limited period of time. Some spots, having been seen easily, apparently disappeared—only to reappear years later and be reported as new discoveries.

The minute markings, according to E. Neison's *The Moon* (1876), include 10 craterlets, six doubtful craterlets, and 20 spots not represented as craterlets. T. G. Elger's authoritative The Moon (1895) states that there are 40 or more spots. "They are extremely delicate objects, which vary in visibility in a way that is clearly independent of libration or solar altitude."

Pickering mapped 71 craterlets and spots discovered by him and earlier observers, but was never able to see more than 39. He commented that large craterlets sometimes disappear.

An interesting comparison was made by T. L. MacDonald of three charts of Plato's spots, two by Dr. Wilkins for 1936-39 and 1941-42, and an independent map by Walter H. Haas for 1935-40. In the July, 1943, <u>Journal</u> of the British Astronomical Association, MacDonald noted that the contemporary Wilkins and Haas charts were definitely comparable, but the later Wilkins map differed from both. His cautious conclusion was, "To that extent there is quite definitely a case for variations."

In 1950, Dr. Wilkins was still undecided about the riddle of the vanishing craterlets, stating that the variations observed could be due to libration and poor seeing, but that the possibility of real changes warranted further observations.

The latest but certainly not the last word comes from Moore in his book, "The evidence is conclusive and we are bound to accept a certain amount of activity on the floor of Plato."

Plato's Third Riddle:
Domes that appear and disappear

Plato's third riddle may confront us at any time without warning. Suppose you have been looking at this feature for several months. The half dozen most conspicuous craterlets and spots have become familiar and are almost always seen, except when poor seeing converts the floor into a shimmering, shapeless blob. Then one night, with Luna riding high in a cloudless sky, you cross your fingers, mutter the astronomer's prayer, unlimber the scope and turn it tentatively on the earth's companion, hoping that tonight you can shove the Barlow clear in, pulling the eyepiece way out for highest possible power.

If you're like me, you may want to approach Plato gradually, saving it as a main course after nibbling at other formations. Perhaps Copernicus is emerging after sunrise. It is a good feature for careful focusing and study of its terraces and central peaks. And to test the seeing you'll turn west to the chain of craterlets, which you find standing steady and clear. Then you look farther west to Archimedes and Aristillus. North down the rugged Alps and a side swing along the Alpine Valley, for perhaps tonight you can definitely find out whether that darkish spot nestled next to the southern cliff is a craterlet or a rockslide down the wall. It does look like a crater—

very round. You test again on those two tiny craterlets just south of Plato—with a little focusing they are clear and steady—it's a good night.

Now to Plato. You look, and look again, and see nothing! Yes, the walls are clear and detailed, and that landslip on the east stands out. But the floor appears smooth, flat, and featureless, perhaps with a faint flickering glimmer of something where you know the comparatively prominent central craterlet should be. You see nothing, but this nothing is the something that has puzzled lunar observers for a century, the apparent obscuration of the floor of Plato at times when floor features should be readily visible.Δ

§§§

Whether or not there are clouds, water vapor, frozen water, underground springs, or even rivers on the Moon has spurred much speculation in the past, and this continues to this day. Many modern authors, including contactees who claimed to have gone to the moon, have said that the Moon has a thin atmosphere, and there is water and some clouds in the otherwise dry environment.

An article on whether or not there might be water on the Moon was conservatively addressed in this 1967 article in the scholarly British journal *Nature* (216:1094-1095, 1967) by the British astronomer H.C. Urey.

WATER ON THE MOON

by H.C. Urey, H. C.
The possibility that water has existed on the Moon for varying lengths of time, both in liquid and in solid form, and both beneath the surface and on the surface, has been widely discussed during the past 10 years. The subject has been discussed repeatedly at scientific meetings and has been received mostly with great skepticism. Evidence supporting this view has recently become quite overwhelming and, in fact, no communication seems necessary to point out the evidence from the Orbiter 4 and 5 pictures. Because many people are not aware of this evidence and suggest that the effects are caused by other liquids, that is, lava, dust-gas or possibly even vodka, a brief discussion of the evidence may be in order.

Gold pointed out that it was unreasonable to believe that all the smooth areas within the craters and between the craters were caused by lava flowing from deep in the Moon, and he suggested that dust produced by particle erosion was the origin of the material filling these craters and the maria. Because of the lack of dust river valleys, I disagreed with this and suggested that dust from the great collisions and temporary rains washed the dust into the low areas, and the water escaped into space or sank below the surface. Gilvarry postulated much more extensive oceans lasting for billions of years. Although many of Gilvarry's observations are reasonable, the long length of time assumed, with no evidence for mature river valleys, unfortunately led to definite non-acceptance of his ideas. Gold and Kopal have suggested that water has escaped from the lunar interior and formed permafrost similar to that found in the arctic regions of the Earth. Safronov and Rouskol argue that water could not have escaped slowly from the lunar interior and formed oceans because the escape rate of water from the Moon would be so great that only a very small atmosphere of water could have accumulated. This conclusion is correct, and sources of surface water, which have been suggested, have been of a catastrophic kind, that is, a degassing of the lunar surface and the colliding objects in the great collisions on the Moon, a great splash from the Earth during the period of accumulation of the Earth, comet head collisions, etc. I suggested that the lake-like areas near and on the walls of Alphonsus were indeed caused by water (see under Moon, Encyclopaedia Britannica, plate III, for pictures of these). Gold suggested that the great central mass in Alpetragius is a pingo.(In regions of permafrost, that is, northern Canada and Siberia, great cones of ice covered with soil are formed by water and ice being extruded from the lower regions. They often look like small volcanoes with sloping sides and a depression like an irregular volcanic cone at the top. In some cases the ice has melted leaving a crater much like lunar craters but of much smaller diameter.)

I have argued that the carbonaceous chondrites may come from the Moon, for those of the type 1 variety, particularly, show that they were once immersed in water and that the Moon has certainly had liquid water on its surface.

Evidence of water on the Moon

21

Schroeter's valley, to the west of Aristarchus, has been known since the late eighteenth century, but terrestrial observations could not establish its origin. Orbiter 4 and 5 pictures show this valley in great detail as well as many neighboring valleys. Schroeter's valley begins in a mountainous region in an enlarged area called the "Cobra Head", and extends in a generally westerly direction into a smooth maria area. Its greatest width is some 8 km and its depth some 600 or 700 m. Other smaller valleys with "cobra heads" are found north of Aristarchus and Prinz. Branching occurs in a few cases but mostly there are no tributaries and no deltas. Possibly there are small deposits at the maria ends, but they are much too small to account for the materials eroded from the valleys. South of Aristarchus and northerly from Marius is a valley extending to more than 160 km in a very smooth maria area. It decreases gradually and uniformly in width from the south-easterly end to the north-westerly end where it runs off the picture available to me (Orbiter 4, frame 150, high resolution). Near the larger end it is about 900 m wide and apparently goes to near zero at the other end. It is a very crooked rille and cannot possibly be a physical fracture. It has no tributaries. Similar rilles are found in many places, for example, within and near the Alpine valley and many other areas. They seem to be a general lunar feature.

But why are there no sediment deposits at either end of these valleys and no tributaries? (There are a very few examples of tributaries.) The walls seem to be formed by slumping, and north of Krieger there is a row of craters which seem to form an initial stage of such slumping. Water must have run below the surface and formed a tunnel which then caved in. But where did the excavated material go? If the maria are underlaid with ice, it is only necessary to melt the ice and let the water drain into the desert sands. (The explanation offered here was suggested by Gold.) But could it have been lava? Would lava flow in a narrow stream for hundreds of kilometres and disappear without a trace? I believe that the answer to both these questions is "No". But the details of these valleys are very varied.

While flying over northern Greenland on September 9, 1967, I saw crooked rille-like structures in the Greenland ice cap. Some of these looked like fractures but others, at least over limited regions, looked much like the crooked rilles on the Moon.

Krieger, north of Aristarchus, is an irregular crater with a recent smaller collision crater on the southern wall, a curious depression in the plane south of the crater and an irregular mass covering the north wall and an area north of the crater. There is a break in the western wall, and from this break an irregular gully or stream bed extends a short distance to the west. This seems to have been a surface stream, and a suggestion of a sediment deposit can be seen at its western terminus. This appears to be a surface stream bed quite different from the other rilles discussed. North of Prinz one of the small rilles of the Schroeter valley type crosses an elongated sunken area, transverse to this valley. It has a flat floor, and a small stream bed, similar to that coming from Krieger, crosses it. These two stream beds indicate that streams flowed on the surface and thus that an atmosphere had a pressure equal to and probably much greater than the vapour pressure of water at its melting point, that is 4.6 mm of mercury. Could Krieger be a pingo that has melted and collapsed? If so, it is a very large example as compared with terrestrial pingos. Krieger is 25 km in diameter. I have found a picture of a terrestrial pingo 300 m in diameter. But in a billion years, say, it may be that pingos get very much larger. Are there unmelted and uncollapsed pingo areas on the Moon? Probably some of these volcanoes which are referred to so confidently are pingos.

South of Aristarchus is a crater similar in size to Krieger (name unknown; it appears on Orbiter 4, picture frame No. 150, 1 of 3 high resolution). There is a break in the northern wall and there is a rather smooth pile of sediment outside the crater at this point. Some liquid drained out of the crater and left this material. Possibly this was lava, or mud, or a flow of dust and gas. In view of the overwhelming evidence for water as the agent producing the other valleys, I favour the view that effects seen in this crater as well as Krieger are caused by water.

Water was once present on the Moon.

In fact, as mentioned here, several serious students of the Moon concluded, or at least surmised and suggested, that water was present on the Moon at some time in the past. This evidence for lake-like structures has been presented repeatedly, each author discovering for himself the same evidence previously recorded by others. The suggestions were reasonable and the evidence valid. The fact that there seem to be no mature river valleys anywhere argues that these seas were present for only a short length of time. It is not possible to give the time at which they were present. Was it 4.5 x 10(9) yr ago when the Moon was captured by the Earth, and may the Moon have captured some water from the Earth at that time, or was it some 2 x 10(9) yr ago when the Moon's orbit changed from retrograde to direct and when the Moon was near the Earth? Or has the surface water appeared repeatedly? Thus water may have been acquired by the Moon early in its history; it escaped into space leaving water below the surface; the atmosphere was lost and low temperatures below the surface were established. Then a comet collided with the Moon, gave it an atmosphere, the temperature became warmer as on Earth, water melted and flowed out of the surface in springs. The atmosphere escaped and the water froze again until the next comet collision. The Safronov and Rouskol arguments seem to be valid and only a catastrophic origin for the water on the Moon seems possible.

Undoubtedly, someone will eventually measure and record these stream beds in great detail. This communication is to point out that the maria of the Moon are dried-up or frozen seas and that water has aided in forming the final features of the Moon. These conclusions in no way determine what the composition of the solid materials in the maria may be or whether this material had a volcanic or other type of origin.Δ

NASA photo shows astronaut footprint on the moon.

This is a view of the side of Lobachevsky crater as photographed by the Apollo 16 astronauts. Note the dark anomaly in the side of the crater. The white streak is an artifact produced by the digital scanning process, but there is a very bright white cap or bright round feature which can be seen in the Clementine images, as well as the unusual dark area. NASA identifies the dark feature as a lava flow. However, this feature exhibits apparent shading suggesting that it may be a crevass. There is also an unusual bluish 'pillbox' object to the right of the rim, in the base of the crater. The coordinates of the dark anomaly are 10.0 N latitude, 111.6 E longitude.

These are two stereo images of the anomalous feature in the side of Lobachevsky, from Clementine. Note the cave-like appearance of the feature, which is not completely dark as would be expected with a lava flow. Notice the several linear features which appear to form a bridge from the rim of the crater to the 'island' in the center of the feature. There is also a spherical object at the top of the island, as well as two small dark spots at the base of the 'island', which appears to have a horizontal linear feature just below the two dark spots. Also, note the two bright spots below the dark feature which correspond to the blue objects in the image from Apollo. The shape of this part of the crater appears to have changed significantly since the Apollo image was taken over 20 years earlier. Could this area have been changed as the result of excavation or mining operations being conducted in the area?

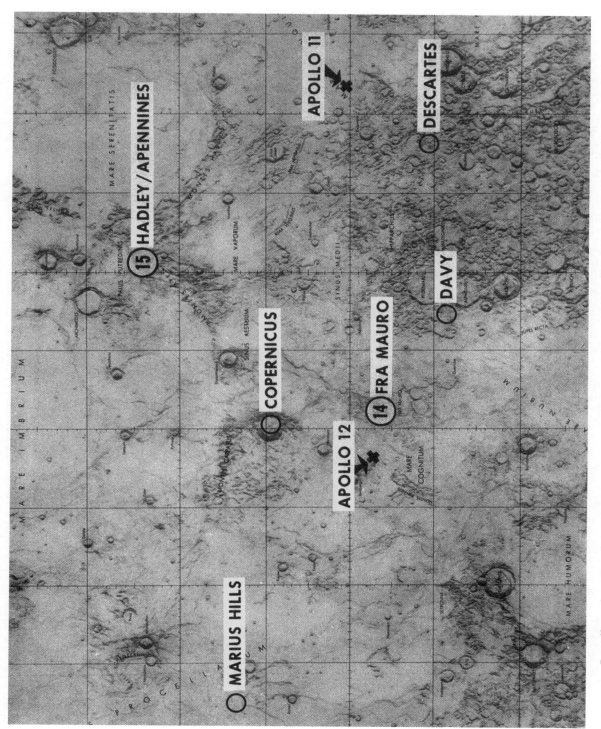

Landing sites for the Apollo series. At the time the map was prepared, only Apollo 11 and 12 had completed their missions. Apollo 11 in July of 1969 and Apollo 12 in November of that same year.

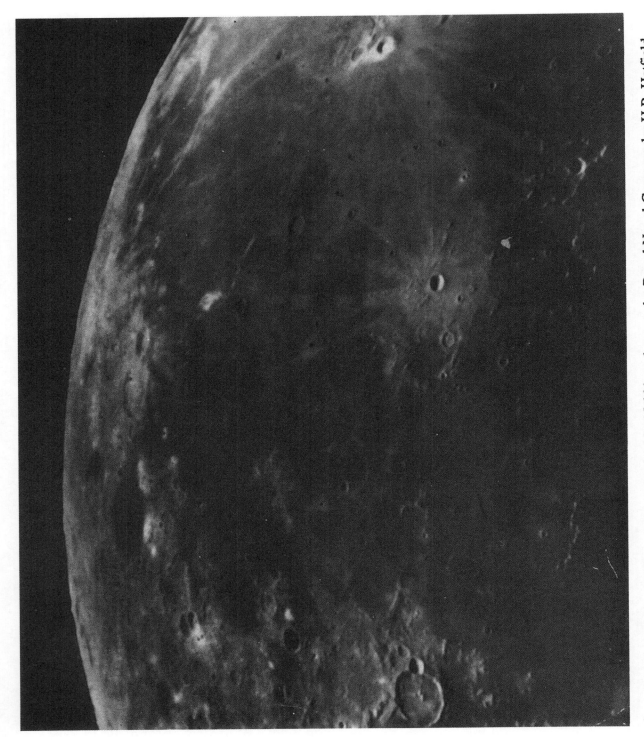

The Oceanus Procellarum, photographed in 1966 by telescope by Royal Naval Commander H.R. Hatfield. Various rays are seen clearly. The central rayed crater is Kepler. Note the crater to the left, Marius, and the rectangular ramp-plateau just out side the upper rim.

THE LUNAR CRATER DARWIN

| SCHMIDT | NEISON | BOUGON | WILKINS |

| BARKER | BALL | BURRELL | EMLEY |

Various drawings by astronomers of the unusual markings in the Crater Darwin.

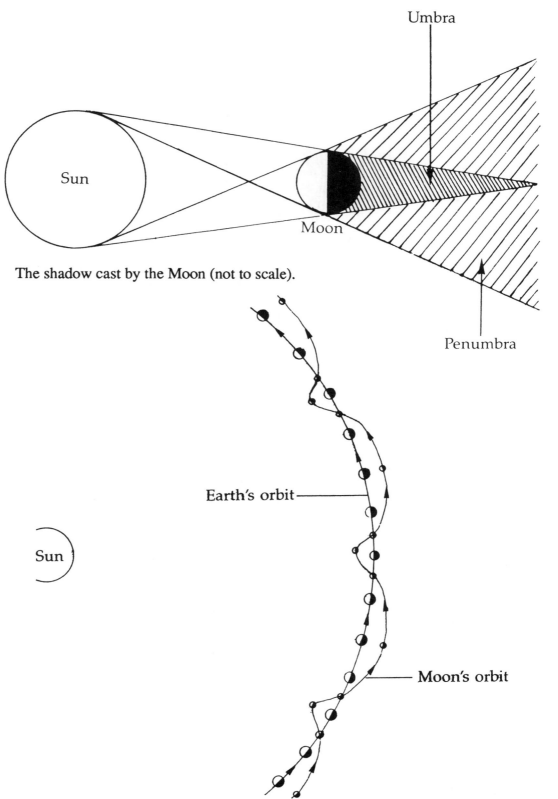

The shadow cast by the Moon (not to scale).

Umbra

Moon

Penumbra

Earth's orbit

Sun

Moon's orbit

Path of the Moon in space (not to scale).

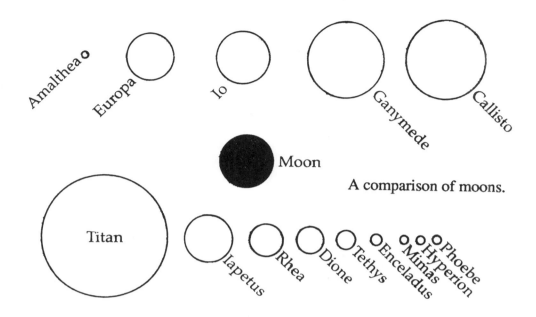

Amalthea Europa Io Ganymede Callisto

Moon

A comparison of moons.

Titan Iapetus Rhea Dione Tethys Enceladus Mimas Hyperion Phoebe

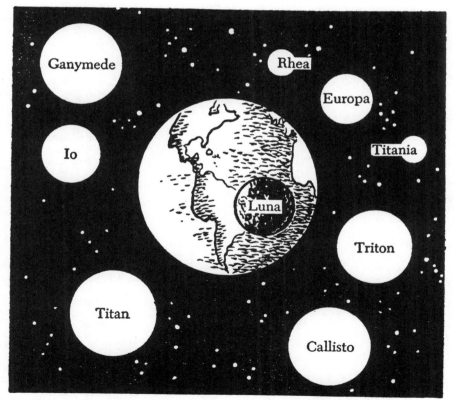

Ganymede Rhea Europa Io Titania Luna Triton Titan Callisto

Principal moons of the Solar System compared with Terra

A MAP OF THE MOON

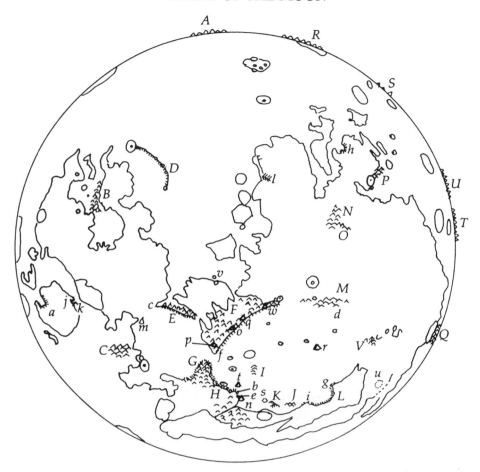

Key

Mountain ranges

H. Alps
D. Altai scarp
F. Apennines
M. Carpathian Mts
G. Caucasus Mts
U. Cordillera Mts
T. D'Alembert Mts
R. Doerfel Mts
E. Haemus Mts
V. Harbinger Mts
Q. Hercynian Mts
L. Jura Mts
A. Leibnitz Mts
P. Percy Mts
B. Pyrenee Mts
N. Riphaen Mts

S. Rook Mts
I. Spitzbergen Mts
J. Straight Range
C. Taurus Mts
K. Teneriffe Mts
O. Ural Mts

Capes and promontories

a. Prom. Agarum
b. Prom. Agassiz
c. Prom. Acherusia
d. Cape Banat
e. Prom. Deville
f. Cape Fresnel
g. Prom. Heraclides
h. Cape Kelvin
i. Prom. Laplace

j. Prom. Lavinium
k. Prom. Olivium
l. Prom. Taenarium

Peaks and isolated mountains

m. Mt Argaeus
n. Mt Blanc
o. Mt Bradley
p. Mt Hadley
q. Mt Huygens
r. Mt La Hire
s. Mt Pico
t. Mt Piton
u. Mt Rümker
v. Mt Schneckenberg
w. Mt Wolff

Chapter 2

Mystery Structures on the Moon

Many phenomena observed on the lunar surface appear to have been devised by intelligent beings. Now, U.S. and Russian moon probes have photographed two such "constructions" at close range.

—Dr. Ivan T. Sanderson

Of the bases the visitors might have from which to conduct their explorations of Earth, none holds more logical or intriguing possibilities than our Moon.

—John Magor,
editor, *Canadian UFO Magazine*

Gruithuisen's 'Lunar City'

The German physician and astronomer Baron Franz von Paula Gruithuisen (1774-1852), shocked the astronomical world in 1824 when he announced that the discovery "of many distinct traces of lunar inhabitants, especially of one of their colossal buildings." [11] The area in question is a series of parallel "mounds" just to the north of Schröter crater, which is near the center of the near-side of the Moon, and is easily found on all Moon maps.

The finding of a lunar city by a well-known astronomer caused a great deal of excitement at the time, though many astronomers were understandably cautious. Much later after Gruithuisen's paper was issued in 1824, the astronomer T.W. Webb described the fabled 'lunar city' from his own observations as: '...a curious specimen of parallelism, but so coarse as to carry upon the face of it its natural origin, and it can hardly be called a difficult object." [11]

The astronomer Elger in his book *The Moon* (1895), refers to a drawing by the astronomer Gaudibert which appeared in the *English Mechanic,* 18 p. 638 (1874) and purports to show his version of the 'lunar city.'

Gaudibert's original 1874 is worth reprinting below in its entirety to help the set the stage for Extraterrestrial Archaeology for more than a century to come.

CURIOUS LUNAR FORMATION

by C. Gaudibert.

Perhaps you will find a corner for the inclosed sketch, which is the rough outlines of that formation which Mr. Webb tells us, p. 94 of "Celestial Objects," third edition, "attracted so much attention" in 1822; and not at that time only, but much later also, as the reader will gather in reading in that invaluable book the precise history and description of the object my sketch roughly represents. Doubtless drawings of this object exist, and it would be interesting to compare them with its present state. It seems almost certain that Gruithuisen found changes here in the disappearance of the east "ribs," with the exception of the north-west "rib," which seems to have been covered by a meridional wall. At the extremity of the next "rib," instead of a wall I see a depression, and beyond a prolongation of the "rib." The third and fourth "ribs" have no prolongation, but the south one has just a depression, and then what seems to be a continuation of the "meridional" wall; so that we have the two extremities of this wall without the middle. It would be interesting also to know whether the east side is now in the same state as it was after Gruithuisen lost the "ribs," and also if the three craterlets north of this object have been observed. They seem of recent date. Observing this object with a power of 550, I saw its surface covered with minute hillocks, with a larger mound at the latitude of the second "rib." The terminator was passing through Stadius when I made my observation.

§§§

The British astronomer and television personality, Patrick Moore picks up subject of Gaudibert's city with an article in the *British Astronomical Association, Journal,* (87:363-368, 1977).

THE LINNE CONTROVERSY: A LOOK INTO THE PAST

Moore, Patrick; *British Astronomical Association, Journal,* 87:363-368, 1977.

Linne lies on the Mare Serenitatis, one of the most famous of the regular lunar seas. There are no really large craters on the Mare; Bessel is the most prominent of them. Naturally, the Mare was drawn and described by all the early observers. Schroter can tell us little (no doubt his main sketches perished with his observatory), but both Madler and Lohrmann are quite definite. I think it will be best to quote their descriptions. Bear in mind that the old German mile which they use is equal to about 4-1/2 English miles or 7 km.

First, Beer and Madler, in their classic work *Der Mond*, which was completed in 1838-39: "According to a measurement by Lohrmann and seven by ourselves, this crater lies at latitude 27o 47' 15" and longitude 11o 32' 28". It is 1.4 miles in diameter, brightness 6 degrees, borders not well defined at full moon." Lohrmann's account reads: "The second most conspicuous crater on the plain. . . it has a diameter of somewhat more than 1 mile, is very deep, and can be seen under all angles of illumination."

Nothing could be more positive, particularly as Madler added that "the deepness of the crater must be considerable, for I have found an interior shadow when the Sun has attained 30 o. I have never seen a central mountain on the floor". Both Lohrmann and Madler actually used Linne as a reference point.

Oddly enough, the great map by Beer and Madler (and it really was a great map, even though the instrument used was a mere 95 mm Fraunhofer refractor) actually held selenography back to some extent. Unlike Schroter (and other observers, much more fanciful, such as Gruithuisen) Beer and Madler regarded the Moon as inert, and contemporary astronomers tended to the view that since an accurate chart had been compiled there was really very little point in observing the lunar surface further. Neither Beer nor Madler did much more lunar work after 1839, and for the next quarter-century the only active selenographer of any standing was Julius Schmidt, yet another German, who went to Greece and carried out most of his work during his spell as Director of the Athens Observatory. Schmidt drew Linne in 1841 and 1843, and apparently agreed with the descriptions given by Madler and Lohrmann. Then came his observation of 1866 October 16, when he found that the old crater had disappeared, to be replaced by a small whitish patch. It was a startling discovery, but Schmidt had no doubt about it, and his announcement caused a major sensation. Telescopes were directed back to the Moon, and it was widely thought that a real change had occurred. Systematic lunar observation began once more, and has continued ever since.

Of the "three greatest selenographers" (Lohrmann, Beer and Madler) only Madler remained alive in 1866. He accepted the change as real, but he added a disquieting comment. He wrote: with the Bonn heliometer in 1867 May he "found it shaped exactly and with the same throw of shadow as I remember to have seen it in 1831. The event, of whatever nature it may have been, must have passed away without leaving any trace observable by me." In other words, to Madler, Linne looked the same in 1867 as it had done in 1831, which immediately weakens the evidence in favour of change. By no means everyone was satisfied, and there is an interesting comment by T. G. Elger, the first Director of the BAA Lunar Section, in 1895: "It is anything but an easy object to see well, as there is a want of definiteness about it under the best conditions, though the minute crater, the low ridges and the nebulous whiteness described by Schmidt and noted by Webb and others are traceable at the proper phase . . . There are still many sceptics as regards actual change, despite the records of Lohrmann and Madler; but the evidence in favour of it seems to preponderate."

What, then, must we conclude? In my view, at least, we can at last reject the idea that any variation in Linne has occurred in telescopic times. No TLP events have been recorded in the area; it is not an active region. And perhaps the early results are not so surprising as has often been thought—and as I once thought myself. Schroter can tell us nothing; Beer and Madler used a telescope which was, by any standards, tiny; and when Schmidt drew Linne as a crater he was still young and inexperienced. Linne is a small object, and it is not hard to believe that observers of the years following 1866 were deceived into reporting changes which did not really occur. Unconscious prejudice may well have played a major role.

The Blair Cuspids: An Alignment of Obelisks on the Moon

On November 2nd, 1966, NASA published an unusual photo of the Sea of Tranquility taken by the Lunar Orbiter 2. William Blair of the "Boeing" Institute of Biotechnology noticed that the photo had a number of unusual objects depicted on it which cast very clear shadows. These objects appeared to be obelisks, and they threw distinct shadows from the early morning sun, similar to that which is thrown by the Washington Monument.

The highest of the obelisks measured about 213 meters, while the lowest must have had the proportions of above-average size spruce trees. Blair analyzed the photo and came to the conclusion that seven obelisks, an extremely tall one with four smaller ones to the lower left of the larger, and then a sixth was even further back, in alignment with the first. A seventh obelisk formed a triangle with the other "corner" obelisks. Furthermore, a rectangular "depression" could be seen in the lower right of the photo.

Triangulation of the photo showed that three outer obelisks formed an equilateral triangle, while triangulation with the other four obelisks created a pyramidal-prismatic form.

Dr. Richard Shorthill of NASA spoke of the objects, now dubbed the "Blair Cusbids" as the "result of some geophysical event."[37] Blair himself responded by saying, "If the cuspids really were the result of some geophysical event, it would be natural to expect to see them distributed at random: as a result the triangulation would be scalene or irregular, whereas those concerning the lunar objects lead to a basilary system, with co-ordinates x,y, z, to the right angle, six isosceles triangles an two axes consisting of three points each."

What Blair calls "a highly speculative analysis in its use of the hypothetical co-ordinates" includes a "ditch" or rather a vast rectangular depression to the west of the biggest spire. "The shadow thrown by such depressions," he stresses, "seems to suggest four angles at 90 degrees, and the structure persuades one to think it is like an excavation whose walls have been eroded or fallen inwards."

Other students of the moon have asked if Blair means by these remarks that the cuspids are perhaps the work of intelligent beings, observation or navigation instruments, or a direct communications system? "Do you want me to confirm it so that you can discredit me?" replied Blair, "well, I will tell you this: if a similar thing had been found on Earth, archaeology's first concern would have been to inspect the place and carry out trial excavations to assess the extent of the discovery."

The sceptics can only reply by suggesting that there could be special conditions where the structure of the natural phenomena is odd enough to make one think of symmetrical formations. "But if this 'axiom' had been applied to similar on Earth," retorts Blair, "more than half the Maya and Aztec architecture known today would have still been buried under hills and depressions covered in trees and woods ... 'a result of some geophysical event'; archaeology would never have developed and most of the facts relating to human evolution would have remained veiled in mystery."[37]

Back in the seventies, two pulp paperbacks were published by Dell books on anomalous structures on the Moon. These were Our Mysterious Spaceship Moon and Secrets of Our Spaceship Moon by science writer Don Wilson. Wilson's work, and that of George Leonard's and Fred Steckling's, will be discussed throughout the book.

Don Wilson's: LUNAR MYSTERY SPOTS WORTH VISITING.

"Although it is not probable that man will return to the Moon within this decade and possibly not even within this century, he will eventually go back to his neighboring world. If and when he does, here are some places worth investigating that may help prove whether or not the Moon is what our two Soviet scientists Vasin and Shcherbakov say it is — a hollowed-out asteroid-spaceship." [20]

1. THE STRAIGHT WALL

An area of great interest and worthy of immediate investigation is the nearly seventy-mile-long straight wall, "a feature so artificial in appearance," says one recent modern astronomy guide, "that in the late nineteenth century it was referred to frequently as 'The Railway.' In past centuries many astronomers felt that it was indeed an artificial creation made by alien intelligence on the Moon. But today astronomers generally agree that it is merely a huge fault line, though a very unusual one, for it seems almost as though something here were pushing up through the surface of the moon.

The two scientists authoring the "spaceship" theory offer this speculation: No doubt one of the most splendid features on the lunarscape — a straight "wall" nearly 500 yards high and over 60 miles long — formed as a result of one of the armour plates bending under the impact of celestial torpedoes and raising one of its straight, even edges.

The edges do present a steep cliff which rises steadily for about 1200 feet at about a 45-degree angle outward from the Moon. Intriguingly, scattered around the huge structure are those large whitish domes, that have, it seems, been appearing in larger numbers in recent years on the surface of this strange world.

2. THE GREAT CRACK IN THE MOON

On the backside of the Moon, strangely almost directly opposite the straight wall, is a huge crack 150 miles long and five miles wide in some places. If the Moon is indeed a spaceship with an inner metallic-rock shell beneath miles of dirt and dust and rock this vast opening certainly might be very revealing. Another question more theoretical than practical: Could this great crack formation on the far side of the Moon, which science claims is merely a fault, be somehow related to the straight wall in its formation?

3. THE STRANGE ELONGATED SPIRES

We have discussed in detail these strange enormous spires which cast large elongated shadows for miles.

Are these spires artifacts, as some speculate, or are they natural? El Baz, as we previously pointed out, maintains that some are "taller than the tallest buildings on Earth." What could they be? Natural or artificial? Alien artifacts or just another natural lunar oddity?

4. THE ENIGMATIC DOMES OF THE MOON

A close examination of the strange domes of the Moon might be beneficial. Are they natural caverns, gaseous blisters as scientists maintain, or artificial constructions as some science writers speculate? As science writer Joseph Goodavage notes: "In the past few years more than 200 white, circular dome-shaped structures have been observed on the Moon and catalogued, but for some strange reason they often vanish from one place and reappear somewhere else." (1)

Has there been that much volcanic activity or such large amounts of inner gases escaping on the surface of this world as to cause hundreds of huge cavernous dome-like blisters to rise on the face of this pockmarked planet? Firsthand investigation would dispel all doubt, and at the same time, if Dr. Wilkins (who theorized they are the latter) is right, the investigation might prove whether or not they would be useful to our space colonization program.

The British astronomer made this observation about these strange domes: "It is possible that the first men to land on the Moon will consider some of these natural caverns suitable shelters from the extremes of temperatures and from space hazards inherent to exposure on the surface. Some of the numerous domes resemble bowler hats; may be largely cavernous in their interiors, since they are certainly of volcanic origin as is clearly proved by the little pits on the summits of many of them. They would only require an opening to be cut in their sides to make safe, ready-made surface bases, superior to the artificial plastic domes favored by many space-fiction writers." (2) Surely an investigation of these strange domes would have high priority.

5. BRIDGE OVER THE SEA OF CRISIS?

Is the huge, bridge-like structure that many outstanding astronomers have seen over the Sea of Crisis area, and which they estimate to be about 12 miles long, actually a natural structure or artificial? Dr. H.P. Wilkins, in a BBC radio interview, claimed:

It looks artificial. It's almost incredible that such a thing could have been formed in the first instance, or if it was formed, could have lasted during the ages in which the moon has been in existence. You would have expected it either to be disintegrated by temperature variation or by meteor impact. (3)

And the question remains: Is this "bridge" over the Sea of Crisis area artificial or natural?

A trip to the spot should resolve this problem once and for all.

6. WILKINS'S GREAT PLUGHOLE "THE WASHBOWL" — IS IT AN ENTRANCE TO THE INNER CAVERNOUS WORLD OF THE MOON?

Dr. Wilkins believes extensive caverns might exist inside the Moon and that these could be "connected" to the outer surface by plugholes like the one discovered by the great astronomer himself. Dubbed "the Washbowl," this huge round hole in the Moon is inside a white crater (Cassini A) which is one and a half miles across.

In his book Our Moon Wilkins writes: "Its inside is as smooth as glass with a deep pit, or plughole, about 200 yards across, at the centre." (4)

Here is a wild speculation that might be worth investigating to prove one way or another. If UFOs exist and if they emanate from inside the Moon as evidence indicated, then they might be coming and going through these "connecting" plugholes.

This particular plughole dubbed "the Washbowl" is over 600 feet across, and as wide as two football fields laid end to end!

And undoubtedly others exist that are even longer. Here is surely a place of high priority on our investigatory trek.

7. "THE THING"

At a press conference in 1972 astronaut Stuart Roosa showed a photo of a mysterious greenish flat area. "This is a new feature — a sharp depression," Colonel Roosa explained. "It's not a rille. It's not a fault line. No one knows what it is at this time. I'll call it "The Thing'." (5)

This would be an area well worth watching!

8. AN ALIEN ARTIFACT OR A NATURAL ODDITY?

Another intriguing early moon photograph that has drawn interest and comment from some scientists shows a miniature crater peak that has in its summit a piece of glass that glints like a diamond on a stickpin. Dr. Thomas Gold, astronomer and NASA scientist, says that he has no explanation to offer for this phenomenon though "he had an idea which was too far out to mention." (6)

Was Dr. Gold referring to the fact that this might be an alien artifact purposely placed on our Moon? Or is it just another peculiar happenstance, another quirk of nature?

9. THE HUGE BULL'S-EYE ON THE MOON!

One of the weirdest and most prominent features on our neighboring world is the Orientale Basin which consists of a series of concentric rings that some scientists think were caused by faulting. It looks like a huge bull's-eye target of concentric circles, created when a huge stone was tossed into an immense pool of lava. A few scientists have indeed conjectured this is the way the peculiar formation might have come into being —   only in this case it must have been a huge meteor smashing into a lake of lava.

There are areas in and around Orientale that record strange negative gravitational anomalies called negative mascons. Could it be, as some scientists speculate, that huge cavities exist under the surface causing these gravitational deviations? Interestingly, this area is where Apollo 17 astronaut Ron Evans spotted a strange light. He reported to Mission Control: "I see a light over the edge of Orientale. I just looked down and saw the light flash again." A UFO over Orientale?

10. THE STRANGE LIGHTS AND GLOWS OF ARISTARCHUS

Many strange lights have been seen on the Moon, and one spot where they have been sighted often is the area of the crater Aristarchus. Dr. Wilkins vividly describes one such sighting: "The moon was a crescent . . . Aristarchus was a faint whitish patch . . . Suddenly Aristarchus began to glow or lighten up until not only the central hill but also the details on the inner slopes were clearly revealed. There was no misty appearance. Everything was sharp and distinct." (7)

What was the cause of this strange light? Wilkins ventures: "The only natural explanation would seem to be that, in certain regions, the moon's surface consists of material which emits electrons under the influence of light or electronic impact, or considerable deposits of metals, for example, iron, which acts as deflectors of free electrons. The fluorescent effects may be due to electronic bombardment." (8)

Although Aristarchus is one of the areas where lights have been seen many, many times, a number of other areas, as we have seen in the first chapter, have been the center of light observations. In fact, science writer William Corliss says: "The Moon, however, unquestionably luminesces over its entire sunlit face and reddish glows over areas as large as 50,000 square miles have been reported. These displays are most easily attributed to solar-induced luminescence. The high localized, ruby-red spots seen by Herschel, Kozyrev, Greenacre, and many others may be either luminescence, volcanism or some phenomenon we do not yet recognize. Only time and investigation will tell." (9)

Our Apollo 11 astronauts also spotted what they described as "peculiar fluorescence on its [the crater's] wall." Luminescent glows have been unquestionably verified through our space program. Interestingly, at the same time the astronauts were reporting these luminescent glows, the Institute for Space Research in Bochum, Germany, saw similar glows for about six seconds. They were reported to have been observed also in Brazil, Ireland and other far-flung places on the planet Earth. This proves it was not a "trick of the eye." Indeed, observatories in Northern Ireland reported a "series of bright pulsations there." (10) Another observatory station reported "a blue flash."

In fact 97 similar cases of such glows and lights were seen from 1960 to 1965 in this area alone! As one study concluded about them: "The nature of these events remain a mystery." (11)

11.   A CROSS AT FRA MAURO, AND A LETTER X AT ERATOSTHENES?

Another lunar curiosity is the sighting of a cross at Fra Mauro, according to the astronomical journal Sky and Telescope. Walter Hass, director of the Association of Lunar and Planetary Observers, thinks this cross may "consist of some sunlit mountain spurs or ridges, that the appearance might be of very brief duration, vanishing as the sunlight reaches the lower slopes." (12)

In the crater Eratosthenes there exists "a group of hills in an acute-angled triangle connected by three lower embankments," and also "a geometric object shaped like a cross," as reported by the Astronomical Register (Volume 20). Some who describe this particular cross as "shaped like the letter X," believe it to be merely an optical illusion!

The west side of the Moon seen under nearly full illumination. Note the sparsity of mare flooding in the Orientale basin (arrow). The Rook and Cordillera scarps appear as bright rings under the high sun (USSR Zond 8 photo 12-306, 2525 H).

Gruithuisen's Lunar City as he drew it.

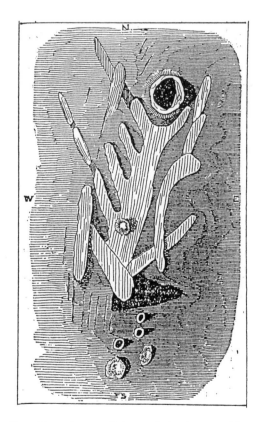

Gaudibert's rendition of the Lunar City.

THE PLATEAU/DOME
N.E. OF LINNÉ [L.N.803]

S
E
(I.A.U)
W

10" Reflector F/10 ×190
×286
Seeing. 6-7/10 Transp. 2-3/5
Moon's Decl. -12° 45'

1987 November 27
1720 - 1745 u.T.
O's { Col. 352°7 - 352°9
{ Sel. Lat -1° 39

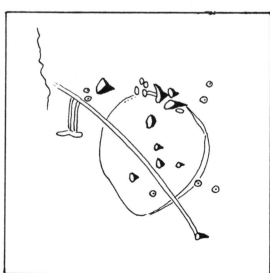

The crater Linne observed by Alika K. Herring on June 25, 1966 (61 inch rfl. x900) Note the pyramidical objects in the top drawing. What is the streak that is observed crossing the plain and dome-plateau?

The crater Dadalus on the far-side of the Moon. Proponents of the "inhabited Moon theory," claim that this cluster of dome-shaped objects are huge geodesic domes which enclose a lunar facility of some sort. Other possible structures may be seen on the inside crater rim at about 4 O'clock.

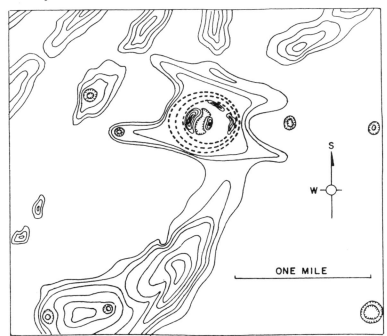

ONE MILE

Topography in the vicinity of Linne as drawn by P.Fauth in 1906. The dashed ellipses indicate the present white spot of Linne, within which are a craterlet and some small ridges. Has the Linne area been strip-mined for some valuable metal?

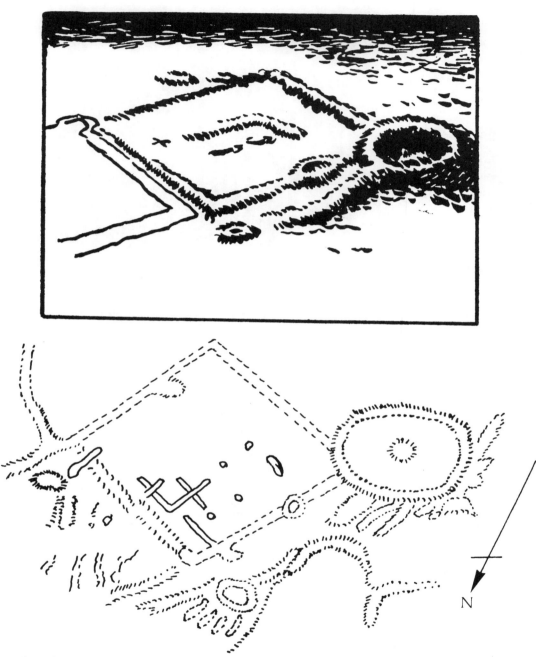

Two drawings of Mädler's Square, the unusual angular-shaped enclosure the appeared in many early books about the Moon It is a remarkable geometrically regular square-shaped enclosure foreshortened into a lozenge shape immediately west of the crater Fontenelle, to the north-east of Plato, on the north 'shore' of the Mare Frigoris.

The famous alignment of obelisks, called the "Blair Cuspids." Above: The early satellite photo showing seven tall, pointed objects, like obelisks, casting long shadows. To the lower right is a rectangular depression. Below: Triangulation of the seven obelisks and the rectangular depression area is outlined.

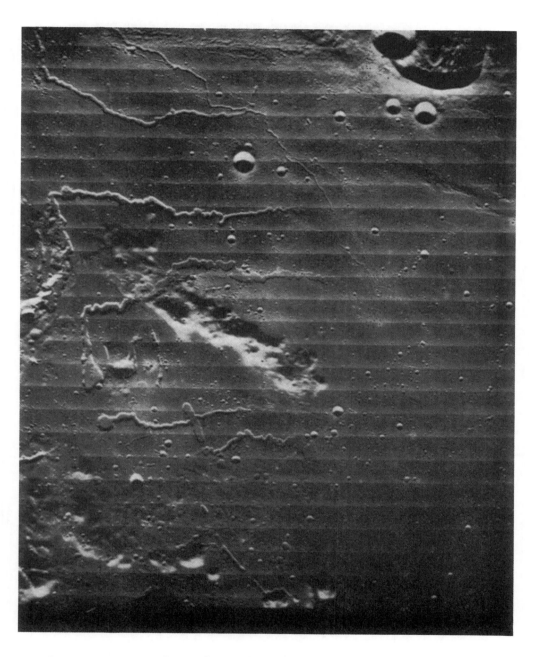

Rivers or Lava Channels on the Moon? A group of winding canyons *(sinuous rilles)*, photographed by Lunar Orbiter 5, cuts across the surface of Oceanus Procellarum, near the crater Prinz. The long dimension of the photograph covers about 110 kilometers (70 miles) of the moon. *(NASA Lunar Orbiter photograph V–191–M)*

A Strange and Mixed-Up Lunar Rock. Looking like a well-mixed marble cake, a ten-foot boulder of breccia from the Fra Mauro Formation waits on the lunar surface to be sampled by the Apollo 14 astronauts. The dark material which makes up the upper part of the boulder is mixed with the white material which makes up most of the lower part. Both the light and dark parts are complex microbreccias which record a very complicated history for the whole rock. *(NASA photograph AS14–68–9448)*

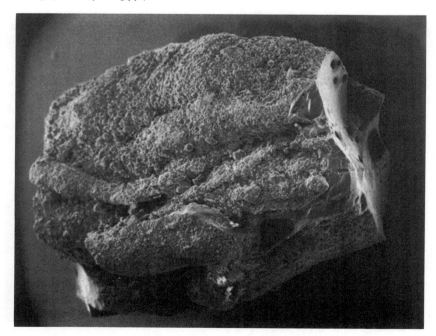

"Magic Component" in the Lunar Soil. This small fragment of ropy, yellow-brown glass, less than a millimeter across, is typical of the material called KREEP, a type of lunar rock which contains unusually high amounts of potassium (K), rare-earth elements (REE), and phosphorus (P). This specimen, returned with soil samples collected by Apollo 12, is shown here in a photograph taken with an electron microscope. Chemical patterns in the KREEP material were apparently established more than 4.4 billion years ago, thus providing a partial record of very ancient lunar history. *(Reprinted with permission from D.S. McKay et al., in* Proceedings of the Second Lunar Science Conference, *vol. 1, p. 755, © Pergamon Press, Ltd., 1971)*

Building Blocks of a Lunar Basalt (top of ι____ page). A thin slice of a lunar basalt returned by Apollo 11 shows the interlocking crystals of different minerals that make up the rock. The rock (sample 10047) is composed almost entirely of three minerals: pyroxene (gray crystals with numerous cracks); feldspar (clear, lath-shaped crystals); and ilmenite (black opaque crystals). (*NASA photograph S–69–47907*)

The Last Bit of Liquid in a Lunar Basalt (below). A spectacular photograph shows the glass droplets formed from the last bit of liquid remaining when over 99 percent of the rock was solid. The tiny droplets of glass (gray), less than a tenth of a millimeter across, are greatly enriched in silica (SiO_2) in comparison to the original basalt. The droplets were trapped in a crystal of the mineral pyroxferroite (a new mineral found only in lunar rocks) which forms the white background. Apollo 11 sample 10003. (*Reprinted with permission from E.L. Roedder et al.*, in Proceedings of the Apollo 11 Lunar Science Conference, *vol. 1, p. 815,* © *1970 by Pergamon Press, Ltd.*)

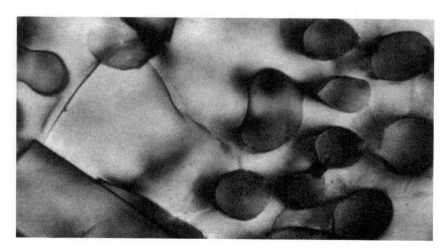

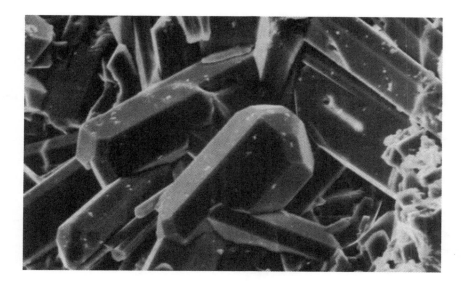

Crystals Formed from a Lunar Vapor. Delicately perched in a small cavity in a breccia collected by the Apollo 14 mission, small crystals of the mineral *apatite* (calcium phosphate) formed directly from the vapor that filled the cavities when the rocks were formed almost four billion years ago. The perfect shapes of the crystal faces are shown in this view with an electron microscope; the longest crystal is only 0.05 millimeters long. *(NASA photograph 72–H–35)*

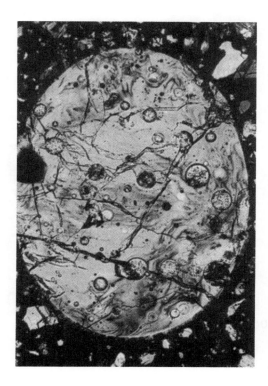

A Glass Drop from a Meteorite Impact (left). A very small glass bead, about half a millimeter long, was formed by the sudden melting of rock struck by a small meteorite. The melted drop was ejected from the crater as part of a spray of droplets to become part of the lunar soil collected by the Apollo 11 mission (sample 10065). The bead shows irregular flow lines produced by the incomplete mixing of glasses of different chemical compositions produced by melting different minerals in the original rock. The very tiny black specks in the glass are small spherules of nickel–iron, probably parts of the meteorite that produced the melting. The droplet is surrounded by black lunar soil which contains smaller fragments of glass and broken crystals of minerals. *(Reprinted with permission from E.C.T. Chao et al., in Proceedings of the Apollo 11 Lunar Science Conference, vol. 1, p. 302, © 1970 by Pergamon Press, Ltd.)*

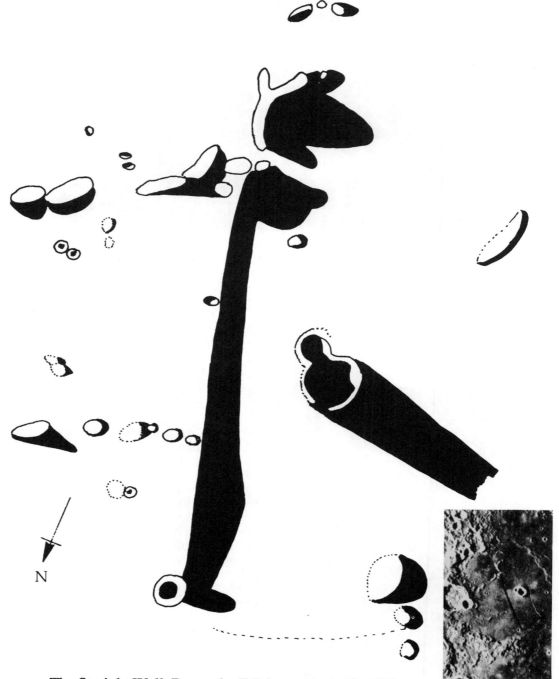

The Straight Wall. Drawn by F.Price on June 18, 1983
with an eight-inch reflector telescope.

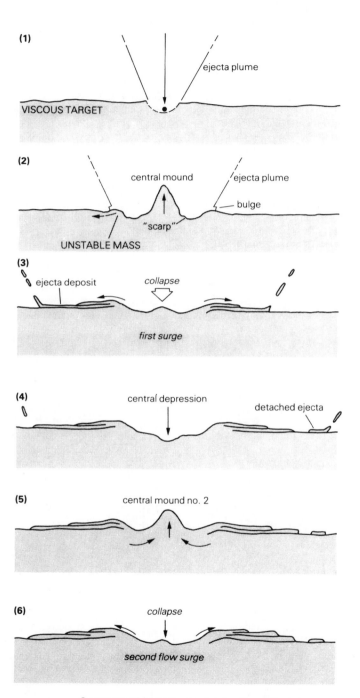

Sequence of impact cratering in viscous targets, derived from analysis of laboratory experiments (from Greeley *et al*. 1980).

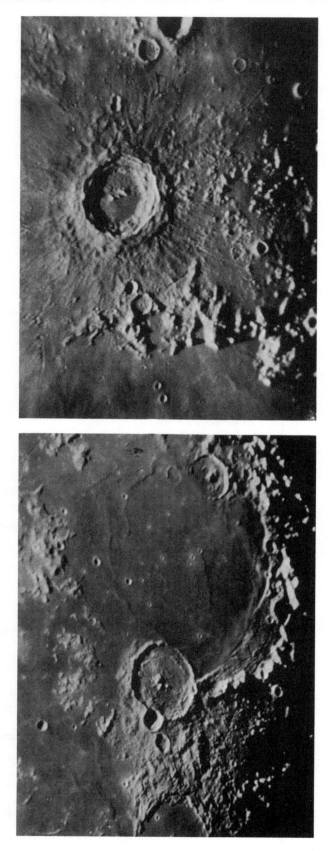

Top: Copernicus and the Carpathian Mountains at Sunrise.
Bottom: The Mare Humorum & Gassendi at sunrise. Note
the curious pyramids in the various craters.

The Lunar Alps: Apennines, Caucasus Mountains and Mare Imbrium at sunrise. Note the flat plain with a number of sharply pyramidical objects suddenly coming from the surface. Several very symmetrical objects, casting sharp and interesting shadows, can be seen towards the top of the photo, and others toward the bottom.

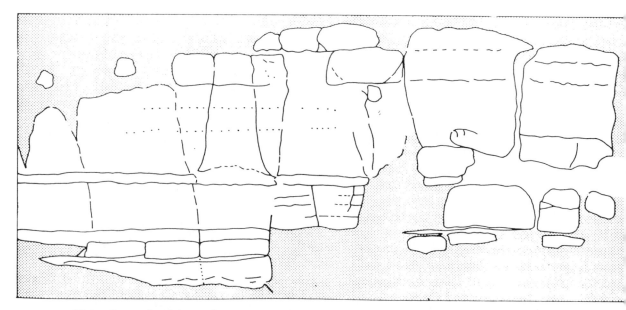

Drawing of a layered outcrop of rock near the Apollo 15 landing site. The outcrop is about 8 meters high. Note its similarity to the polygonal building style used at the massive wall of Sacsayhuaman in the Andes of Peru. Walls like this on Earth can be artificial. Can they on the Moon as well?

Detail of a megalithic wall at Sacsayhuaman. Each oddly-shaped block fits perfectly with the others, making the wall earthquake-resistant.

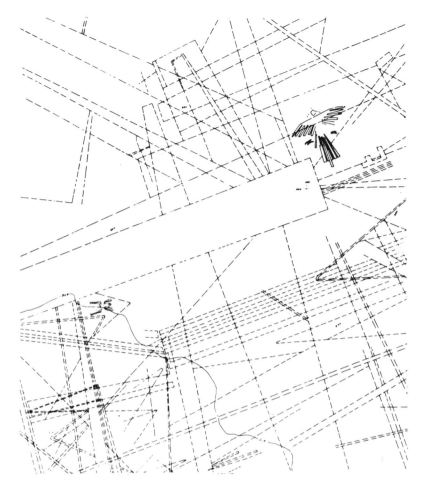

Lines at the Nazca Plain in the Atacama Desert of southern Peru.
Here we see how lines and "rays" on a gigantic scale can be part
of the archaeology of a dry, desert region, including our Moon.

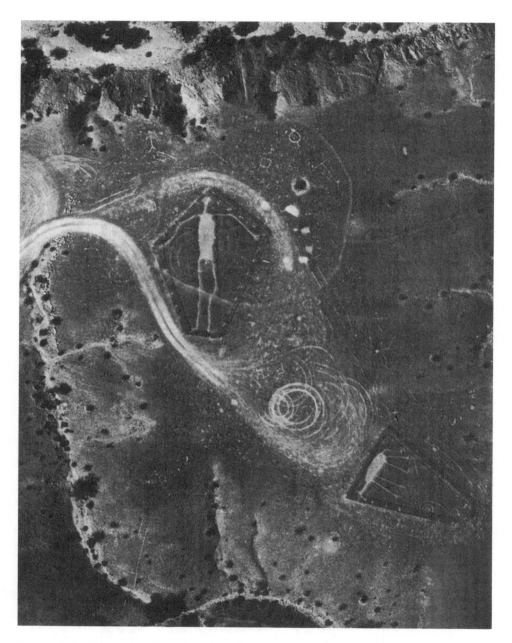

An aerial photo of the gigantic figures etched in the desert near Blythe, California. Of particular interest here is the tracks of vehicles on the desert floor, including the "cookie-cutting" of the vehicles. Are similar markings on the Moon, and other moons and planets, the work of large "Lunar Rovers"?

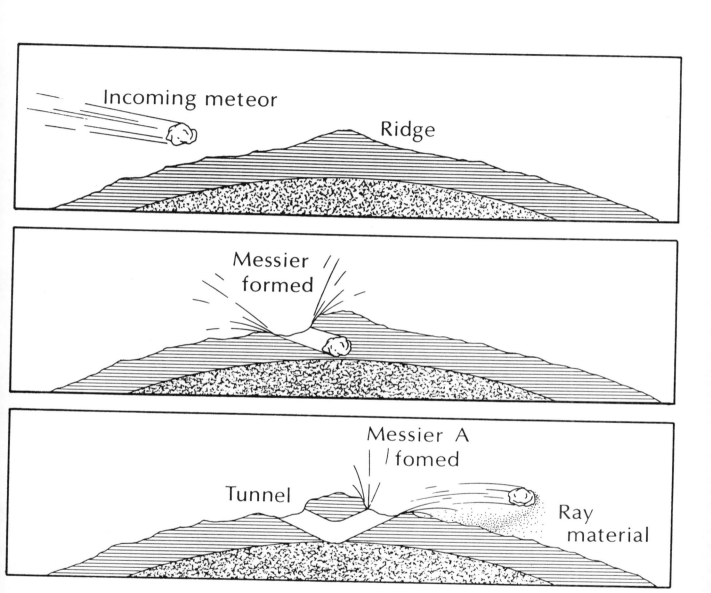

The Lunar Tunnel Theory: As early as 1837, astronomers wrote that the craters Messier and Messier A were exactly alike. In 1952 the astronomer Dr. H.H. Nininger, an American specialist in meteorites, suggested that the two craters were part of a tunnel on the Moon, created naturally by meteor impact. Others have postulated that the tunnel may be one of many artificial constructs on the Moon, while modern astronomers tend to dismiss the idea of a tunnel altogether.

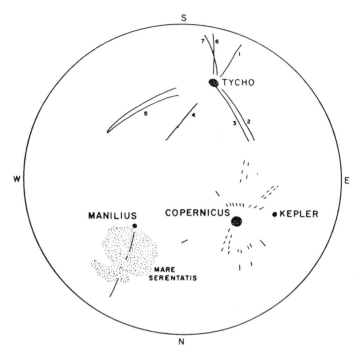

Selected rays from Tycho and Copernicus, illustrating how some
do not converge on the craters, and therefore may not be part of
'ejecta' from the crater.

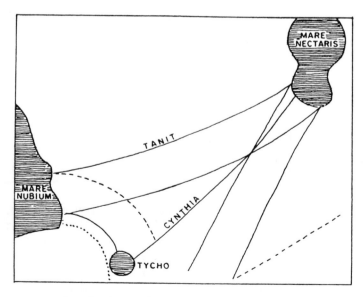

Some reported naked-eye lunar canals between Tycho and the
Mares Nubium and Nectaris. Some modern authors claim that
irrigation and cultivation take place on the Moon. Do the "canals"
of Tanit and Cynthia have to do with this irrigation?

Drawing of a lunar industrial complex from the 1961 book, *Mars*.[26] According to the original caption, it was to extract liquid hydrogen, oxygen, and other propellants from rocks found on the Moon. The processing of rare and expensive metals, abundantly found on the Moon, would be another important industry, but this is not mentioned in the article.

A 1961 artist's conception of a future base on the Moon, designed to be largely underground while its twelve-man crew in experiments and astronomy.

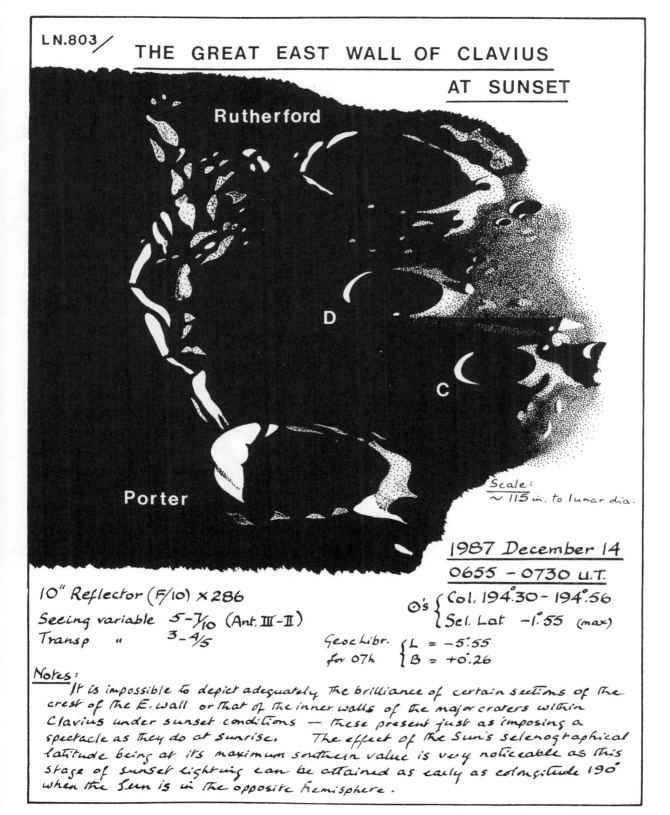

THE GREAT EAST WALL OF CLAVIUS

AT SUNSET

Rutherford

D

C

Porter

Scale:
~ 115 in. to lunar dia.

1987 December 14

0655 – 0730 U.T.

⊙'s { Col. 194°.30 – 194°.56
{ Sel. Lat. –1°.55 (max)

10" Reflector (F/10) × 286

Seeing variable 5 – 7/10 (Ant. III – II)

Transp   "   3 – 4/5

Geo Libr. { L = –5°.55
for 07h   { B = +0°.26

Notes:

It is impossible to depict adequately the brilliance of certain sections of the crest of the E. wall or that of the inner walls of the major craters within Clavius under sunset conditions — these present just as imposing a spectacle as they do at sunrise.   The effect of the Sun's selenographical latitude being at its maximum southern value is very noticeable as this stage of sunset lighting can be attained as early as colongitude 190° when the Sun is in the opposite hemisphere.

Drawn by Howard Hill.

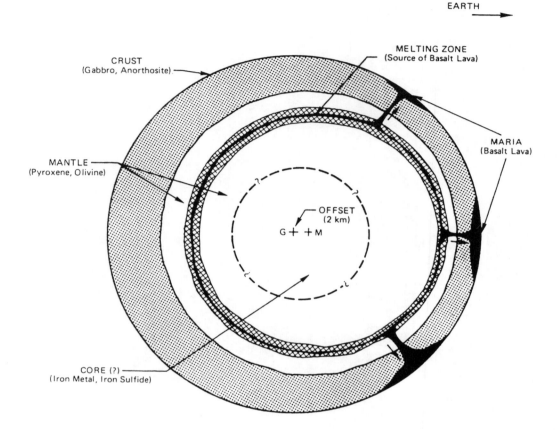

EARTH →

CRUST
(Gabbro, Anorthosite)

MELTING ZONE
(Source of Basalt Lava)

MARIA
(Basalt Lava)

MANTLE
(Pyroxene, Olivine)

OFFSET
(2 km)

G + + M

CORE (?)
(Iron Metal, Iron Sulfide)

A Slice through the Moon. The internal structure of the moon, as determined by the Apollo Program, is shown in this cross section. The moon's diameter is about 3,500 kilometers, and the different layers are not drawn to scale. The outer crust (dotted) is thicker on the far side of the moon (about 100 kilometers) than it is on the near side (about 60 kilometers). This crust is rich in calcium and aluminum and is composed of such rocks as gabbro and anorthosite. Beneath the crust is a denser mantle (white), rich in magnesium and probably composed mostly of the minerals pyroxene and olivine. A small iron-rich core (dashed boundary) may exist at the center of the moon. The moon's center of mass (M) is offset about two kilometers toward the earth from its geometric center (G). The maria (black) on the near side are filled with basalt that formed in a deep zone of melting within the moon's mantle and then rose to the surface (arrows).

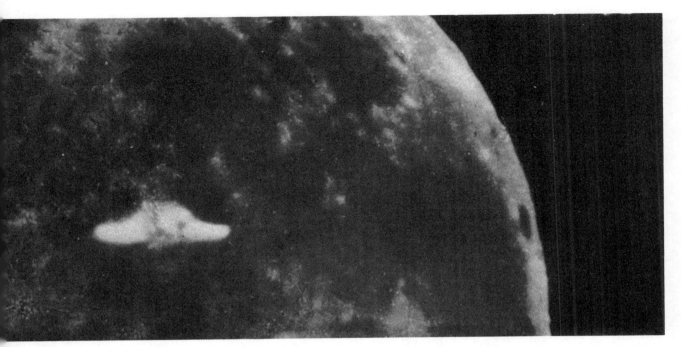

George Adamski's 1950 photo of disc-shaped spacecraft coming from the Moon's surface, presumably on its way to Earth. Though Adamski originally claimed to have taken this photo from a telescope, he later claimed to have gone to the Moon as well. This photo was one of the first to be used in the classic book, *Flying Saucers Have Landed* (Desmond Leslie & George Adamski, 1953).

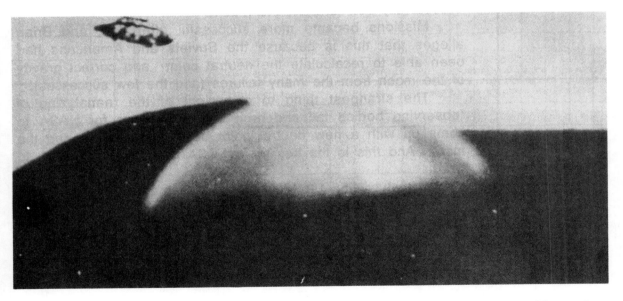

Howard Menger's classic 50s photo of what he claimed was a dome-shaped building taken on the Moon by him. From his 1959 book, *From Outer Space to You.*

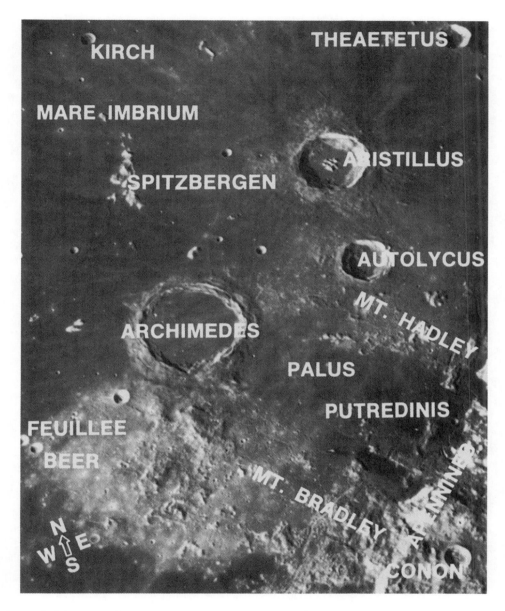

Left and Above: The Mare Imbrium region, with the curious crater Aristillus and the seven or more "pyramids" in the center.

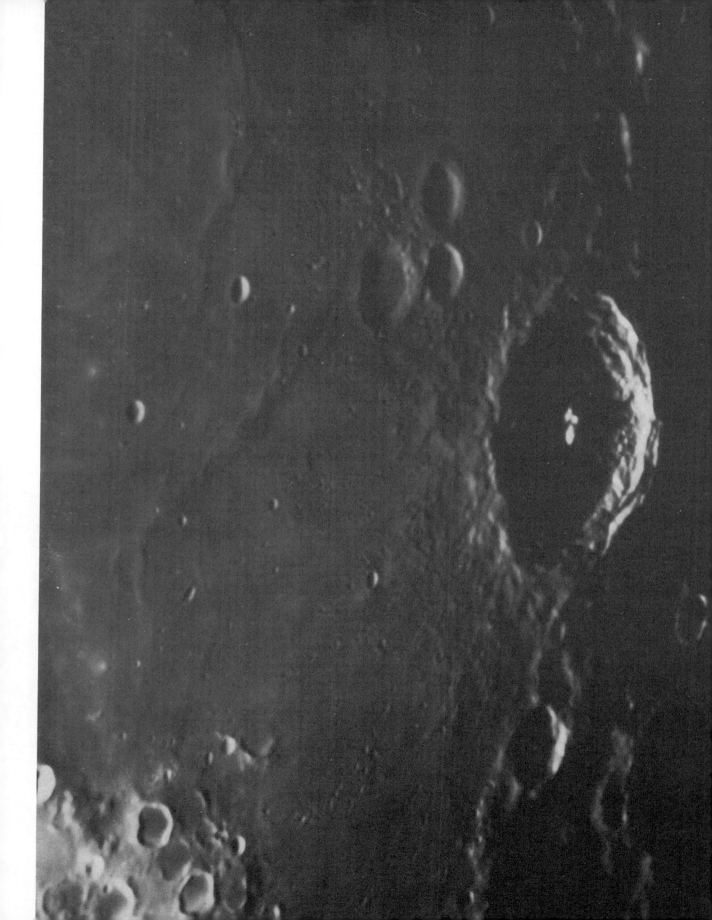

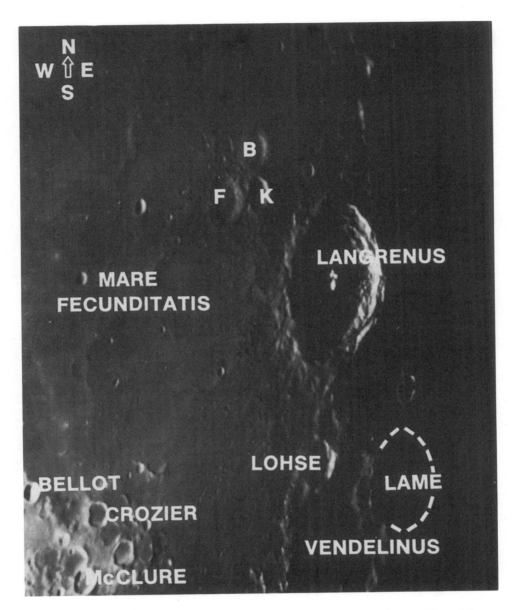

Left and Above: The crater Langrenus at sunset. Are dome-like objects reflecting the early morning sun?

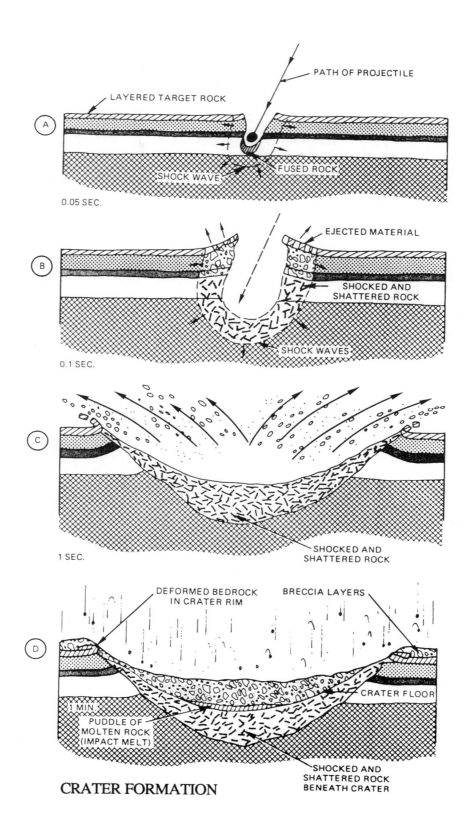

CRATER FORMATION

Chapter 3

LUNAR LANDING
PHOTO PACKAGE

This package of 17 photos was given to the Apollo 15 crew for study during the July, 1971 mission. Questions beneath each photo were instructions to the astronauts on what to observe and describe.

Why these unusual areas of the Moon? Note that some of these photos show some highly unusual features of the Moon: walls, craters, "lakes," gulleys, and other odd-ball structures.

Note the strange resevoir-crater on photo V-9 and the strange elongated oval depression, with a "rile" running across it on the left side of photo V-10.

NATIONAL AERONAUTICS AND SPACE ADMINISTRATION

LUNAR ORBITAL SCIENCE
VISUAL OBSERVATION SITE GRAPHICS

APOLLO MISSION 15
JULY 26, 1971
LAUNCH DATE

PREPARED UNDER THE DIRECTION OF
DOD BY ACIC (USAF) FOR NASA

V-1A TSIOLKOVSKY REGION (128.5°E, 20°S)

Describe pertinent details relative to:
1. Structures and possible layering on the central peaks of Tsiolkovsky.
2. Nature of light-colored floor material and relationship to surrounding units.
3. Variations in texture and structure along segments of the wall of Tsiolkovsky.
4. Rim deposits due south of the crater and possible volcanic fill of the crater Waterman.
5. Origin and inter-relationship of crater pair due north of Tsiolkovsky.

1ST EDITION JUNE 9, 1971 (ACIC)

V-1B NW RIM OF TSIOLKOVSKY (126.5°E, 20.5°S)

Determine the nature of the flow units on the northwest rim of Tsiolkovsky in terms of:

1. Structural control.
2. Relationship to the crater Fermi.

1ST EDITION JUNE 9, 1971 (ACIC)

V-2 PICARD REGION (54.8°E, 14.7°N)

1. Describe subtle color-tones within western Mare Crisium, if any.
2. Is there a difference in the color of the crater Picard and the surrounding mare material?
3. Describe the similarities and/or differences between the craters Picard, Lick, Yerkes and Peirce; compare to the multi-ringed craters of Mare Smythii.

1ST EDITION JUNE 9, 1971 (ACIC)

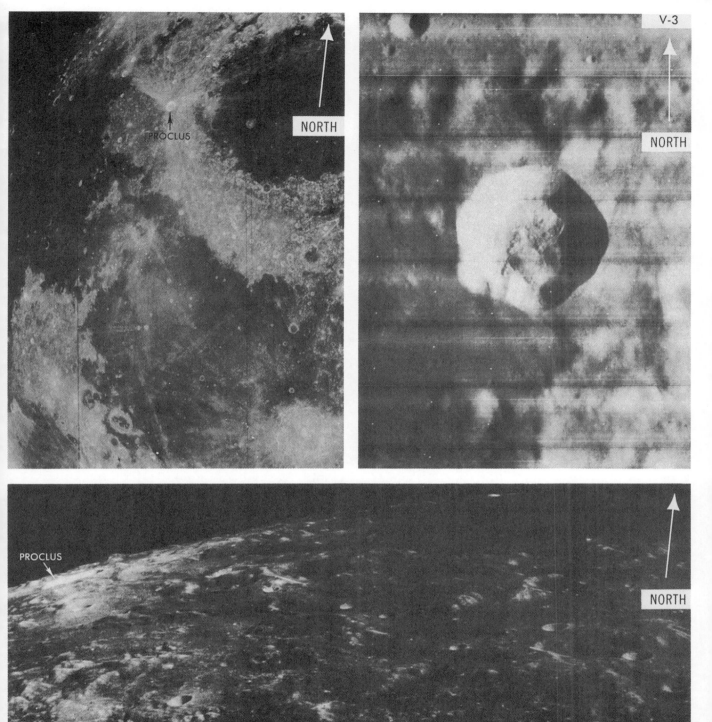

V-3 PROCLUS (47°E, 16.4°N)

Observe the crater Proclus and its environs both vertically and obliquely to determine:
1. What are the major differences between the surrounding units?
2. Does the crater Proclus straddle two different surface units?
3. Are there any topographic features which would indicate that shadowing was responsible for ray-asymmetry?

1ST EDITION JUNE 9, 1971 (ACIC)

V-4 CAUCHY RILLES (38.7°E, 9.7°N)

1. Use monocular to investigate the graben walls. Note particularly the possibility of layering.
2. Describe the domes in the mare material and their probable origin.

1ST EDITION JUNE 9, 1971 (ACIC)

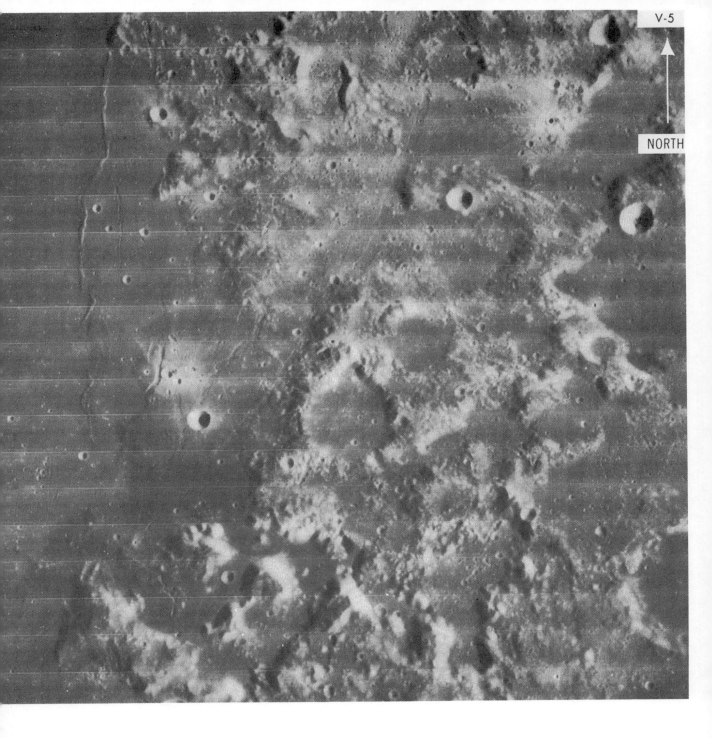

V-5 LITTROW AREA (31.3°E, 21.8°N)

Use photograph to locate and describe the following:
1. The highland units on the eastern rim of Mare Serenitatis.
2. Three mare units which may be distinguished by relative albedo.
3. Sources of the darkest mare unit which mantles older highland and mare materials.
4. Floor fill and wall structure of Rimae Littrow.

1ST EDITION JUNE 9, 1971 (ACIC)

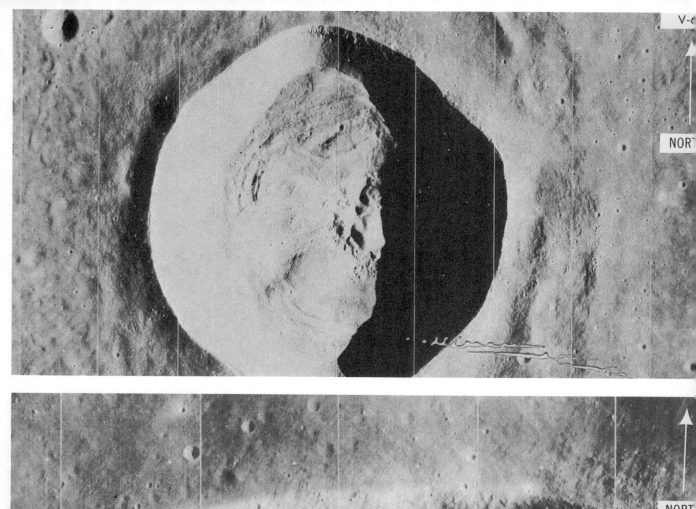

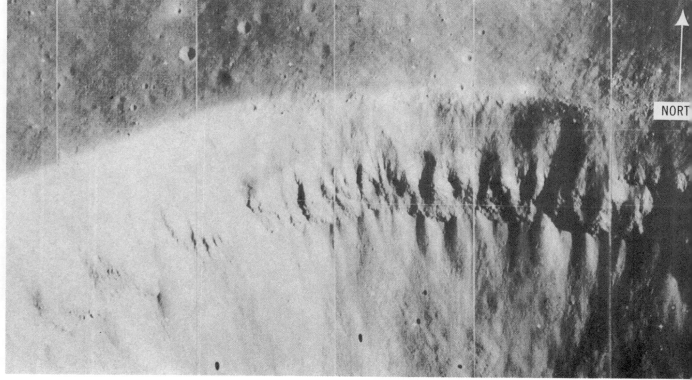

V-6 CRATER DAWES (26.3°E, 17.4°N)

Describe the rim, wall and interior of the crater Dawes in context of probable origin of its features.

1ST EDITION JUNE 9, 1971 (ACIC)

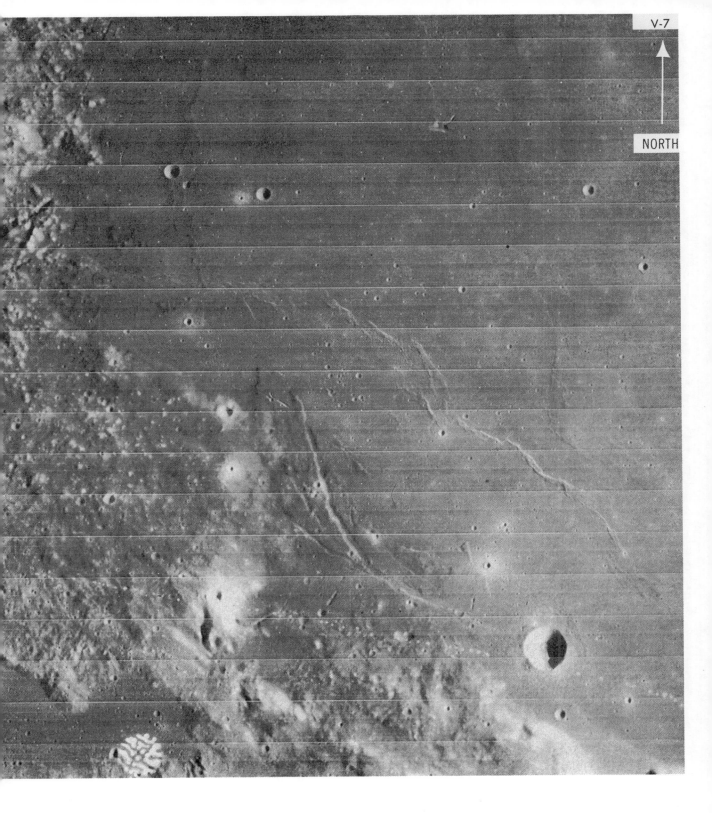

NORTH

V-7 SULPICIUS GALLUS AREA (11.6°E, 19.6°N)

Observe the arcuate rilles, Rimae Sulpicius Gallus I, II and III and their relationship to the surrounding dark deposits; compare the setting to that of Littrow Area (V-5).

1ST EDITION JUNE 9, 1971 (ACIC)

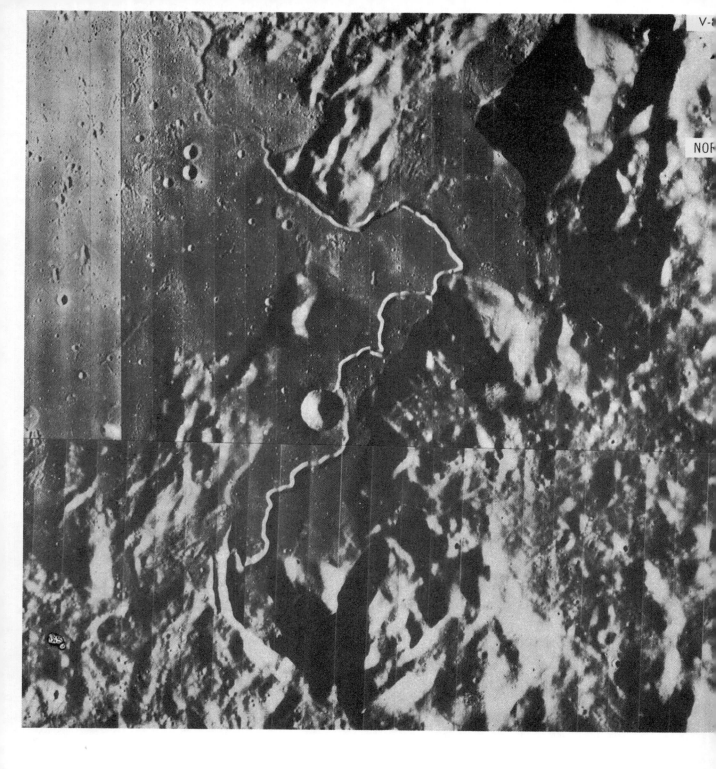

V-8A HADLEY/APENNINES (3°E, 25.8°N)

Record differences and/or similarities between landing area and surrounding region. Note specifically:
1. The crater of origin of the "Secondary South Cluster" (Autolycus versus Aristillus).
2. The probable color boundary, which may correspond to a flow unit, east of the landing area.

1ST EDITION JUNE 9, 1971 (ACIC)

V-8B LANDING SITE HADLEY RILLE (3.65°E, 26.1°N)

Use photograph to locate the LM and make observations relative to the local geology of the site.

1ST EDITION JUNE 9, 1971 (ACIC)

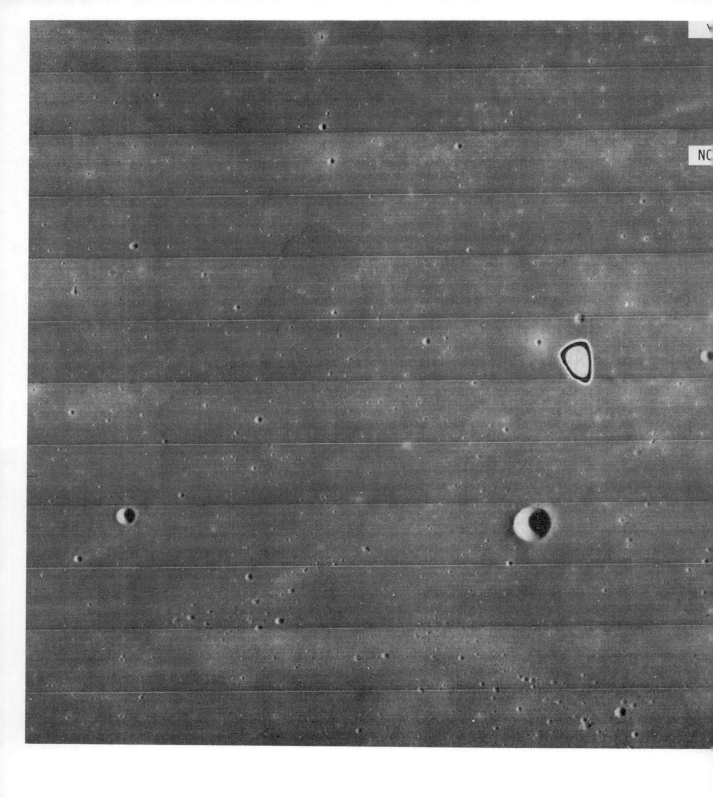

V-9 IMBRIUM FLOWS (21.5°W, 31.5°N)

Observe the flow front in Mare Imbrium obliquely and record observations relative to its nature and color.

1ST EDITION JUNE 9, 1971 (ACIC)

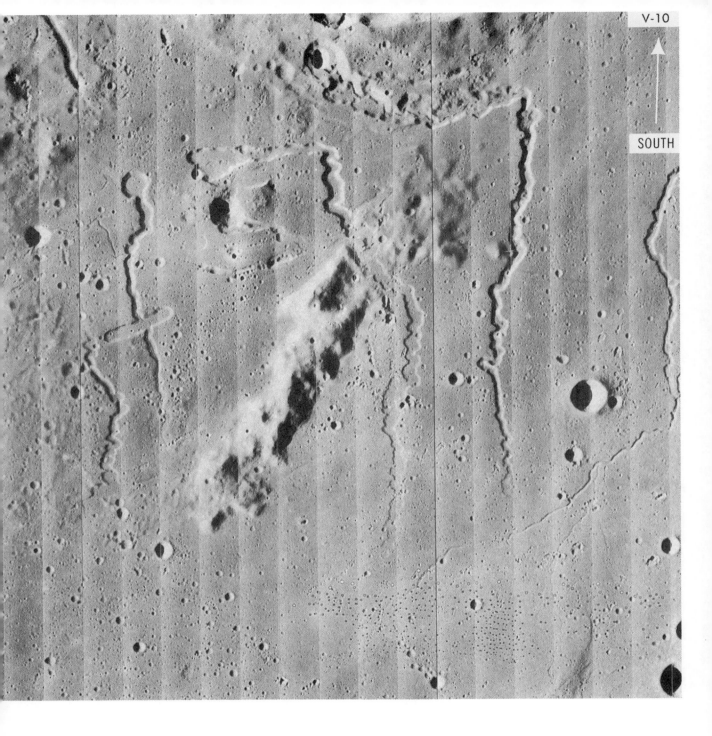

V-10 HARBINGER MOUNTAINS (43.5°W, 27.5°N)

Study the features of Rimae Prinz especially in reference to:
1. Probable deposits at the terminal portions of the sinuous rilles.
2. Layering along the walls of the rilles.

1ST EDITION JUNE 9, 1971 (ACIC)

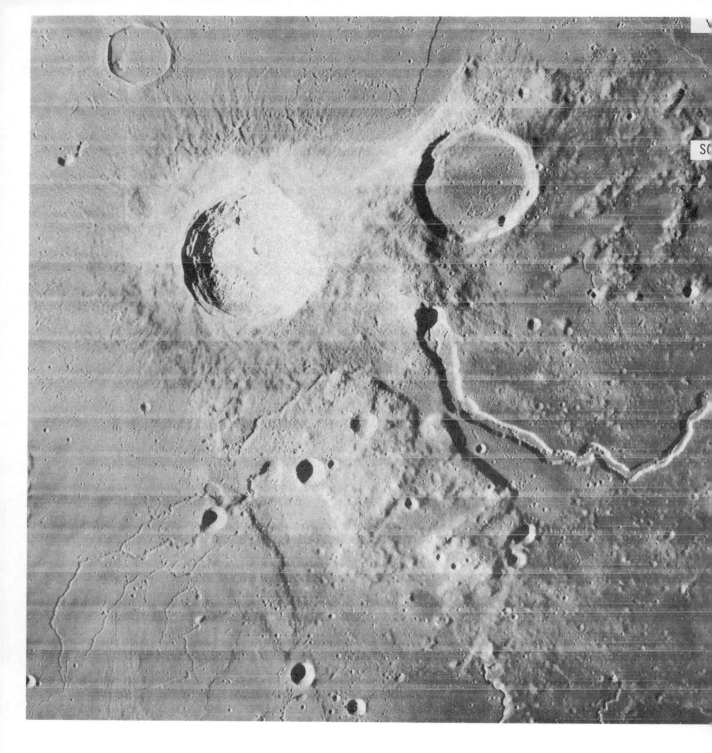

V-11 ARISTARCHUS PLATEAU (48.5°W, 25°N)

Describe the major units of the Aristarchus Plateau (as viewed in earthshine and in sunlight) . Note particularly the following:
1. The domical structures and dark deposits.
2. The Cobra Head and its vicinity.
3. Schröter's Valley and its wall structures.
4. The Aristarchus rim and related volcanics.

1ST EDITION JUNE 9, 1971 (ACIC)

SEA OF SERENITY

LITTROW AREA →

SEA OF TRANQUILITY

SEA OF CRISES

SEA OF WAVES

BORDER SEA

SEA OF FERTILITY

FOAMING SEA

OF NECTAR

SMYTH'S SEA

V-12 EASTERN MARIA

Use color chart to:
1. Compare and describe the color tones of the major maria at varying sun angles.
2. Following TEI, list the maria in order of decreasing color tones (starting with the darkest).

1ST EDITION JUNE 9, 1971 (ACIC)

Within the image, the following labels appear:

LITTROW AREA
PROCLUS
SEA OF TRANQUILITY
TARUNTIUS
CENSORINUS
SEA OF FERTILITY
SEA OF NECTAR
LANGRENUS
PETAVIUS B
PETAVIUS
STEVINUS A
HECATAEUS
HUMBOLDT
SOUTHERN SEA
CURIE
GIBBS
LA PEROUSE
SEA OF WAVES
FOAMING SEA
SEA OF CRISES
HUMBOLDT'S SEA
GAUSS
NO
FAB
JOLIOT
LOMONOSOV
BORDER SEA
GODDARD
NEPER
SMYTH'S SEA
MOISEEV
HIRAYAMA
SKLODOWSKA
PASTEUR
HILBERT

V-13 MAJOR LUNAR FEATURES

Following TEI, use photograph to identify observable lunar surface features.

1ST EDITION JUNE 9, 1971 (ACIC)

V-14 MARE INGENII (163.5°E, 32.5°S)

Examine the high albedo surface materials; are there any topographic expressions to these features?

1ST EDITION JUNE 9, 1971 (ACIC)

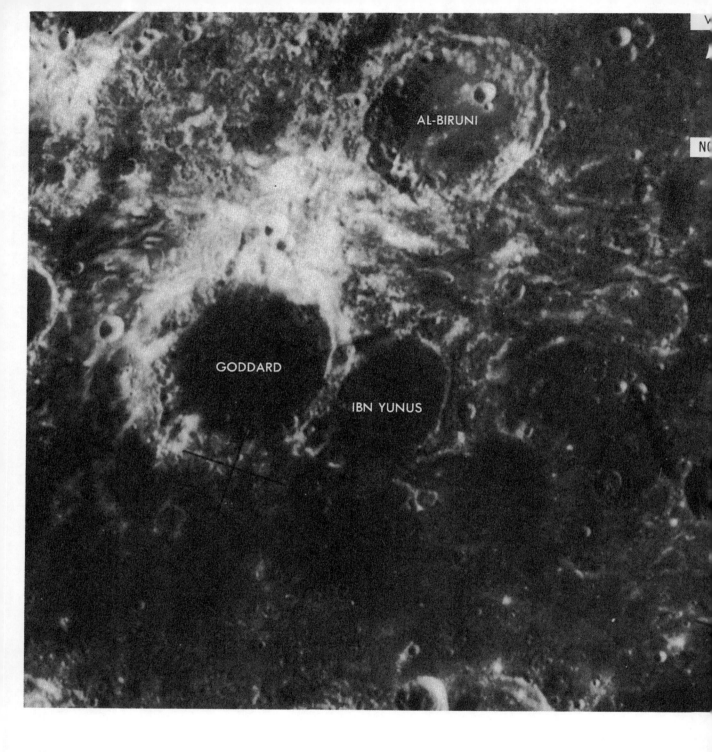

AL-BIRUNI

GODDARD

IBN YUNUS

V-15 IBN YUNUS AREA (91.2°E, 13.7°N)

Examine the swirls of high albedo materials; compare with those of Mare Ingenii (V-14).

1ST EDITION JUNE 9, 1971 (ACIC)

Chapter 4

More Mystery Structures on the Moon

The Moon must be cavernous with an atmosphere within, and at the centre of its caverns a sea. One knew that moon had a lower specific gravity than the earth...one knew, too, that it was sister planet to the earth and that it was unaccountable that it should be different in composition. The inference that it was hollowed out was as clear as day.
—H.G. Wells (1901)

Before man journeyed to our Moon, many scientists of Earth were intensely interested in the possibility of finding evidence of alien beings having visited our satellite. Joseph F. Blumrich, a leading design engineer at the Marshall Space Flight Center in Huntsville, Alabama, concluded after an eighteen-month study on this subject that the Earth and the Moon have been visited regularly by extraterrestrial beings. He claimed that eventually we would find their artifacts on the surface of our lunar neighbor.

Why, despite half a dozen manned trips to the Moon, haven't we? To begin with, the area of the Moon's surface we have explored in six Apollo manned missions is minuscule. Another problem in our search for such artifacts is that they could be placed anywhere and might be in forms we have never imagined.

Science reporter Joseph Goodavage once quoted a high-ranking General Dynamic Corporation executive who worked closely with NASA on the many Moon projects as stating: "An object or artifact placed by an alien civilization on the Moon could be something as obvious as a small pyramid sitting atop a mountain peak. We'd literally have to stumble over it before anybody would recognize it for what it is." He added "But nothing less than a full-scale exploration of the Moon will turn up whatever is there." (*Saga*, April 1974.)

Probably such exploration will not take place until the twenty-first century at the earliest.

Actually, even without full-scale exploration, we have discovered a number of structures which appear to be artificial during the few manned and unmanned space probes we have sent to our Moon. In fact, of the many mysteries uncovered in our journeys to this neighboring world, none is more mystifying than that of the strange structures discovered there.

Ø Ø Ø

In the book *Our Mysterious Spaceship Moon* [20] (Dell, 1975) the author discuss many different discoveries that have been made on the Moon—both American and Soviet. The amazing thing is that, as startling and seemingly important as they are, little is known of them by the public.

In fact, even before man journeyed to our satellite, reports of structures sighted on the surface of the Moon were numerous. Astronomical literature is crammed with them. One of the most startling is the huge bridge-like structure seen over the Sea of Crisis in 1954 by John O'Neill, former science editor of the *New York Herald Tribune.* This oddity was confirmed by other leading astronomers who also saw it through their own telescopes. Some estimated it to be 12 miles long.

Of course the big question is whether it was a natural structure or an artificial construction? The eminent British astronomer H. P. Wilkins, head of the Lunar Section, British Astronomical Association, made this startling statement in a BBC radio program: "It looks artificial." (Donald Keyhoe, *The Flying Saucer Conspiracy,* Holt, 1975.)

When he was asked what precisely he meant by the term "artificial," Dr. Wilkins answered: "Well, it looks almost like an engineering job." This lunar expert added that it was more or less regular in outline and even cast a shadow under a low Sun. He startled everyone when he exclaimed: "You can see the sunlight streaming in beneath it."

In the entire radio interview, not once did Wilkins refer to this structure as being a "natural" bridge. Instead, he used words which indicated that he thought it might be artificial. The fact that the bridge had not been seen before, although the area was well known and often studied, increased the possibility that it might indeed be a construction made by beings apparently inhabiting the Moon—and fairly recently.

Many other seemingly intelligently constructed "structures," like walls that formed squares or rectangles and even strange dome-like structures that appeared out of nowhere and at times seemed to disappear, led many observers to believe that they are the work of alien intelligence.

The chances are, admittedly, that many apparently artificial constructions are nothing but natural formations, misinterpreted by Earth observers due to the vast distance between us and our nearest neighbor. Space photos of Earth teach us a lesson here. From outer space, orbiting vehicles have taken photographs that lend to many natural Earth formations an aura of artificiality. For instance, from the depths of space the Barringer crater of Arizona looks like an artificial construction. Similarly, photos of an area at the southern edge of the Sahara Desert in northern Nigeria show what appears to be a sprawling series of structured walls—but we know that these are merely natural formations. So man must be extremely careful in his conclusions

SIGNS ON THE MOON?

One of the strangest of all such lunar reports comes out of Japan, where *Mainichi,* one of Japan's largest newspapers, reported the unusual discovery by Dr. Kenzahuro Toyoda of Menjii University, while studying the Moon through a telescope on the night of September 29,

1958 of what appeared to be huge black letters, so pronounced they were easily discernible. The letters seemed to form two words: PYAX and JWA. No one to this day knows what these letters seen on the Moon mean or can give an explanation to the experience.

It should be emphasized that these are the kinds of reports made by observers whom Wilkins, former director of the Lunar Section of the British Astronomical Association, calls "people who have been observing the moon too long to be easily deceived."

Dr. Wilkins adds: "In any case it is incredible that all were the victims of hallucination. We must accept the records even if we cannot explain them. Our knowledge and opinions are the products of existence on the earth; it is reasonable to suppose that on another planet conditions exist and events take place which have no counterpart on our planet. If there are intelligent creatures on other worlds, they are most unlikely to have bodies, or minds like ours; it would be very surprising if they did."

Wilkins concludes: "The moon is an alien and foreign world and much of what happens up there must remain a mystery until men actually land on its warty surface." (*Our Moon*, [42] p. 139). The objection might be made that man has gone to the Moon, photographed it completely at close range, and even landed and explored some of its surface. And no evidence of intelligently made structures or activities was uncovered. Or was it?

The surprising answer to this objection is that it was! Photos, both American and Soviet, reveal that seeming non-natural, artificially made structures do exist on the Moon. Incredibly, the Moon itself is one huge artificial structure in an artificial orbit around the Earth.

⌀⌀⌀

SOVIET DISCOVERY OF "MONUMENTS" ON THE MOON
The Soviet space probe Luna-9 took some startling photographs (February 4, 1966) after the vehicle had landed on the Ocean of Storms, one of those dark, circular

"seas" of lava on the Earth side of the Moon. The photos revealed strange towering structures that appear to be lined up rather than scattered randomly across the lunar surface.

Dr. Ivan T. Sanderson, the late director of the Society for the Investigation of the Unexplained and science editor for *Argosy* magazine, observed that the Soviet photographs "reveal two straight lines of equidistant stones that look like markers along an airport runway. These circular stones are all identical, and are positioned at an angle that produces a strong reflection from the Sun, which would render them visible to descending aircraft." (*Argosy*, August 1970.)

But Sanderson was not the only reporter revealing these strange structures to the world. The Soviet press also carried articles on them. The Soviet magazine *Technology of Youth* gave an extensive report on them, calling them "stone markers" which were unquestionably "planned structures," and suggested that these "pointed pyramids" were not natural formations but definitely artificial structures of alien origin.

After examining the photographs of these objects, Dr. S. Ivanov, winner of the *Laureate State Prize* (which the Soviets consider equivalent to the Nobel Prize), calculated from the shadows cast by the spire-like structures that at least one was about 15 stories high.

Ivanov, who is also the inventor of stereo movies in the Soviet Union, pointed out that by luck—perhaps the space probe landed on a spot where the ground had settled, or set down upon a small stone or rough spot—"a chance displacement of Luna-9 on its horizontal axis had caused the stones to be taken at slightly different angles." This double set of photographs allowed him to produce a three-dimensional stereoscopic view of the lunar "runway."

The result of this bit of good fortune, as Ivanov reports, was that the stereoscopic effect enabled scientists to figure the distances between the spires. They found, much to their surprise, that they were spaced at regular intervals. Moreover, calculations confirmed that the spires themselves were identical in measurement. Says Ivanov: "There does not seem to be any height or elevation nearby from which the stones could have been rolled and scattered into this geometric form. The objects as seen in 3-D seem to be arranged according to definite geometric laws."

This discovery must be heralded as among the most important discoveries made by either the American or Soviet space program. But, strangely, for the most part they have been ignored. As we shall soon see, other discoveries, equally important, have been covered up by NASA.

In fact, Art Rosenblum, head of the Aquarian Research Foundation, who says he learned of the Soviet discovery from Lynn Schroeder and Sheila Ostrander, the authors of *Psychic Discoveries Behind the Iron Curtain,* before their work was published in America, claims they indicated that authorities at NASA "were not at all happy about its publication." Why not? What is NASA trying to hide? asks Rosenblum in his book *Unpopular Science* (Running Press, 1974).

The key quetion is what is the purpose of these gigantic structures? Ivan T. Sanderson once speculated: "Is the origin of the obelisks on the Earth and those on the Moon the same? Could both be ancient markers originally erected by alien space travelers for guidance of late arrivals?" He pointed out that it seems hard to understand why man ever started making obelisks anyway, since it is a very difficult job and seemingly purposeless. Or did obelisks have a purpose other than Earthly? Could these spire-like structures actually be signals for the coming and going of spaceships, as some have speculated?

If the "energy grid" and antenna system of New Zealand's Bruce Cathie from is correct, could it be that the obelisks, pyramids are part of an energy grid or geometric energy pattern around the Moon? Antennae like Bruce Cathie has described may well exist on the Moon, but it is probably too small to have been located by photograph—yet!

Intriguingly, on the edge of this same Sea of Storms is a strange opening that leads down into the Moon. Dr. H.P. Wilkins, one of the world's leading lunar experts before his untimely death some years ago, was convinced that extensive hollow areas did exist inside the Moon, perhaps in

98

the form of caverns, and that these were connected to the surface by huge holes or pits. He discovered such an opening himself—a huge round hole inside the crater Cassini A. This crater is one and a half miles across, and the opening which leads down into the Moon is over 600 feet across—more than two football fields laid end to end. Wilkins writes in his definitive work, *Our Moon*: "Its inside is as smooth as glass with a deep pit or plughole, about 200 yards across at the centre."[42,20,21]

As we shall see in the coming chapters, hundreds, in fact thousands, of UFOs have been seen on or around the surface of the Moon, and a concentration of them has been spotted in the Sea of Storms. Could they be coming and going through this huge opening or one like it?

⌀⌀⌀

The Moon's composition is not at all what it should be had the Moon been formed in its present orbit around the earth.
—Dr. Harold Urey,
Science News, October 4, 1971, p. 246

PYRAMIDS ON THE SEA OF TRANQUILITY?

First and foremost, the strange pyramidal, obelisk-like structures that appear to be artificial and which Soviet space engineer Alexander Abramov claims are positioned exactly like the major pyramids around Giza near Cairo, Egypt. These have probably been closely examined by NASA, since our astronauts went to the very same Sea of Tranquility on our first trip to the Moon, though the results have never been released and probably never will be unless enough public pressure can be applied to our government.

Secondly, the site of the Soviet-discovered monolith, that mysterious rectangular block of stone that appears strangely to be like the monolith of *2001: A Space Odyssey*, Arthur Clarke's famous book and movie.

Thirdly, the inside of "Ranger" Crater. The controversial

"Ranger 7 Crater" would be a good place to concentrate our Moon look, this time without the veil of secrecy covering up our findings.

The first phase of our Moon exploration the Ranger series returned thousands of photos of the Moon's surface-close-up pictures that revealed a great deal about the surface of this strange satellite. One of these taken by Ranger 7 just before it smashed into the Moon has produced a storm of controversy. The photo was taken about three miles on the last leg of its crash dive and appears to show some objects inside a crater. NASA officials claim they are just "a cluster of rocks." Other investigators are not so sure.

No one knows for sure but some investigators like (now deceased) Riley Crabb of the *Borderland Science Research Organization* claim that their circular symmetry indicates that whatever they are, certainly they are "intelligently constructed."

Crabb believes that this conclusion is "confirmed by the sharp, straight black shadow cast" by one of two "brilliant white shafts" inside the crater. He points out that this August, 10, 1964, photo published in *Missiles and Rockets magazine* (p. 22), shows "clearly outlined in between the bases of the two shafts a perfect circle, perhaps 40 or 50 feet across. The hole itself is pitch black, as though it led into the interior of the moon; but the edges are bright, like the edges of a gigantic bubble or lens."

Crabb goes on to explain: "As we looked at the Missiles and Rockets reproduction of the Ranger photo we became aware of two more perfect black holes in the crater, one to the left of the left-hand shaft, and one in the top of the little cone to the south of the shafts..." He concludes: "You can be sure that military and civilian photo analysis have devoted hundreds of hours to this particular 'rock' formation, but in view of the continuing 'silence policy' on Flying Saucers such technical analyses will be classified secret for years to come." (*Journal of Borderland Research*, November-December 1964.)

Some see in this photo UFOs sitting inside this mysterious crater. One such investigator is George Leonard, author of *Somebody Else Is On the Moon*,[19] an amateur astronomer who claims that through an ex-NASA scientist friend he got to look at a composite photo of several Ranger 7 pictures, that proves this is precisely what they are. This photo, says Leonard, put together by NASA's Jet Propulsion Lab in California, shows a large object in the crater with a "dull metallic finish." The object is "smoothly rounded, symmetrical, and has what appears to be a turret-shaped protuberance, which is also remarkable for its perfection."

Asks Leonard, with an obvious eye on UFOs: "What looks like that?"

He also is convinced that on its gleaming back he can discern a strange marking that looks something like an English letter Y with a line beneath it. He says a study of the world's alphabets indicates that it is very much like the ancient Semitic Z found on the famous ancient Moabite Stone.

If there is any validity to Leonard's conclusion, its implications are staggering. This remarkable investigator is convinced that whoever is on the Moon was intrinsically involved in mankind's past. Whether ancient Atlantean in their *vimanas* or the *Watchers* of the Bible themselves, someone in on the Moon.

"They've watched us develop since at least the Bronze Age. They've had a catbird seat on all our wars and pettinesses. They've architected and built big things here and left signs all over our Earth." So Leonard concludes.

Without hesitation Leonard in his intriguing book *Somebody Else Is On the Moon* speculates: "The Moon is a logical seat for all the UFOs skipping around the fringes of our cultures since the dawn of time." And in Ranger 7 photos he believes he has found evidence of such lunar UFOs, or at least of constructions on the Moon.

The Moon is ancient—evidently an foreign structure brought here from another solar system. Possibly to observe the Earth?

Ø Ø Ø

THE STRANGE TUNNEL ON THE MOON

Another oddity of the Moon is a strange tunnel about 20 miles long which is apparently lined with walls of glass!

Dr. H. H. Nininger, director of the American Meteorite Museum in Winslow, Arizona, announced this discovery back in 1952. He claims that through a good telescope not only can the tunnel be seen but the entrance and the exits of that tunnel are clearly discernible.

Located on the western part of the Moon in the Sea of Fecundity are two unusual craters Messier and W. H. Pickering. These two strange craters are very close together but they differ greatly from other lunar craters in that the rim or lip of each crater is "noticeably extended in the same direction." (*Science Digest*, November 1952.)

Dr. Nininger points out that the tunnel starts here with these two odd-looking formations, one the entrance and the other the exit. They are on the opposite sides of a towering mountain ridge, which is several thousand feet high and 15 to 20 miles wide.

The shape of the respective holes or entrances suggests that the same force has created a tunnel through this mountain.

Is this an artificial construction on the Moon? Dr. Nininger suggests that it was created by a "meteorite." This magical meteor "moving 20 to 30 miles per second would vaporize the powdery dust on contact," melting instantaneously and cooling quickly, thus forming a glazed tunnel.

It seems impossible that any meteor would do this. Most meteors would explode on contact. Even at the slow speed Nininger assigns to this slow-moving meteor it would still be travelling at 72,000 miles per hour! How could it then perform its miraculous job of vitrification? Is the tunnel actually vitrified?

Another serious problem is that it is difficult to comprehend how it could travel horizontally to perform its tunneling job. But Nininger believes that a large meteorite could sweep low enough, skimming the Moon's surface, tunneling its way through solid rock mountain, dropping from the skies hitting and then ricocheting through this hard submantle, burning its way through, and leaving in its miraculous wake enormous holes that now "mark its entrance and exit." (*Science Digest*, November 1952)

∅∅∅

UFOs are astronautical craft, or entities. If they have a fixed base of any kind, that base is likely the Moon.

—Morris K. Jessup, popularizer of
The Philadelphia Experiment.

THE MYSTERIOUS HOLE IN THE MOON

If we really wanted to get at the heart of the matter, there are the strange "plugholes," huge round openings which Dr. H.P. Wilkins of the British Astronomical Association is convinced may connect with extensive inner hollows of the Moon's cavernous interior. Are such connecting holes the passageways for aliens coming into and out of their hollow Spaceship Moon?[20]

Wilkins claims that he discovered one such huge hole using one of the most powerful telescopes in Europe. He dubbed it the "Washbowl," since it looks like one. This huge round opening into the Moon is located in Crater Cassini A and is over the length of two football fields across.

In his classic book *Our Moon*,[42] Dr. Wilkins gives us this remarkable description of this "hole" in the Moon: "Its inside is as smooth as glass with a deep pit, or plughole about 200 yards across, at the center."

An opening like the mouth of a bottle certainly gives the appearance of having being constructed. What startling discovery could be made here? Could this be one of the openings to the inner world of this Spaceship Moon?

THE PUZZLING STRAIGHT WALL

The straight wall is a ridge over 60 miles long which was so remarkably straight it was nicknamed "The Railway." The Soviet scientists who formulated the spaceship theory of the Moon speculated that it might have been caused when the inner metal shell was ruptured. Thus, a huge armor plate inside the Moon, bending under the impact perhaps of a huge celestial torpedo, might have raised this straight, unnatural fault line of rock, pushing it outward.

The edges do present a steep rock cliff which rises from the surface of the Moon in a steady climb for over 1,200 feet at about a sharp 45-degree angle. The area around it shows the ghost of a huge crater that may have crashed here eons ago. Intriguingly, all around are large, whitish domes.

Speculating on a mystery spot such as this can cause the imagination to soar. On the back side of the Moon, strangely enough, nearly directly opposite the Straight Wall is a huge crack 150 miles long and at places more than 5 miles wide.

If the Moon does have that inner metallic rock shell beneath its outer crust this vast opening could be very revealing. The position of this crack intrigues us into this speculation: could the gargantuan crack be related in formation to the Straight Wall? But this question is theoretical. The practical significance of the great crack in the Moon is that it might be a great crack in the veil of rock enshrouding the hull of our mysterious Moon.[19,20,21]

NASA COVERS-UP PHOTOS?

A letter to the editor in the UFO journal, *Notes From the Hanger*, edited by Jim Keith, had this to say about NASA photos of the Moon:

> Dear NUFOM,
> Hey! Is everybody asleep? Shape up. Pay attention.
> After an avalanche of reports, photos, imprints, even fatalities no one cares or wonders where they come from. Even the late Dr. Hynek said, like a babe in the woods, "we don't know where they come from."
> Okay. Now let's determine where the DON'T come from, and this is from outside the solar system. My letter in the January 1982 *National Geographic* reads:
> A spacecraft traveling at 1000 times the speed of astronauts on their way to the moon (fifteen million miles per hour) would require 192 years to reach Proxima Centauri, the very nearest star."
> So, let's look closer in, very close: the Moon.

Several years ago an item in the legitimate press *(New York Daily News)* stated that NASA had refused to release 125 lunar photographs to an investigative group. Imagine! 125 photos showing things that NASA doesn't want the public to see!

Why does NASA flout the freedom of Information Act and get away with it? Why doesn't this investigative group keep the pressure on NASA and publicize their plight? This news far outweighs Balboa's discovery of the Pacific Ocean.

I have several lunar photos that NASA may have deemed "borderline."

NASA # 67-H1179 and 67-H-1206-B (taken on different orbits) show a cloud formation over Tycho crater that can only be artificial. 67-H-1206-B shows increase in translucence in certain areas.

67-H-327 shows a half mile wide hole (not a crater) as seen from an altitude of 32 1/2 miles. Inside is a colossal skyscraper size object of manufactured appearance.

These photos were obtained in 1979 from NASA supplier *BARA Photographic, Inc.* P.O. Box 486, Bladensburg, MD 20710.

Later I wrote to NASA to inquire if the photos were still available as I feared that they might have been put on the "forbidden" list. They sent me copies of some and believe thee me, you should see the difference between the BARA photo of 67-H-327 that is clear with good resolution and the NASA samples that are dark, fuzzy with poor definition, not conducive to closer scrutiny.

We are surrounded by the NASA-Air Force-Pentagon-White House conspiracy of silence.

Sincerely,
John Zueblin

∅∅∅

THE HOLE IN THE MOON & THE GIANT LADDER

The "Giant Ladder" is George Leonard's impression of an oblique view from the Apollo 8 spacecraft of a large area on the lunar far side. In it is an almost obliterated crater with many parallel markings running through it. One set of these parallel markings continues in the air from the rim of the crater on into its bottom. It appears to be an enormous rope ladder or, conceivably, the tread from a very large vehicle. NASA does not identify the size of the crater or give a

105

good bench mark for judging the distance, but my guess is that the "rope ladder" is about four miles long.

The object seems to cast a shadow on the floor of the crater. If this is a shadow, then the phenomenon is not a tread but more analogous to a leaning ladder. The phenomenon is very real but it almost defies description. This is perhaps because we lack real analogies from our reality-structure, and therefore find it necessary to rely on crude correspondences to our experience such as "the giant ladder." I do not, for example, know how to describe the stringy piece of ground which has woven itself through the ladder. Nor can I account for the way in which the ladder itself seems to have no beginning or end, but is part of the ground.

Not only is there a large grid pattern sharply defined in some places, the Moon also appears to have a smaller pattern of filaments which cross one another at right angles to form a mesh. At least one qualified person has argued that the skin of the Moon, beneath a superficial layer of breccia and dust, may actually be an artificial protective cover—a cover which has been exposed in some places long ago due to a horrendous battle..

"Have you ever kicked over an anthill and watched the mega-myriad creatures work feverishly to repair? Is this the activity which we are glimpsing on the Moon?" asks George Leonard, author of *Someone Else Is On the Moon*.[19]

LUNAR RAYS: THEIR FORMATION AND AGE

Extracted from Louis Giamboni's article in *Astrophysical Journal* (130:324-335, 1959):

The nature of the rays of Tycho and Copernicus suggests that they were laid down at a time when the angular velocity of the moon was markedly different from that observed today. The rays of Tycho indicate that the lunar sidereal period was between 0.5 and 6.8 days and that the poles were in approximately the same position then as they are today. These rays were created within 8×10^7 years of the time the moon was formed. The rays of Copernicus support these observations and indicate that the rotation of the moon at the time that these rays were formed was similar to the rotation which existed at the time that Tycho was formed.

Several observers have noted that the rays in the vicinity of a lunar crater, if extended, do not always pass through the center of the crater. Many extended rays would be tangential to the crater; other rays would miss the crater entirely. Observers have also noted both single rays and pairs of rays. No consistent explanation of these phenomena has yet been advanced. This paper presents a possible explanation for both these phenomena in terms of the lunar sidereal rotation and the equations of motion for a body moving in a vacuum. The theory is developed for the rays of Tycho and Copernicus."

THE NEW THEORIES ON RAYS FORMATION

There is evidence to show that some rays may not be ejecta from the crater. Authors like George Leonard and Don Wilson maintain that the rays are a combination of "moon rover" tracks and the dust of cargo ships moving from one crater to another. In this theory the "ghost rings" of the moon are explained as moon-rover mining vehicles doing "cookie-cutter" effects while the rays are main routes from one base or mining site to another.

Don Wilson in his books sums up the case for literal "roadways" on the moon:[20,21]

"Whenever one proposes a theory to explain a phenomenon, he must be certain that it covers all examples. We must list all known properties of the rays; we must describe all types; and only then can a new theory be compared with the list to see if important areas are covered or left out." Summarizes Wilson:

(1) Rays do not appear to have sufficient depth to cast a shadow.

(2) They are white, and do not show up well under oblique sunlight (i.e., when there are pronounced shadows). On the other hand, the rays become very enhanced under full midday sun.

(3) Rays typically cross the darkened smooth maria,

ridges, mountains, and valleys with no interruption. Where they stop suddenly, there is usually another crater at that point. While most rays are reasonably continuous, a few can be found which stop, start again in a few miles, stop, and start again.

(4) There are some "oversystems" of rays, notably the system of crossing rays from Copernicus, Kepler, and Aristarchus.

(5) Some rays do not emanate from exactly the center of a large crater, but are tangential to it.

(6) There are many examples of craters which have pronounced rays coming from one, two, or three directions only. More than one crater can be found with a single ray streaming from it.

(7) Many rays (e.g., from Copernicus) seem to end in a tiny white craterlet.

(8) Rays range in width up to ten miles.

(9) They appear to consist of dustlike particles which are perfectly spherical, judging by their appearance from all angles, and which cling to everything touched.

(10) They sem to have the same albedo (reflective quality) as white rocks from inside the Moon's crust.

Textbook Theories as to the Origin of Rays

Velikovsky, that insightful genius who confounded the orthodox scientists with his *Worlds in Collision,* was, of course, vilified in return. But he had the sense to admit that the rays were a mystery, and did not create an explanation merely to explain all phenomena within the context of existing knowledge. He said, "Bright streaks or 'rays' up to ten miles wide radiate from some of the craters; their origin, too, is not known."

All observers are not as cautious. *The Flammarion Book of Astronomy* supposedly put the matter to rest with these words: "When a crater is formed...dust is flung out in all directions. The particles describe long parabolic jets in the vacuum, their length being enhanced by the fact that the lunar force of gravity is 6 times smaller than on the Earth. They fall to the ground and form long rays diverging from the crater. The haloes of the fine recent craters Tycho and Copernicus can be seen in a small telescope; the rays are a fine white and stretch to considerable distances."

Fred Whipple, in *The Nature of the Moon* (3rd Edition, 1968), writing from the vantage point of more experience following several Moon probes, makes a statement which may be in accord with the old orthodoxy but clashes violently (as we shall shortly see) with the observations of the Apollo 12 astronauts: "The huge rays from the great new craters such as Tycho cannot, however, be explained by white dust alone.

The U.S. Ranger VII pictures have confirmed Kuiper's telescopic observation that the rays are rough and rocky. White rocks, such as appear in the Surveyor pictures, could cover the surface of the rays sufficiently to keep them relatively white for long periods of time until they were slowly covered by debris thrown from more distant parts of the Moon. Their increase in relative brightness at full Moon, however, requires further explanation."

The extent to which scientists will go to protect (a) the orthodoxy and (b) one another is astounding. Whipple's statement reveals his concern over the fact that dust from whatever sources is always falling on the Moon, and even if it is only a few particles a century over a given area, in time—and time is what the Moon has had plenty of-a surface whiteness would become obliterated. If you assume that the rays were caused by splash-out from meteoric impacts, or volcanic ash thrown up and out, or a whiteness showing through cracks in the Moon's surface resulting from alternate heating and freezing, then you must have an explanation for the fact that they still show white and get even whiter during a full Moon.

Suffice it to say, while a few astronomers have flatly

stated that they did not know the source of the rays, most have been content to accept the easy (but unscientific) explanation that splash-out from either meteorites or volcanic eruptions has been responsible.

Why Old Explanations for the Rays Cannot Be Correct

A meteorite hitting the Moon and making a crater would tend (unless it were a very oblique hit) to create a ray pattern all around the crater. There are as many craters which have only partial ray systems as there are those which are fully patterned.

An oblique hit by a meteorite would not create a single ray. The splash-out would be more general over the direction of flight.

Says George Leonard, "I have sketched below a few good examples of odd ray systems around some craters. These ray systems are not peculiar to small craters or to large craters; they occur in all sizes (e.g., craters of half-mile diameter on up to many miles in diameter).

"Another strong consideration not examined in the books I have read is that of overlapping ray systems; a new impact would, if this theory is the true explanation of rays, tend to partially obliterate another nearby ray system. But this is never the case. All rays seem to show up clearly, even in the case when three ray systems, from Copernicus, Kepler, and Aristarchus, overlap."[19]

One of the most striking arguments against the splash-out from meteorite or volcanic-ash theory is the fact that the rays do not always stream from the center or the main body of the crater, but sometimes from a point tangential to it. Dinsmore Alter in *Pictorial Guide to the Moon* (Crowell, 1967) writes:

A simultaneous study will show many peculiarities in the ray system of Copernicus. One is the fact that the major rays are not radial to Copernicus. The second is that in Mare Imbrium, north of the crater, there are many plume-shaped short rays which are radial to Copernicus. The points of the feathers are toward that crater. In a few cases a craterlet is observable on the pointed end of such an elementary ray and in nearly all cases a brightish spot can be seen there that can be assumed with some confidence to contain a craterlet. Examination of the two major rays extending northward into Mare Imbrium shows that they have a complex structure. Despite overlapping, there are places where this structure can be observed as composed of the elemental plume rays, which are radial although the complex rays are not.

∅∅∅

A NEW EXPLANATION FOR CRATER RAYS

So far we have see that evidence for intelligent, purposeful residents on the Moon exists. Artificial structures of various sizes and ages seem to be in evidence. There is evidence that the Moon has been occupied for an extremely long time

If mining operations, from Atlantis or some other solar system, are taking place on the Moon, then how do the occupants of the Moon move around? Don Wilson gives the following answer: Suppose they arrived on the Moon from another point in space by spaceship, perhaps powered by a means totally unknown to our scientists at the present time. By extension, they move from one point on the Moon to another by spaceship. In some of the photographs of the Moon there are objects which may well be these spaceships. They range in size from smaller than a football field (e.g., the objects seen in the small crater near where Ranger Seven impacted the Moon in 1964) to a mile or more in diameter (e.g.,the objects suspended from the side of the cliff in Tycho).

It is but one step now to the new explanation for crater rays. Flying objects on the Moon land at the bottom of big craters having a fine, powdery white dust at the bottom. They go back and forth to other craters, to deliver or to get a supply of something. The fine, powdery white dust sticks to the underbellies of the flying objects. As the flying objects vibrate above the ground, the dust gets shaken off. Because the flying objects have definite places to go, the dust tends to fall as straight rays along certain paths. In the case of

111

very busy craters, the occupants in the flying objects have many places to go in all directions. In the case of some quieter or more specialized craters, there may be interchange only between that crater and a single other point on the Moon—hence one single ray.

Says George Leonard, "I searched the NASA literature for reference to the rays and for new data on them. I talked with Dr. Farouk El-Baz, the geologist who had been so closely associated with the Apollo flights. He confirmed that the rays consisted of a fine white powdery dust or soil. He referred me to the preliminary scientific report from the Apollo 12 flight. This was a manned landing on the Moon."[19]

Says Leonard, "The material [at the ALSEP deployment site] appeared to be loose and fluffy and, according to Astronaut Bean, was difficult to compact by merely stepping and tramping on it [i.e., the material constituting one of the white rays of Copernicus]. The fine-grained surface material had a powdery appearance and was easily kicked free as the astronauts moved on the surface. During the Apollo 11 EVA [i.e., "extravehicular activity"], Astronauts Armstrong and Aldrin noted the ease with which fine-grained material was set in motion while they were walking on the lunar surface.

"The tendency of the loose, powdery surface material to move easily in the lunar vacuum and 1/6 gravity environment imposed operational problems that were augmented by the fact that the same material also exhibited adhesive characteristics that resulted in a tendency for the material to stick to any object with which it came into contact. As a consequence, equipment and spacesuits became coated, and housekeeping problems arose from the dust brought aboard the LM at the conclusion of EVA periods..."[19]

Fine-grained material adhered to the astronauts' boots and spacesuits, the television cable, the lunar equipment conveyor, ALSEP components, astronaut tools, sample return containers, the color chart, and the cameras and camera magazines... It appears that under the shirt-sleeve atmosphere (5 lbs. per square inch pressure) of the command module, the fine, dusty material lost its adhesive characteristics.

Those who hypothesized that the rays streaming from craters consisted partly of boulders were wrong. Those who guessed that the rays shone from cracks in the Moon's surface were wrong. The rays are simply a thin covering of white powdery soil which sticks to everything—including the underbellies of flying objects.

This explanation is totally in accord with the properties of the rays as we now know them. Flying objects would not necessarily emanate from or return to the center of a large crater. Flying objects may well make many stops in their travels—hence, "feathering" of the rays and streaks which sometimes connect two major rays.

The white streaks go right across rilles, ridges, valleys, mountains—as white dust falling from a flying object would. Raymond A. Lyttleton points out in *The Modern Universe* (Harper, 1956): "And there are the strange bright streaks, some ten miles or so broad, that extend out from many of the craters but have no perceptible shadow effects and must presumably be an extremely thin superficial phenomenon. They also run right across all other irregularities without any resulting change in color or width."

I think it is clear to the reader that crater material splashed out in an arching curve at time of impact or volcanic action might be terminated at a high mountain range; whereas a flying object, progressing in a generally straight line and shaking off white powder, will create a continuous ray much as we see crossing mountains and valleys alike.

The most convincing aspect of this new theory is that it accounts for the brightness of the rays after millions of years of space dust slowly accumulating on the Moon. The large craters, such as Tycho and Kepler and Copernicus, which have the largest ray systems, are probably, in Patrick Moore's words, "Pre-Cambrian [i.e., over five hundred million years old], in which they are at least as ancient as the oldest terrestrial fossils." They may perhaps be considerably older.

The Apollo 17 *Preliminary Science Report* infers from the data that "The time of formation of more than 90% of the cratering on the Moon was 4 billion years ago or earlier." The fact that the white powdery soil can be seen today with such brilliance can probably be attributed to a continuing process, that of countless trips made by many flying objects over countless years, rather than to an impact in the Pre-Cambrian or earlier times.

An interesting sidelight on the Apollo flights to the Moon—after several manned landings, thousands of photographs, samples of soil and rocks—is that the great mysteries of the Moon have come no closer to solution. We still do not know the origin of the Moon, the cause of the craters, the nature of its core. Fesenkov and Oparin in *Life in the Universe* (Twayne, 1961) write, "Despite the enormous development in the last decades no new explanation of the formations on the lunar surface has been advanced. The so-called meteorite theory of the formation of lunar craters, first proposed by Gruithuisen in 1824, is still seriously debated today."[19]

One can search the scientific reports of the Apollo flights in vain and still not find a serious inroad to these mysteries. Patrick Moore admitted in *A Survey of the Moon,* written prior to the manned Moon flights, that "The plain unwelcome truth is that we are still very much in the dark as to how the Moon's craters were formed."

In the same book he states clearly how much of a mystery the rays are: "The Moon is full of puzzles, but it is probably true to say that the most baffling problems of all are set by the bright rays. Not even the most casual observer can overlook them when the Moon is near full, but so far nobody has been able to find out precisely what they are." ∅

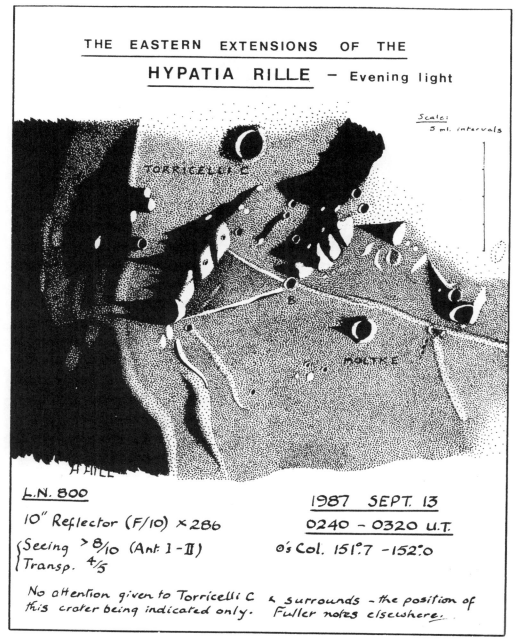

THE EASTERN EXTENSIONS OF THE

HYPATIA RILLE – Evening light

Scale:
5 ml. intervals

TORRICELLI C

B

MOLTKE

A HILL

L.N. 800

10" Reflector (F/10) × 286

{ Seeing > 8/10 (Ant. I - II)
{ Transp. 4/5

1987 SEPT. 13

0240 – 0320 U.T.

0's Col. 151°.7 – 152°.0

No attention given to Torricelli C & surrounds – the position of
this crater being indicated only. Fuller notes elsewhere.

British astronomer Howard Hill's drawing of the fascinating formations
located at the "Eastern Extensions of the Hypatia Rille." These mammoth
walls with their ravines are a baffling set of structures that demand close
attention. Is this the "Monument Valley" of the Moon?

MORETUS

Short

7¼" Spec. ×292

1966: December 4

Geoc Libr. (04ʰ) $\{ L = -2°.64$ $B = -6°.58$

$\{ Seeing. 5 – 6$ $Transp < 4$

03ʰ 15ᵐ to 05ʰ 00ᵐ U.T.

Colong. 167°.8 to 168°.7

1950: Feb 25

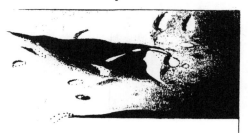

$\{ L = -6°.74$ $B = -6°.54$ Obs. protracted due to much cloud

1950: Feb 26

British Astronomer Howard Hill's drawings of the unusual pyramid in the crater of Moretus. At various times Hill believed he saw a central staircase and possible sand-dune movement around the pyramid.

unar Orbiter 5 recorded this evidence of objects moving on the Moon on the slope of the central peak of itello. In the upper half of this greatly enlarged tiny portion of the original frame, we see two "boulders" hich have rolled down the mountain from left to right. The larger one, just above the small dark crater, is out 75 feet across and sufficiently irregular to have left a conspicuous tread-marked path some 900 feet ng. It shines brightly and casts a long shadow into the crater. Near the upper border a 15-foot object with a angular shadow has left a weaving 1200-foot trail. George Leonard claimed that the upper object rolled up d out of a crater before rolling downhill to where it is seen in the photo. (NASA , VII Gassendi S 2.4)

View obtained by the Apollo 17 astronauts using a telephoto lens to photograph "boulders and boulder tracks on the North Massif at the Apollo 17 landing site. The largest object, making a weaving, tread-like track is about 5 meters across. Illumination is from the right. (NASA photo, AS17-144-21991)

Top: A Russian artist's impression of the Lunokhod 1 Lunar Rover built to move on the surface of the Moon in January, 1973.
Bottom: Moon researcher Fred Steckling's drawing of his impression of the mining vehicle that may be leaving tread-marks on the Moon.

A Rare "Black Eye" on the Back Side of the Moon. The crater Tsiol-kovsky, named after a Russian pioneer in rocketry, contains one of the rare deposits of dark mare material, probably basalt, on the back side of the moon. *(NASA Lunar Orbiter photograph III–121–M)*

NASA APOLLO 8 PHOTO of the Tsiolkowsky Crater on the back side of the Moon. Notice the large "lake" and smaller ones.

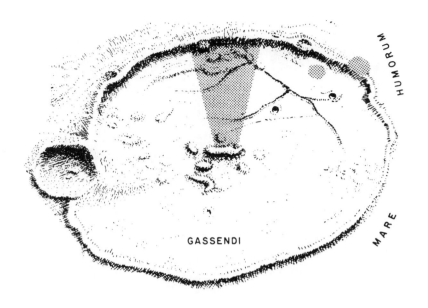

Transient lunar phenomena at Gassendi on April 30 and May 1, 1966.
Shaded areas mark the color phenomena seen to spread across the crater.

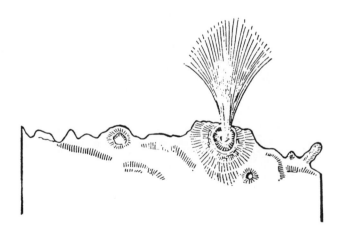

A drawing of a supposed lunar volcano erupting.

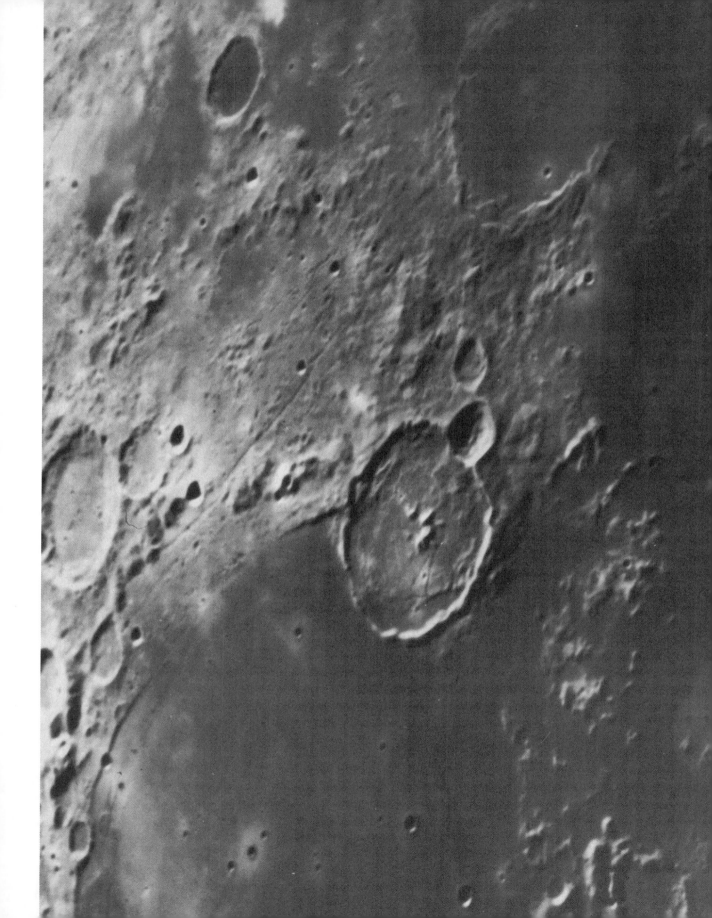

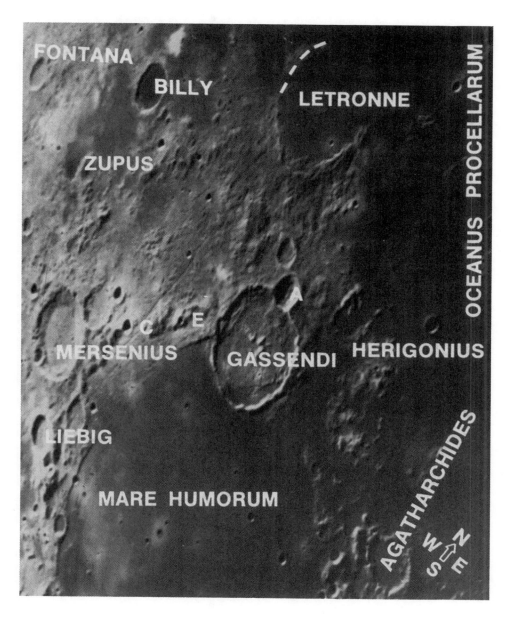

Left and Above: The crater Gassendi and nearby features. Gassendi has attracted Moonwatchers for centuries because of the lights often seen there. Features to note are the four "pyramids" in the middle of Gassendi Crater with the dark lines beneath them, the huge rectangular platform coming up to the crater's edge at site E, the cross near Zupus, and the structure at A in the top corner of Gassendi. At site C is a rille, road or canal. At the very top of the photo, above the crater Billy, is some sort of light phenomenon, possibly a reflecting pond or perhaps a cloud.

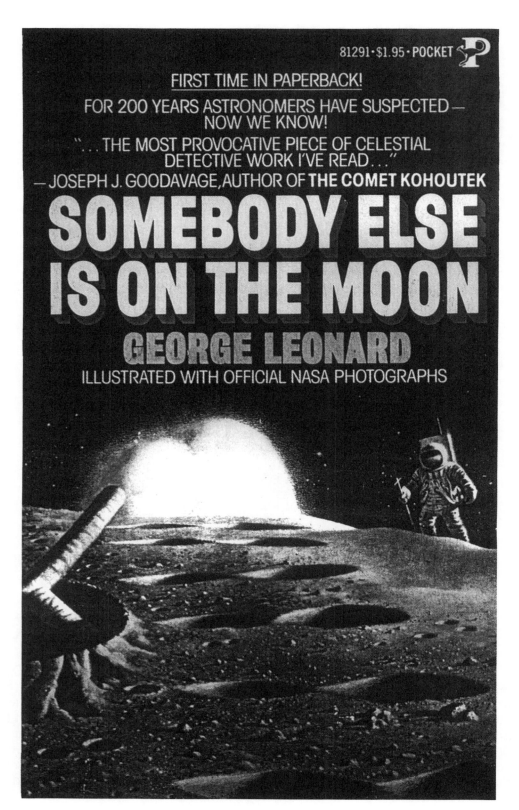

George Leonard's classic book about anomalous structures on the Moon.

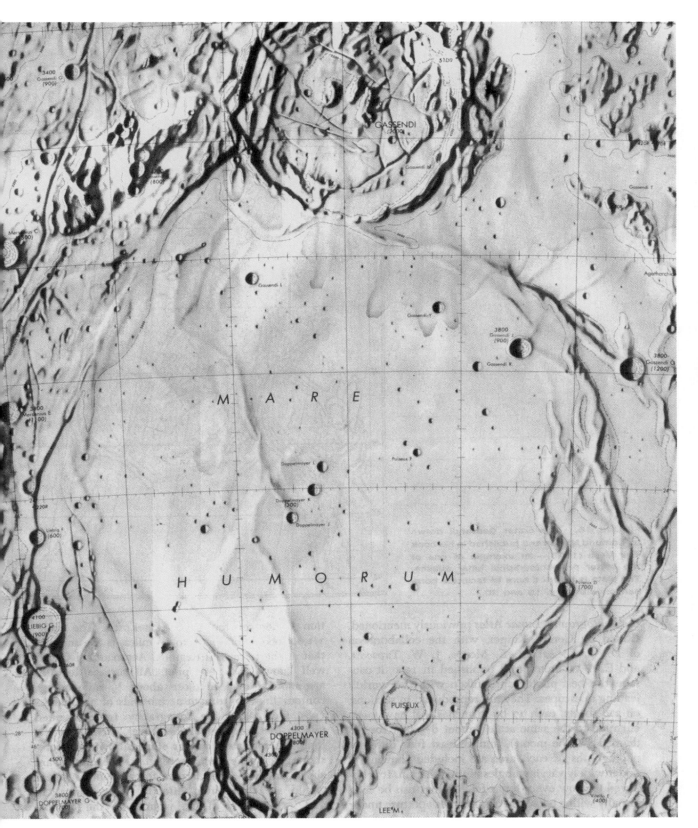

The crater Gassendi and the Mare Humorum in this NASA map.

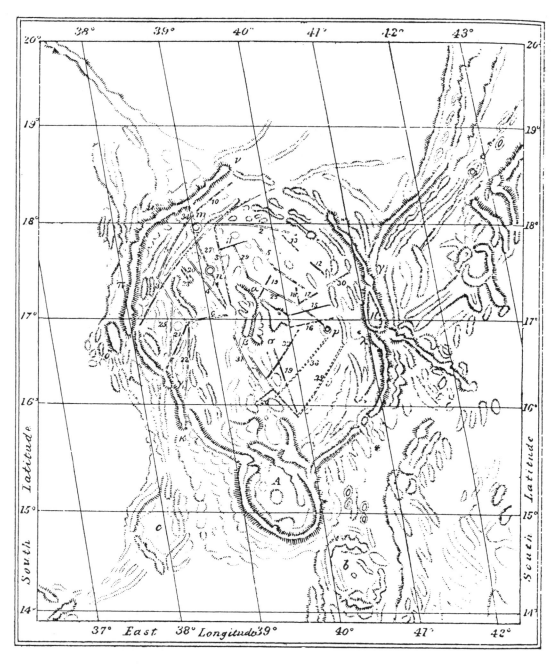

The crater Gassendi drawn in 1876 by Edmund Nelson for his book *The Moon*.
Like other astonomers and mappers of the Moon, Nelson took great interest in
Gassendi and saw structures in the central crater.

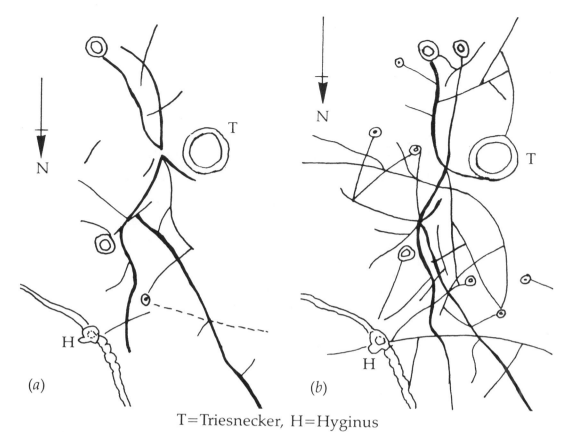

T=Triesnecker, H=Hyginus

Lines and unusual features in the Gassendi Crater.

Gassendi clefts. (a) *Neison's chart,* (b) *Fauth's chart*

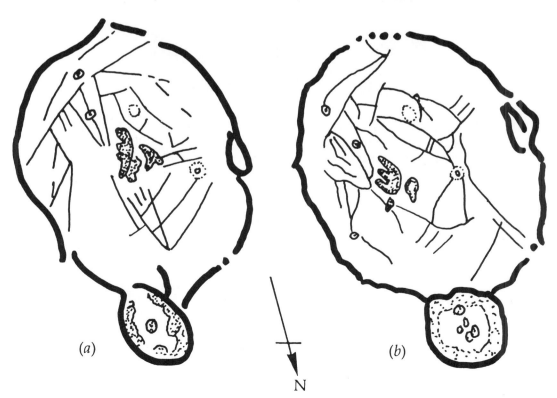

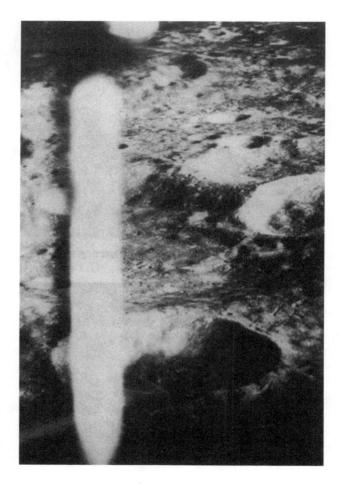

NASA Apollo 16 Hasselblad photo of a cigar-shaped object between the Moon and the camera. Compare this photo to that in the chapter on Phobos. NASA Photo 16-19238.

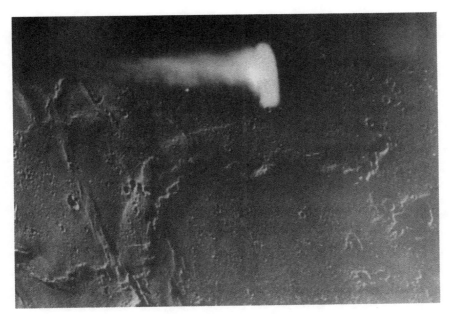

APOLLO 11 PHOTO OF GLOWING CIGAR-SHAPED OBJECT CLOSE TO THE
MOON. NASA No. 11-37-5438.

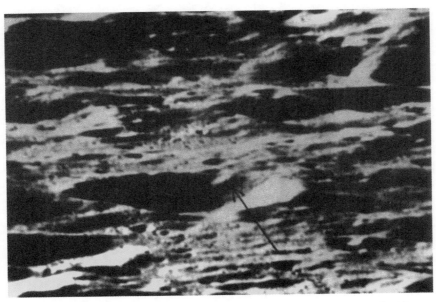

(Area Blow-up) OVAL OBJECT INSIDE THE LARGE CRATER. Apollo 16
Photo No. 16-18918.

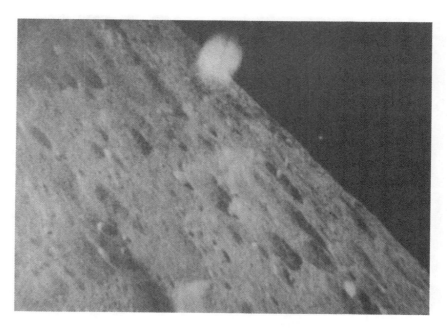

APOLLO 13 PHOTO OF UFO ON THE MOON. NASA No. AS 13-60-8609.

STRANGE WHITE AERIAL OBJECT HIGH OVER THE LUNAR SURFACE. As photographed by Apollo 12. NASA NO. AS 12-51-7553.

Photos and captions courtesy of Fred Steckling.

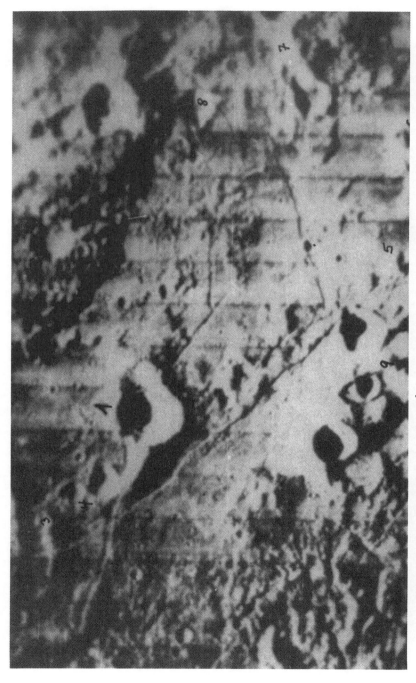

NASA LUNAR ORBITER IV PHOTO No. 161. Southeast of the Crater Damoiseau. (1. Damoiseau D.) (2. Damoiseau) (3. Smoke pillar drifting from west to east.) (4. Clouds over the crater's edge.) (5. Long platform entering hangar.) (6 and 7. Constructions) (8. Large platform extending over riverbed.) (9. More platforms).

Photo courtesy of Fred Steckling

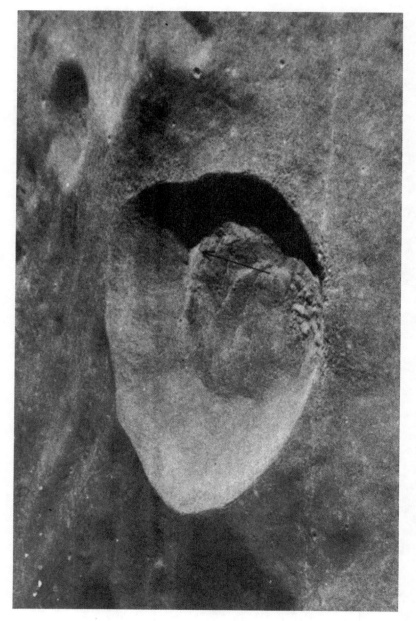

APOLLO 8 PHOTO OF THE HIDDEN SIDE OF THE MOON. Notice white cross on the crater bottom at one o'clock. This crater has not been named.

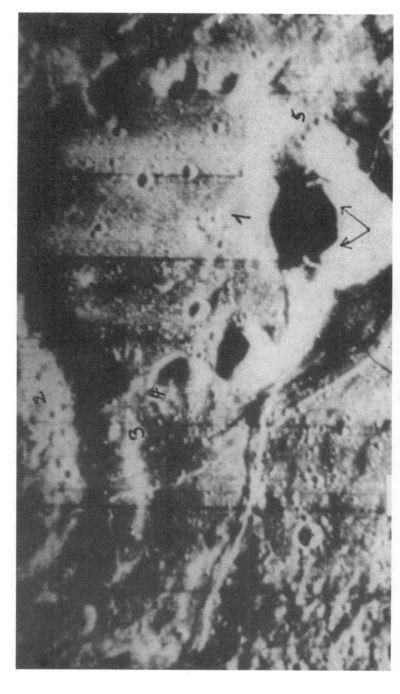

NASA LO. IV. Blow-up of Plate 74. No. 161⌐. Now notice 2 double walls, right and left, in the Crater Damoiseau D. Also notice the riverbed flowing from N.W. to S.E. right through the Crater Damoiseau No. 1.
No. 3 – The smoke pillar.   No. 4 – The cloud over crater's edge.
No. 5 – Is this crater a reservoir dammed up? Count 5 evenly spaced constructions, much like pump stations.

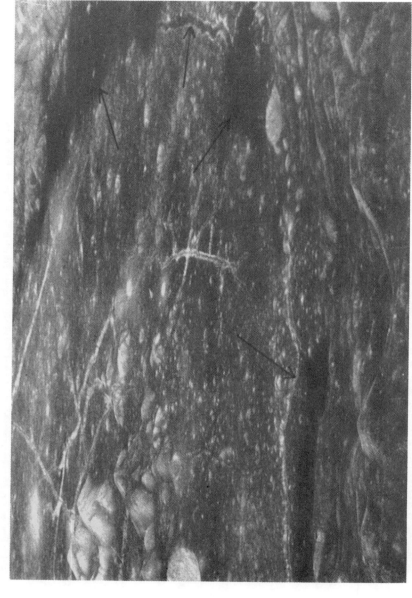

NASA APOLLO 12 PHOTO No. 12-7419. The Crater Humboldt and area. Notice dark patches which look muc like vegetation. Also the dark riverbed between these patches.

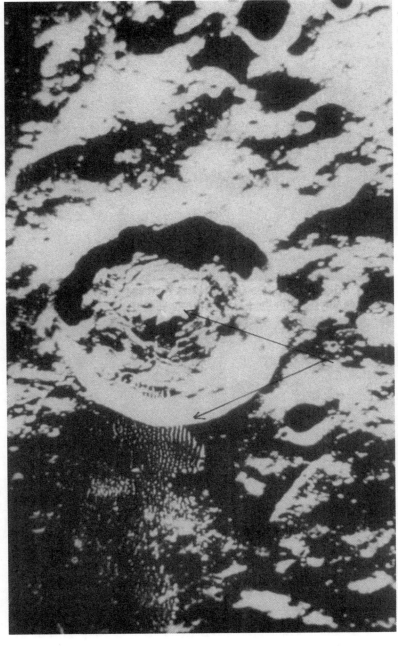

(Area Blow-up) THE CRATER "VITELLO." NASA Lunar Orbiter V. No. MR 168. Notice Macklel type clouds left of "Vitello." Also notice platform in center of the crater.

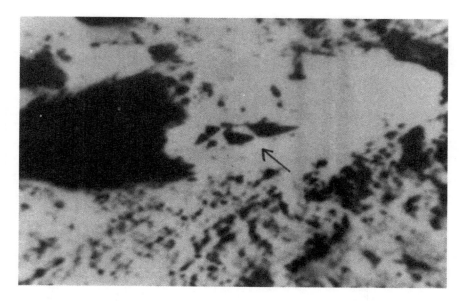

(Area Blow-up) DID APOLLO 16 PHOTOGRAPH PYRAMIDS ON THE MOON? On the bottom of this crater there seem to be 3 of them.

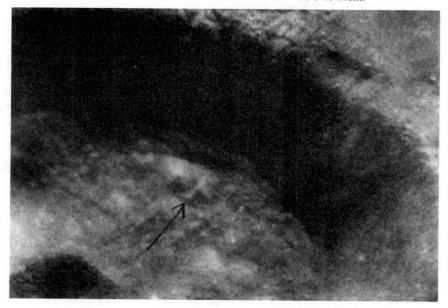

(Area Blow-up) THIS APOLLO 8 PHOTOGRAPH No. 8-17-2704 shows two pyramid-shaped constructions on the moon.

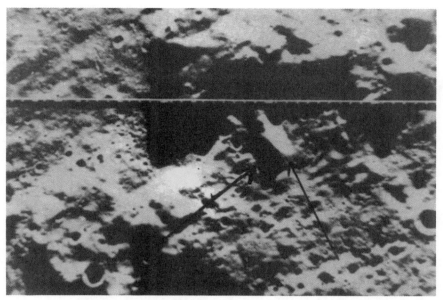

LARGE PLATFORM SOUTH OF THE CRATER ARCHIMEDES. Reported by Mr. Darling. Platform size–5 miles long, 1 mile wide. Elevation–5,000 feet AGL.

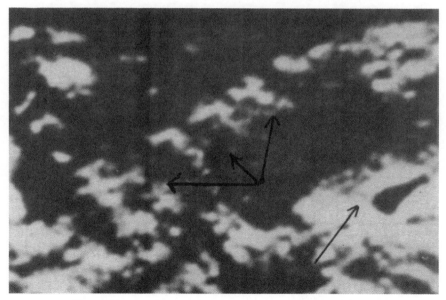

THIRTY MILES OF PLATFORMS CARVED INTO THE MOUNTAIN TOP. South of Archimedes. Each platform seems to represent a letter or symbol. Also notice large construction in the valley below.

Photos and captions courtesy of Fred Steckling.

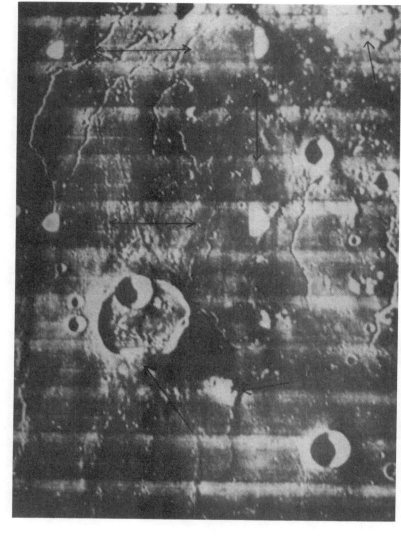

(Area Blow-up) No. 151-3. NASA LUNAR ORBITER IV PHOTO of the crater "Krieger" and area. To the right of "Krieger" notice five triangular white pond-like constructions reflecting the sunlight. Also notice clouds on the edge of "Krieger" as well as 50 Km. southwest of the crater.

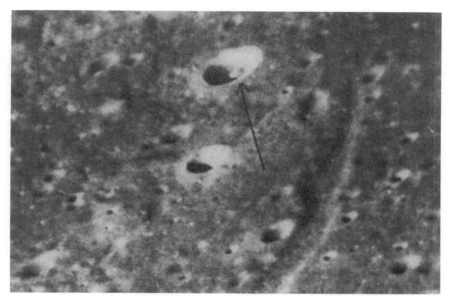

(Area Blow-up) APOLLO 14 Photo No. 14-10116 showing white dome in crater.

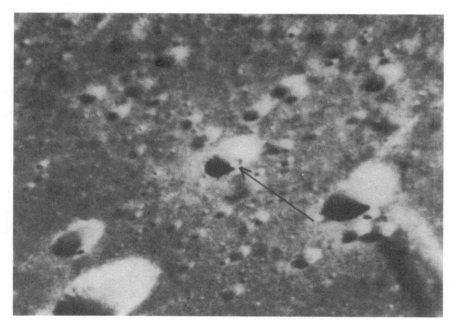

(Area Blow-up) APOLLO 14 Photo No. 14-10116 "Another Dome."

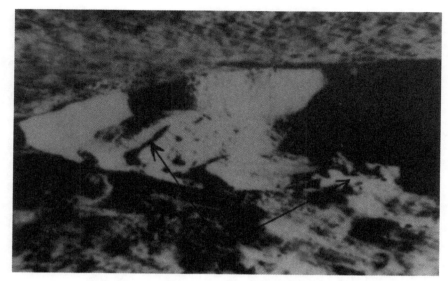

(Area Blow-up) CLOSEUP OF THE CRATER KEPLER IN OCEANUS PRO-
CELLARUM. Notice 3 domes (like large radar domes) located at the crater's rim
to the right of photo. NASA Lunar Orbiter III Photo No. 67-H-201. Also
notice left crater ridge which seems to have been cut or worked on. Kepler
is 20 miles in diameter.

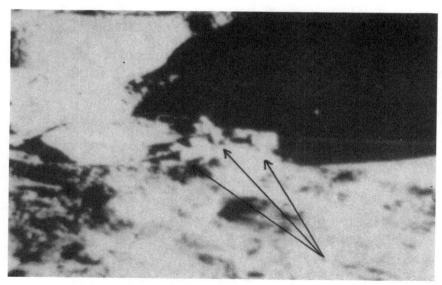

(Area Blow-up) THE THREE DOMES CLOSE UP IN THE CENTER OF
KEPLER. Actually located on a large platform at the crater rim. NASA Lunar
Orbiter III No. 67-H-201.

LUNAR ORBITER III PHOTO No. 6H. Showing smoke rising from the bottom of a crater. Also notice white dome inside crater to the N.W.

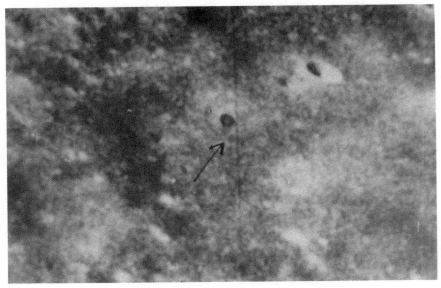

(Area Blow-up) APOLLO 16 No. 16-19386. This photo shows a small pond with an island on the bottom of a shallow crater. Notice the long spiraled pipe run from south to north just by the pond's edge. Are they using the Archimedes screw principal?

LUNAR ORBITER V NASA No. HR 181⊥. Unnamed crater on the Moon's hidden side. Notice from 1 to 12, all seem to be platforms or constructions. Notice objects on platform No. 9. Also notice step-shaped platform No. 12.

Photo courtesy of Fred Steckling

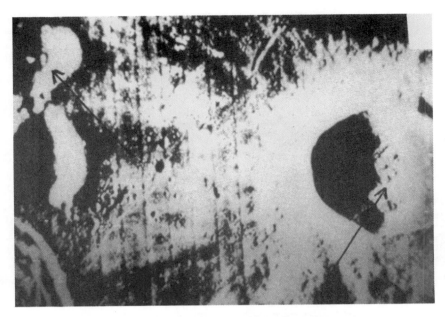

NASA LO IV PHOTO No. MR 81. The Crater Ritter and Ritter C and
D. Notice 2 dome-shaped objects in Ritter and 2 glowing objects in Ritter C.

NASA LO IV PHOTO No. HR 86$\frac{3}{}$. The Crater Posidonius. Notice 2
oval-shaped objects on the bottom of the crater and clouds to the N.W.
covering the big cleft.

Photos and captions courtesy of Fred Steckling.

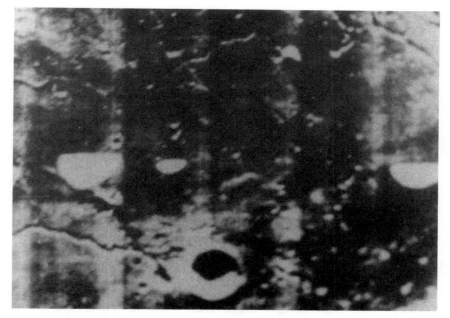

Top: Two artificial-looking installations can be seen in these blow-ups of Lunar Orbiter IV Photo No. HR157 [1] of an area west of the crater Aristarchus. The crater is perfectly shaped and the "hangar" next to it is about 25 miles long. **Bottom:** Possible reservoirs of water on the Moon, reflecting sunlight. In the same area west of crater Aristarchus. Photo No. HR151 [2] LO IV.

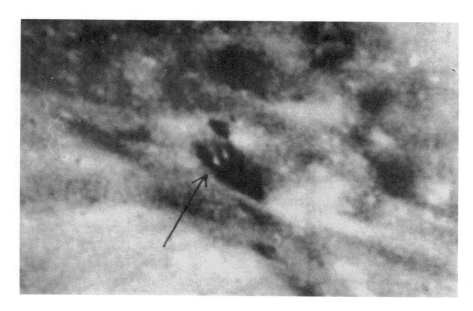

(Area Blow-up) TWO OBJECTS OR CONSTRUCTIONS INSIDE THIS CRATER
TAKEN BY APOLLO 16. No. 16-19386.

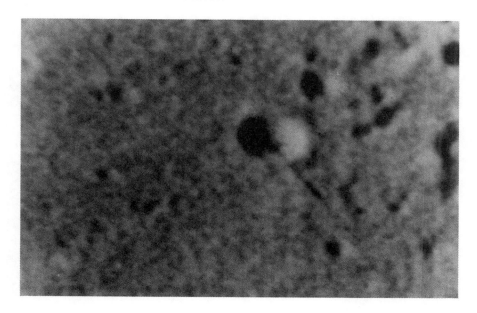

(Area Blow-up) APOLLO 15 PHOTO. LONG TUBE EXTENDING OUT OF A
CRATER.

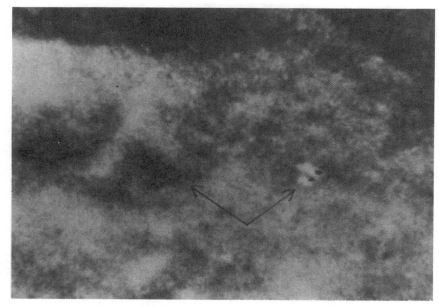

(Area Blow-up) THE SAME 3 FACED PYRAMID-SHAPED CONSTRUCTIONS 14 TIMES ENLARGED. Also notice two dark objects parked on the arrowhead-shaped clearing.

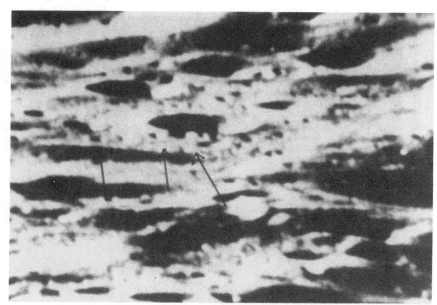

(Area Blow-up) CONSTRUCTIONS MUCH LIKE LARGE TANKS OR TOWERS CAN BE SEEN ON THIS APOLLO 16 PHOTO No. 16-18918.

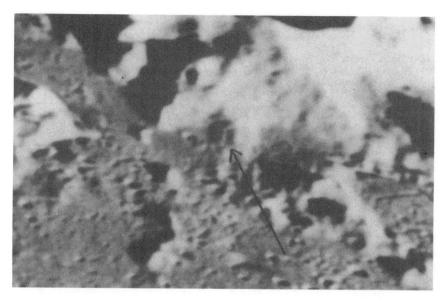

(Area Blow-up) APOLLO 10 PHOTO No. 10-32-4810. 80 miles north
of Triesnecker. Notice the cathedral-like entrance cut into this mountain.

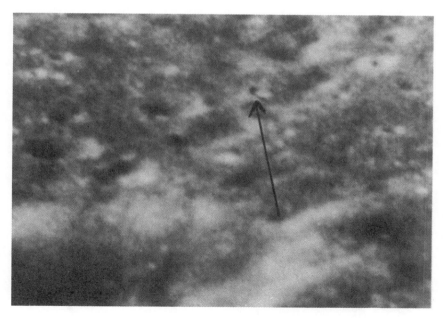

(Area Blow-up) APOLLO 16 PHOTO OF WHITE LONG OBJECT HALF
WAY STICKING OUT OF A CRATER. NASA No. 16-19386.

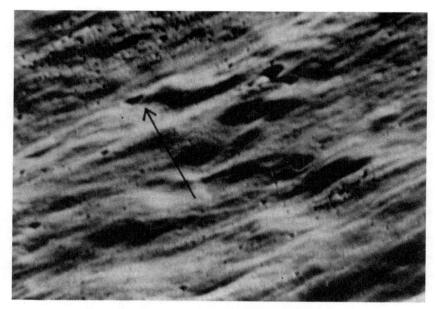

(Area Blow-up) NASA APOLLO PHOTO 16-19273. N.E. of the King Crater. Notice dust blowing out of crater upper left. "Who is mining the Moon?"

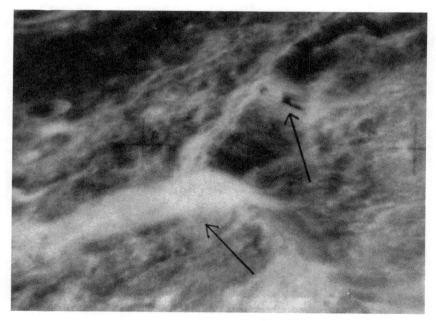

(Area Blow-up) LARGE LOW CLOUD BANK hugging the crater's edge of the Lobachavsky crater on this Apollo 16 No. 16-758 photo. Also notice large oval object on the crater's edge casing a shadow.

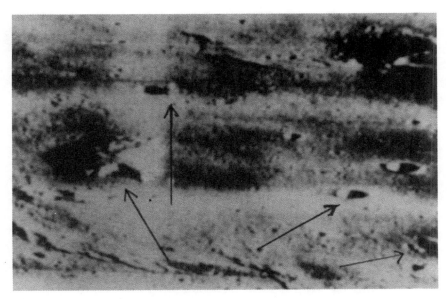

(Area Blow-up) NASA Lunar Orbiter II Photo No. MR 213. Notice hill, left of center, has been cut out like a piece out of a cake. Above the hill, notice large radar-type dome casting a shadow to the left. To the right of photo also notice several perfectly cut holes (or craters?) and two oval objects.

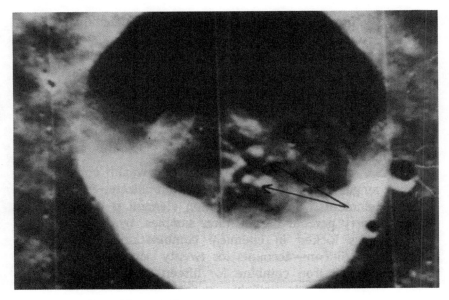

(Area Blow-up) Two Domes on the Crater Floor. NASA photo Lunar Orbiter IV. No. 168-H3 "Lunar Backside."

Photos and captions courtesy of Fred Steckling.

In this blow-up from an APOLLO 8 photo (no number given) the arrow points to three rows, or terraces, which Steckling believes have been done artificially.

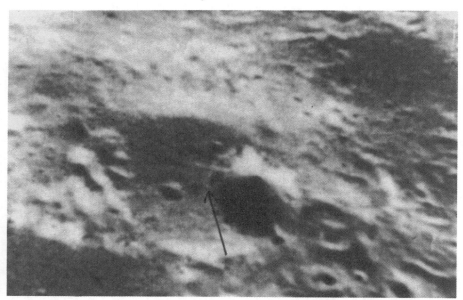

(Area Blow-up) APOLLO 16 PHOTO, KING CRATER AREA. Cross at the edge of the center Crater No. 16-19228.

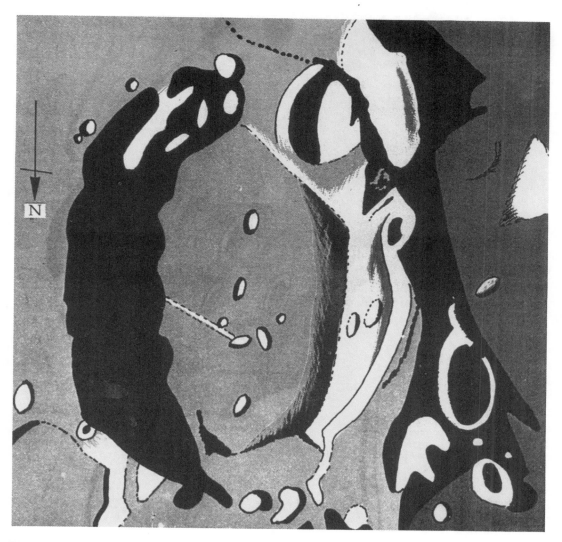

Unusual "pipe-line" object observed by F.W. Price in the crater Mersenius on April 9, 1968. (Eight-inch refractor, Buffalo Museum of Science, NY.)

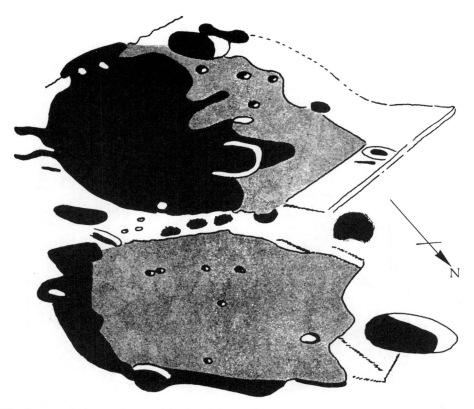

Platform constructions observed by F.W. Price on the northern side of the craters Klaproth and Casatus on March 2, 1966. (Eight-inch refractor, Buffalo Museum of Science, NY.)

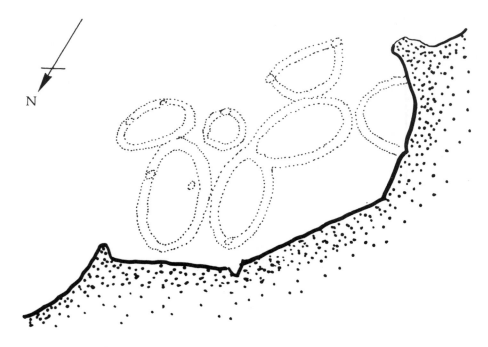

So called "Ghost" rings in Sinus Iridum, redrawn after W. Goodacre.

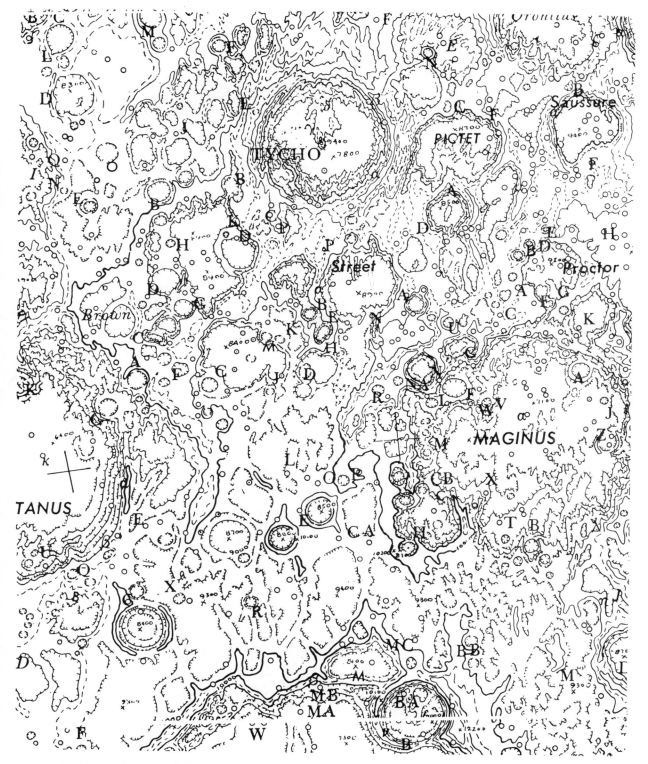

An interesting map of the Tycho area of the Moon. This is a sample of the lunar maps produced by the Army Map Service.

THE MOON THE MOON THE MOON

VOLUME 5. No.2.

DECEMBER 1956.

VOL 6. No 1

OCTOBER 1957

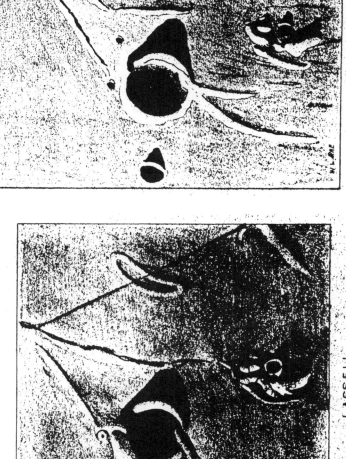

LASSELL AND SURROUNDING AREA
8¼-inch Refl.
W. L. Rae.

LASSELL 8½" Refl. x 340
1886 JANUARY 15. T.G.Elger.

The British journal *The Moon* featured several stories on the straight line that is seen to cross the ovoid crater to the right of both drawings. What is curious is whether this might be the shadow of something else, or is a "ditch" crossing this portion of the Moon.

L.N. 767

LOHRMANN

Not depicted.

E

W

(I.A.U)

CAVALERIUS

HEVELIUS
AND ENVIRONS

1985 : January 4
2140 - 2330 U.T.
⊙'s Col. 68°·46 - 69°·38

for
24h. $\begin{cases} l = -5°·23 \\ b = -2°·54 \end{cases}$ Geoc.
Libr

10" Reflector × 286

$\begin{cases} \text{Seeing. var. } 6\text{-}\frac{8}{10} \text{ (Ant. II)} \\ \text{Transp. } \frac{4}{5} \end{cases}$

A composite drawing based upon two separate observations.
The first covered the upper L.H. part of the frame from Lohrmann A
northwards and westward to Lohrmann (2140 -2210 U.T.) and then
the interior and inner wall details of Hevelius (2215 -2330).

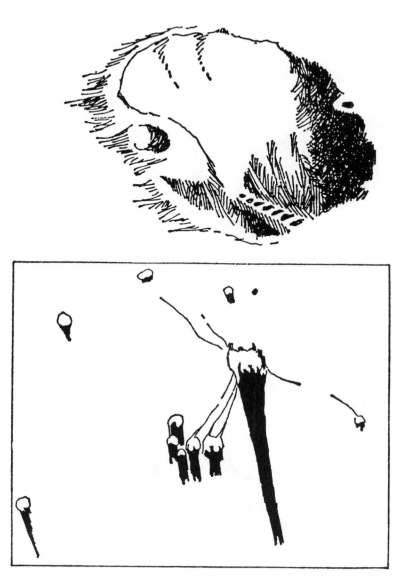

Top: A George Leonard drawing of the "Giant Ladder" that descends into the "bottomless" crater on the opposite page. **Opposite:** The bottomless crater on the Moon, mentioned on pages 105-106 and pages 114-115, can be seen on the lower portions of the photo. This is NASA photo #67-H-327, discussed on page 106—a half-mile-wide hole with a "colossal skyscraper size object of manufactured appearance." **Bottom:** Leonard's drawing of the famous alignment of obelisks, called the "Blair Cuspids" showing seven tall, pointed objects, like obelisks, casting long shadows. Leonard says he drew this from NASA frame 67-H-758.

Top: A George Leonard drawing of constructions in the Tycho area of the Moon. **Bottom:** More structures in the Tycho area according to Leonard. Compare the top photo with that of the installation on Mars taken by the Phobos 2 space probe.

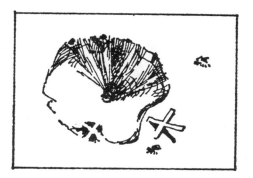 

Top: (left) A George Leonard drawing of an X-drone near a crater on the Moon. (right) Leonard's drawing of spray coming out of a crater. **Bottom:** Leonard's concept of one of the automated mining drones that he believes is scooping up Moon soil, processing the valuable metals, and discarding the waste.

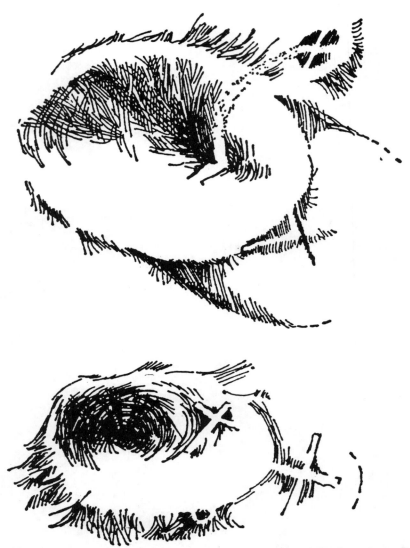

Top & Bottom: A George Leonard's drawings of X-drones and crosses in various crosses as described in his book, Somebody Else Is On the Moon. He claims to has seen them in photos of Tycho, the Alpine Valley, Mare Crisum, Plato and others.

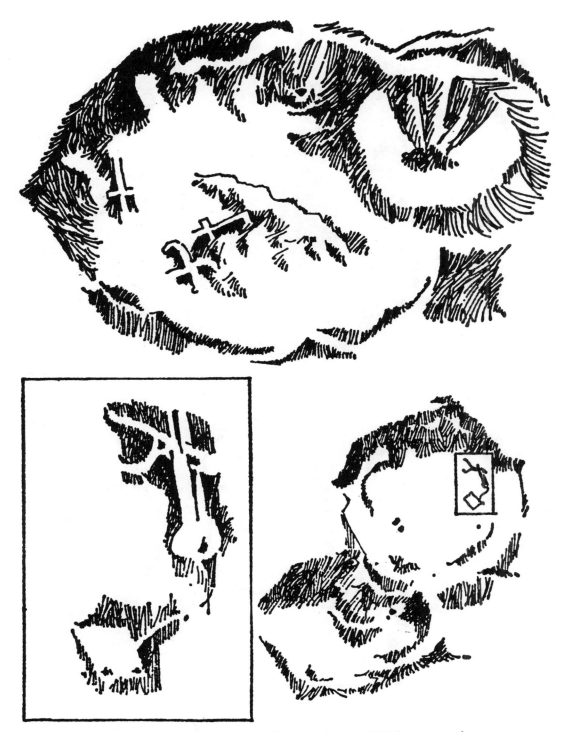

Top & Bottom: A George Leonard's drawings of X-drones and crosses in various crosses as described in his book, Somebody Else Is On the Moon. He claims to has seen them in photos of Tycho, the Alpine Valley, Mare Crisum, Plato and others.

Top: George Leonard's drawings of the huge constructions in the Bullialdus area the Moon. (NASA photo 72-H-1387) **Bottom:** Leonard draws various anomalous craters that he thinks are part of the "Super-Rig" Construction of the Moon—his belief that the Moon is an artificial satellite.

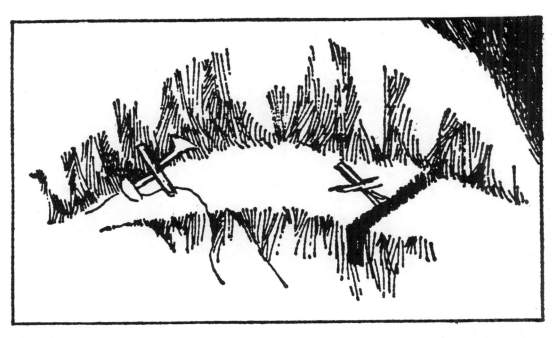

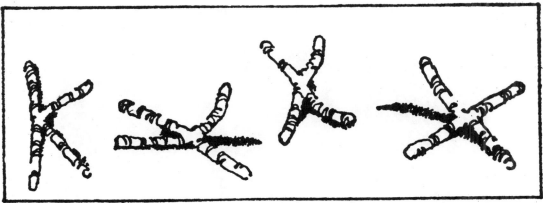

Top and Middle: George Leonard's drawings of the huge "X-Drones" that he said moved about the Moon. **Bottom:** George Leonard's drawings of how the Moon has been "stitched-up" or as possible bridges across chasms.

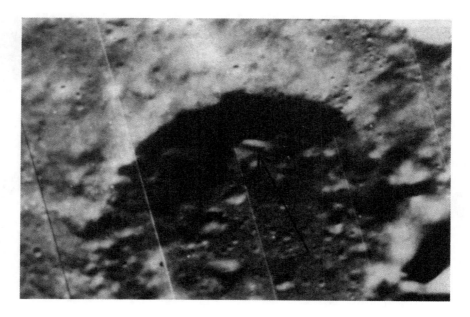

Top & Bottom: A Lunar Orbiter IV photo (No. LO Iv 89-H-3) of a white, reflecting cigar-shaped object near the crater Romer. Courtesy of Fred Steckling.

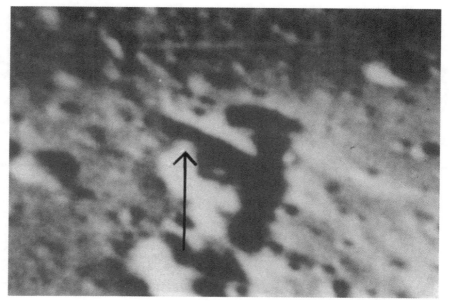

Photos courtesy of Fred Steckling

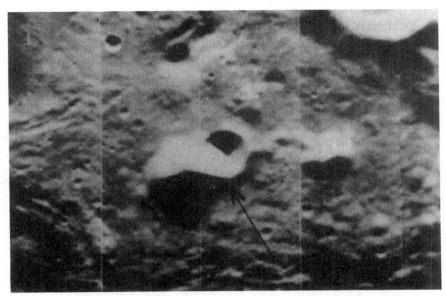

(Area Blow-up) NASA LO IV Photo No. 187H2. The Alpine Valley area of the Moon. Notice large cloudlike object covering half of the central crater.

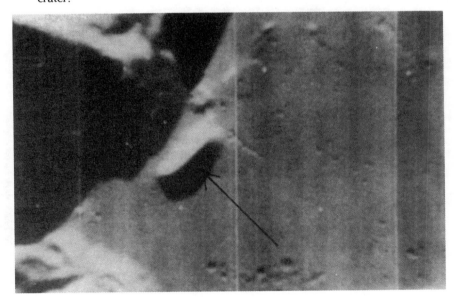

NASA LO IV No. 187H2. Showing large cigar-shaped cloud or object.

Photos and captions courtesy of Fred Steckling.

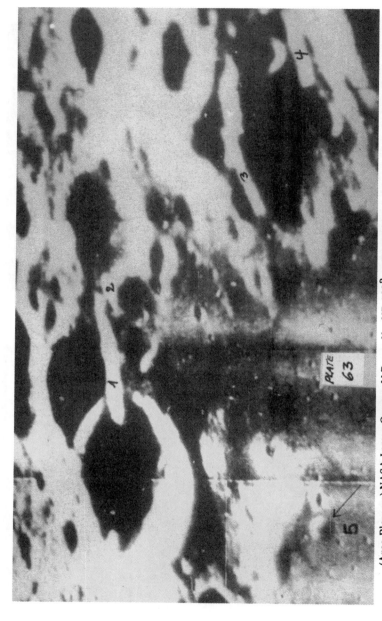

(Area Blow-up) NASA LUNAR ORBITER V PHOTO No. HR 1033. "Mare Moscovience" on the Moon's back side. Notice:
No. 1 A large cloud handing over crater rim.
No. 2 A tadpole-shaped object next to it.
No. 3 and 4 Cigar-shaped airborne objects.
No. 5 A very large dome.

— THE LICETUS–HERACLITUS REGION —

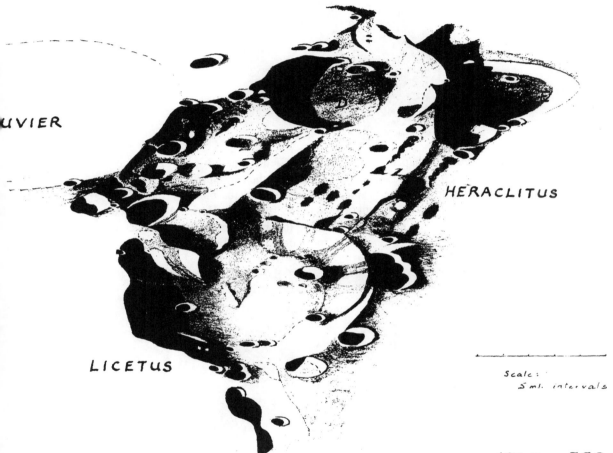

UVIER

HERACLITUS

LICETUS

Scale:
5 mi. intervals

1960 : FEB. 5

{ 0600 – 0705 hrs. G.M.A.T.
{ 0850 – 1000 hrs. G.M.A.T.

O's Sel. Colong. { 9°.9 – 10°.4
{ 11°.3 – 11°.9

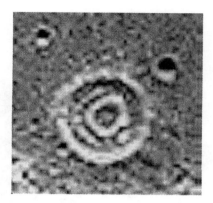

This unusual donut-shaped crater is found in Clementine orbit 150, in images lue5227o_150.gif and lue5228o_150.gif. Notice the symmetrical objects that flank the opening on the left side of the crater, and the bullseye-like inner crater, which contains two bright objects in the lower part. Here is a processed image of the full frame made by combining the high and low gain images to form a composite in order to preserve more detail in the bright areas.

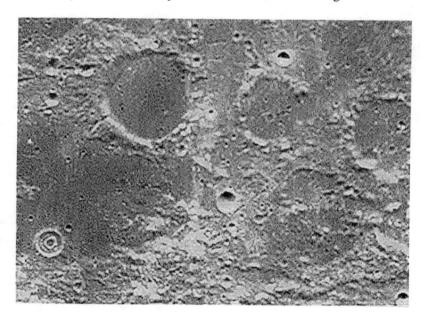

Chapter 5

The Search For Life On Mars

Of the many spectacular achievements of the
Mariner 9 mission, none was more surprising than
the discovery of channels on the Martian surface.
— Michael H. Carr
The Surface of Mars

With its polar ice caps and other features, Mars remains
more Earth-like than any of the other planets in our solar
system. However, at first glance, it is a freezingly cold, barren,
crater-strewn and windswept world, just over half the size of
Earth, some 4,230 miles in diameter—Earth is 7,926 miles. Its
days are 24 hours, 37 minutes long. Like Earth, Mars has
seasonal changes. Clouds come and go and morning fog covers
the floors of some major craters, but the atmosphere is mostly
carbon dioxide. Fierce dust storms rage, fanned by 300 miles-
per-hour winds. The temperature starts at way below freezing,
and seldom goes above it—although the polar ice caps are seen
to advantage and retreat seasonally.

Some of the more breathtaking features of the surface of
Mars include views of such imposing features as the Valles
Marineris, the so-called Grand Canyon of Mars, the largest
natural feature in our solar system, 250 miles across on
average, and stretching from end to end some 3,100 miles, the
distance from San Francisco to New York. Although Mars is
now a dry, hot and dusty planet, there is indisputable evidence
of vast previous water flow that cut immense canyons, flowed
around island features, and left still visible shorelines.
Possibly the most striking of all the singular natural
formations on Mars is the magnificent volcano Olympus
Mons, which is about 75-100 times greater than the biggest

volcano on Earth—Mauna Loa in Hawaii—and the largest mountain yet observed in our solar system. There are also great ice cliffs in the north polar region at the edge of the polar ice cap, which consists of water ice and not frozen carbon dioxide. Any conventional tour of Mars would take one through these mentioned wonders and more, and probably end with a view of the spectacular Martian sunset.

In 1877 the debate on Martian canals and their origins began in the scientific press with the first publication of Schiaparelli and his maps. Below is an article published in 1889 in the British astronomical journal, *Sidereal Messenger:*

MARS AND HIS CANALS
by H.C. Wilson. *Sidereal Messenger.*(8:13-25, 1889.)

Up to 1877 the observers appear to have confined themselves chiefly to delineating the outlines and variation of tint of the dark areas which immediately strike the eye when one examines the disc of Mars with a telescope of sufficient power, and to have neglected to examine carefully and persistently the bright reddish areas. During the opposition of 1877, which was exceptionally favorable, Mars being at its nearest approach to the sun and to the earth at the same time, M. Schiaparelli, the director of the Observatory at Milan, had the happy inspiration to concentrate his attention upon the great brilliant areas of the continents, in order to study their minutest details. He was rewarded by a brilliant discovery, of details so numerous and surprising in character that many astronomers are still, after the lapse of twelve years, incredulous of their reality. It was no less than a perfect network of very narrow dark lines, mostly straight, running across the continents in all directions, connecting the seas. To these Professor Schiaparelli gave the name of "canals," because, I suppose, of their straightness and from the fact of their connecting the seas.

In 1879 he again saw the canals of 1877 and several new ones. No one else was able to see them, although many observers were provided with more powerful telescopes. Two or three saw some narrow markings on the planet, but it was not certain that these were the same that Schiaparelli had seen.

During the opposition of 1881-2 Schiaparelli, following up his wonderful discoveries, struck a last blow to the confidence of the astronomers who hesitated to follow him; this time the canals appeared almost all to be double. A new canal appeared beside the old one, rigorously parallel in most cases, and starting, not from the same point of origin as if the old canal were simply divided into two component canals, but from a different point, as if a new canal had really been formed parallel to the first.

I have prepared a copy of a chart of Mars constructed by Professor Schiaparelli, from his observations made in 1882 and 1886, upon which you can see the network of fine lines, the canals, crossing the continents from sea to sea in all directions. They are somewhat exaggerated in distinctness in the drawing, so that you may see them with ease. This chart is upon what is called Mercator's projection, the regions near the poles being distorted out of all proportion, but the equatorial regions represented accurately.

Will you compare the lines of the chart with Schiaparelli's own words of description:

Schiaparelli's Own description of the canals:

"These lines [the so-called canals] run from one to another of the dark spots of Mars usually called seas, and form a very well-marked network over the bright part of the surface. Their arrangement seems constant and permanent (at least so far as can be judged by the observations of four and one-half years); but their appearance and the degree of their visibility is not always the same, depending on circumstances which we cannot at present discuss with full certainty. In 1879 many appeared which had not been seen in 1877 and in 1881-1882 all those which had been seen the first time were re-discovered, and other new lines as well. Their number could not be estimated as less than 60. Sometimes these lines or canals show themselves under the form of diffused and indistinct shading; at other times they appear as very definite and precise markings of uniform tone, as if they had been drawn with a pen. In most instances their curvature differs very little from a great circle, if indeed it does differ; some others however are much curved. The breadth of the finest can hardly be estimated at less than 2° [70 miles] of a great circle but in some cases it reaches to about 4 o. As to the length, that of the shortest is certainly less than 10 o, others extend to 70 o and 80 o. The color is sometimes as dark as in the seas of Mars, but often it is brighter. Each canal terminates at its two extremities either in a sea or in another canal. I know of no instance where one end remains isolated in the midst of one of the bright areas of the surface without resting on lines and dark spaces.

"Now in many of these lines it has fallen to me to observe the curious and unexpected circumstance of a doubling or reduplication; this happens in the following manner: To the right or left of a pre-existing line, which suffers no change from its previous direction or position, another line appears, nearly equal to the first and parallel to it; in some instances a slight difference of appearance being visible and sometimes also a slight divergence of direction. The distances between the pairs of lines formed in this manner varies from 6 o to 12 o of a great circle; there were also other lines which I suspected to be doubled, but the distance being less than 5 o or 6 o the telescope did not succeed in resolving them, and showed in that place a large, broad, and somewhat confused stripe. Sometimes a line is divided by another which intersects it into two districts or sections of unequal darkness and extent; in this case the companion line is divided into two sections in the very same way, with one exception no sensible irregularity of direction or of shape could be ascertained with the power used in these observations, which was always one of 417. Some of the pairs show so great a regularity that one would say that they were systems of parallel lines drawn by rule and compass. Perhaps however this regularity will not resist the use of a high magnifying power. In various instances, pairs are so connected the one with the other as to form a polygon of double lines with very pronounced angles, and such a series then occupies a great space. Two pairs sometimes cut each other without being interrupted; meeting then three by three they form at the points of triple intersection a network of which our telescope could only give an exact and complete resolution in one or two cases.

"Excluding those cases not well ascertained through the inability of the instrument to resolve objects so minute, the number of reduplications I observed in the last opposition is 20, of which 17 had been established in the course of one month, from January 19 to February 19, the mean date corresponding very nearly to the end of the second month after the vernal equinox of the planet. The phenomenon seems to be confined to a definite epoch, and it appears as if it took place simultaneously over the whole planet's surface occupied by the bright areas. No trace could be ascertained in 1877 during the weeks which preceded or immediately followed the southern solstice of the planet.

Only one isolated case presented itself in 1879, between December 24 and 26, and this was exactly reproduced under similar circumstances between January 11 and 12, 1882; it took place in the two lines named Nile I and Nile II on my chart of 1879. Both of these two epochs being close to the vernal equinox of Mars there is ground for believing that the phenomena of reduplication may be periodical, and perhaps connected with the position of the sun with respect to the axis of rotation of the planet." **End Schiaparelli's description.**

When Schiaparelli's chart for 1882 was published it was received with incredulity and almost ridicule, by many. This was due in part no doubt to a fault in the engraving of the chart, which made the lines of the canals and the outlines of all the markings of the planet hard and unnatural, quite unlike the actual appearance in the telescope. But if you will compare the two charts you will see how difficult it is to reconcile the features of the one with those of the other. The different method of projection and the addition of so many new features, all exaggerated in distinctness, renders the whole aspect unfamiliar. Yet if one will start with a prominent marking as, for instance, Kaiser Sea (Syrtis Major), and follow the coast lines, he will find nearly every feature of the Proctor chart upon that of Schiaparelli and in its proper place. Perhaps the greatest differences apply to the long narrow inlets of Nasmyth, Bessel and Huggins. These are replaced on Schiaparelli's chart by narrow canals or pairs of canals (Protonibus, Ceraunus, Iris and Gigas). In fact if we examine the original drawings of Dawes we find that the appearance of these features corresponds very much more closely with the chart of Schiaparelli than with that of Proctor.

Up to 1886 no certain confirmation of the duplication of the canals or of their existence was obtained by any other astronomer, but in that year Professor Perrotin of the Observatory of Nice, succeeded with a 15-inch telescope in detecting fifteen of them, and witnessed also the duplication of several. It will give one an idea of the difficulty of seeing these objects, to know that Professor Perrotin, armed with so powerful an instrument, at first gave up the attempt after several days' fruitless effort; having renewed his trials still without success, he was about to give them up finally, when he succeeded in seeing the canal Phison which crosses Dawes continent.

During the present year both Perrotin and Schiaparelli were provided with still more powerful instruments, the latter with an 18-inch and the former with a 30-inch refractor, and the results obtained from the study of Mars' surface go to completely confirm Schiaparelli's discoveries. Several drawings of the planet by these two gentlemen have been published in recent periodicals and I have copied two of them for your benefit. The lower on the left hand (Fig. 2) is by Schiaparelli, from sketches made on June 2, 4 and 6. The most prominent marking near the center is easily recognized as Kaiser Sea (Syrtis Major and Nilosyrtis) of the chart. On the right is the curious forked bay of Dawes. The canals of the equatorial regions are drawn very much as they appear in the chart. Some old ones are omitted while several new appear. This (Astaboras) is straight and double instead of curved and single as in the chart. It is not really a separation of the old canal into two, but a new canal is seen starting from a different point of Kaiser (Ismenius). The greatest difference is in the regions around the north pole. The system of canals is extended right up to the polar cap, and we notice across the ice cap itself two dusky streaks. This opposition was very favorable for the examination of the north polar regions, that pole being inclined considerably toward the earth, and the opposition occurring after the midsummer of the northern hemisphere of Mars, so that the polar snows were largely melted and the ice cap reduced to a minimum. It seems quite reasonable to suppose that these dark streaks may be open channels in the frozen polar sea. [Fig. omitted]

What then are these strange markings, and why have they not been seen before?—are questions which naturally arise. The discoveries of Schiaparelli were made with a telescope of only eight inches aperture. Why is it that so many observers armed with more powerful instruments have utterly failed to see them? Partly, perhaps, because their skies were not so transparent as that of Italy; partly because their eyes were not so keen as those of the Italian observer; partly also because the phenomena of the canals are periodic; but more because of lack of persistent, long-continued scrutiny of the planet's disc.

Again Mars can be seen well only when near opposition, that is, about two months in the year and his distance at opposition varies from 34,000,000 to 64,000,000 miles because of the ellipticity of his orbit, so that a really favorable opportunity to observe minute details occurs only once in about fifteen years. Also, it is necessary for such observations that the sky of Mars be free from clouds over immense areas, whole continents in fact, and we can judge from terrestrial analogy that such a condition would be rare.

Several ingenious theories have been suggested to account for the canals. We can hardly admit that they are artificial canals constructed by the inhabitants. Their great width of seventy miles or more would prohibit that hypothesis, although we may suppose, with Proctor, those inhabitants to be of gigantic stature. Mr. Proctor suggested (M. N. xlviii, p. 307), that they might be rivers, the duplication being a diffraction effect, when mists hang over the river bed, but in doing so seemed to ignore their most characteristic features, their straightness, their frequent intersections, and the fact that they connect the seas, running from one to the other, and that the duplication is not the separation of the old canal, but the formation of a new one on one or the other side of the first.

M. Fizeau, the eminent physicist of Paris, explains them by the analogy of rifts in glaciers and considers the whole planet involved in a glacial epoch. He is led to this hypothesis by the presence of the dark canal in the north polar cap. Dr. Terby, of the observatory of Louvain, thinks this would necessitate a greater movement in the system of canals than has been observed. He finds no evidence of any change since they were discovered. Dr. Pebard, a physicist of Geneva, suggests that the canals are immense fissures in the crust of Mars through which the waters flow from ocean to ocean. The mass of Mars, being about one-eighth that of the earth, has cooled off more rapidly, producing great fissures in the crust extending to a very great depth. Another writer suggests for the very same reason that the canals are ridges or wrinkles in the crust, or, in other words, mountain ranges. There are serious objections to each of these and we are still far from a satisfactory explanation. I am rather inclined to the view that these markings are in part, at least, rivers and chains of lakes, that the continents are low and flat and subject to extensive inundations at certain seasons of the Martial year. It seems possible in this way to account for the variations noticed in many of the markings and there appears to be no inconsistency in supposing evaporations and precipitation to be more rapid and abundant on Mars than upon the earth, because of the smaller force of gravity.∆

Another article on the canals of Mars appeared in the British journal *Science* in 1892:

THE LINES ON MARS
by William J. Hussey.(*Science*, 20:235, 1892.)

In <u>Science</u>, Sept. 23, Mr. C. B. Warring communicates a theory to account for the gemination of the so-called canals of Mars. He suggests that the phenomenon may be due to a defect in the eye of the observer by reason of its possessing the power of double refraction in some or in all directions. That some eyes do possess the power of double refraction is a well-known fact. It is a defect which, I imagine, is much more common than is generally supposed. It may be suggested that data representing a large number of cases <u>might</u> show astigmatic eyes to possess the power of double refraction more frequently than others. I do not know that any data have been collected upon this point.

Concerning the existence of the canals of Mars and that they are sometimes really double, I have no doubt. My own recent work at the Lock Observatory has convinced me that they are not illusions due to imperfect eyesight. During the present opposition, I spent about thirty nights in the work on Mars, working with Professors Schaeberle and Campbell. On about half the nights I saw the so-called canals with more or less distinctness, but on only one occasion did I clearly see a canal double. This was August 17, when the canal called Ganges on Schiaparelli's map was clearly seen to be double, and was so drawn in my notebook. That the doubling was real and not apparent is evident from the fact that Professors Schaeberle and Campbell both saw the same canal double on the same night, and drew it so. Other canals, some of them nearly parallel to Ganges, were seen that night, but none of them appeared double.

Our work was done independently. In turn each went to the telescope, and made a drawing of what he saw. We did not see each others' drawings, nor did we talk of what we had seen. It was not until the next morning that we learned that each had seen Ganges double. Δ

The "raw," unprocessed Viking photo 35A72 of the 2-kilometer wide face on Mars and the surrounding terrain. The circle in the upper left corner is a blemish on the television camera. Black and white specks are noise spikes in the data transmission.

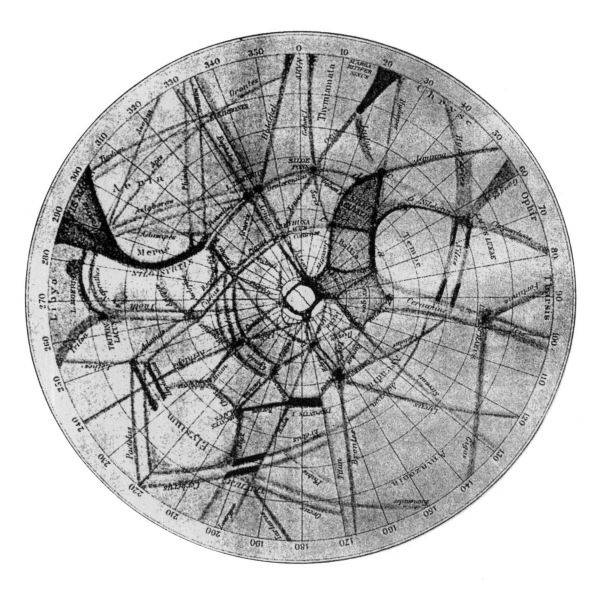

A chart of the Northern Hemisphere of Mars,
by Schiaparelli, 1888

Reproduced by courtesy of the Royal Astronomical Society

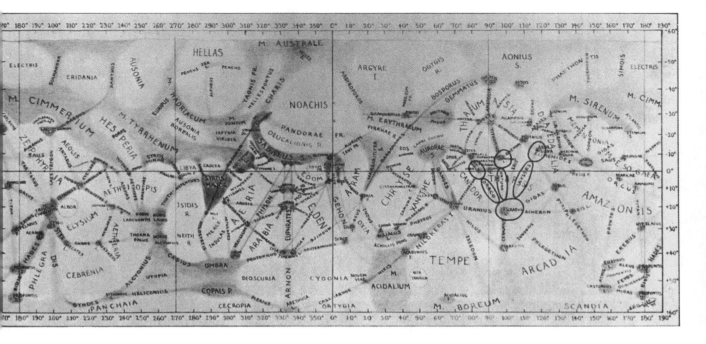

Markings on W observed at opposition of 1958 are transferred to map of Mars. It is seen that the marking coincides closely with canals and oases.

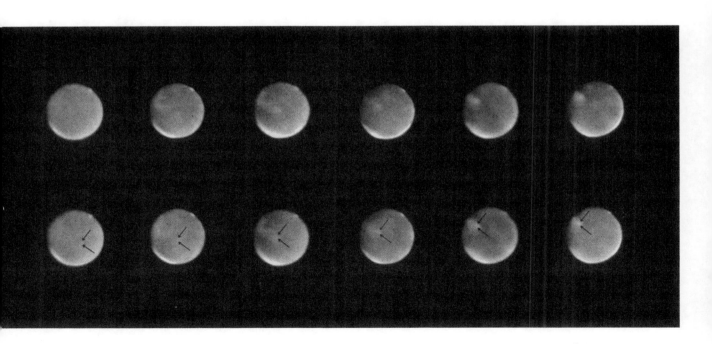

The Formation and Growth of a Cloud during a Martian Afternoon

The photographs, in order from left to right, were secured at intervals through a period of about four hours, during which the planet rotated 55°. The place of the brightest part of the cloud, in the successive positions of the planet, is shown by markers in the lower row, the rotational movement being upward to the left. The cloud is not visible in the first picture, but becomes so in the second and increases in strength as it is carried through the Martian afternoon to sunset. Photographs taken on October 16, 1926, at Mount Hamilton and Mount Wilson. (LICK OBSERVATORY)

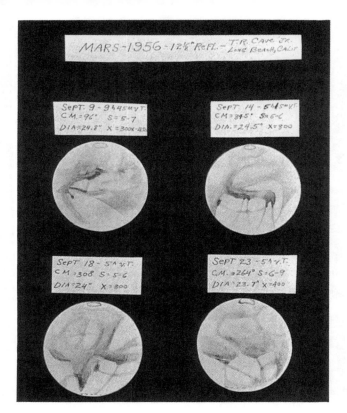

Sketches of Mars at the opposition of 1956, made with a twelve-inch reflecting telescope, showing polar cap, maria, and canals.

(COURTESY OF T. R. CAVE, JR.)

Nomenclature for Mars, adopted by the International Astronomical Union. The main features are designated in accordance with the former classical system. Each name refers to the whole of a district.

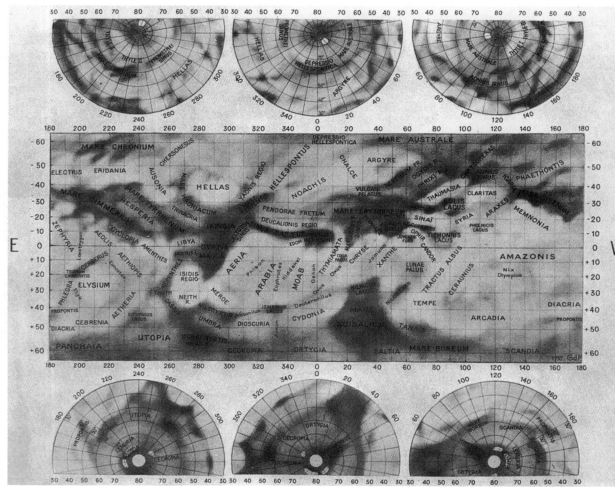

Schiaparelli's map of Mars, based upon his observations during six oppositions from 1877 to 1888. Schiaparelli discovered the canals, shown here as narrow stripes. He changed the names of the Martian features.

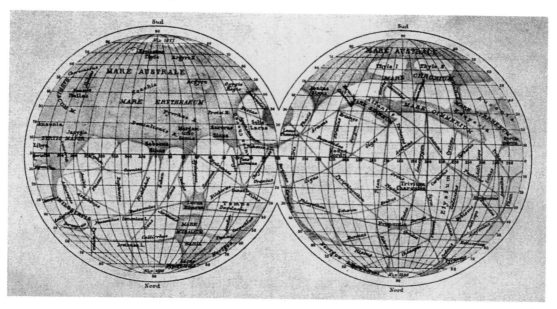

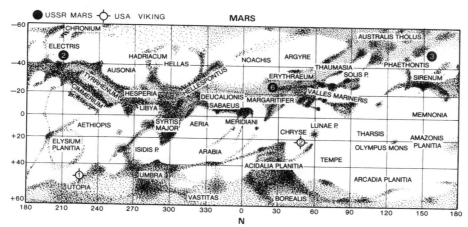

Map of Mars, with impact and landing points of Russian Mars probes and American Vikings 1 and 2.

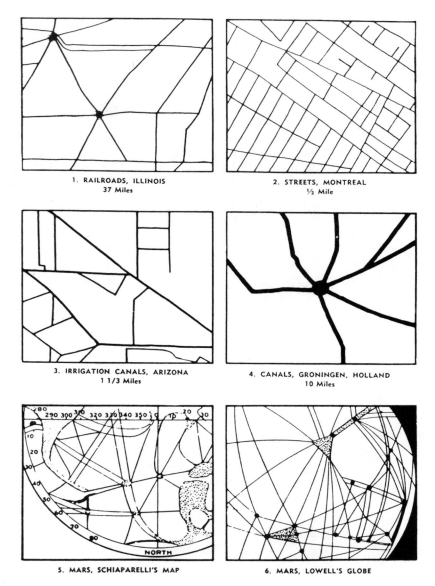

1. RAILROADS, ILLINOIS
37 Miles

2. STREETS, MONTREAL
½ Mile

3. IRRIGATION CANALS, ARIZONA
1 1/3 Miles

4. CANALS, GRONINGEN, HOLLAND
10 Miles

5. MARS, SCHIAPARELLI'S MAP

6. MARS, LOWELL'S GLOBE

Examples of artificial networks showing 5-point and 6-point intersections. Networks that originate by deliberate planning are much more complex than those formed by nature. The complexity of the Martian canal network, as Percival Lowell saw it, would indicate that it was the result of intelligent planning.

(From *Mars and Its Mystery*, 1906, by Edward S. Morse, Little, Brown, and Co., Boston)

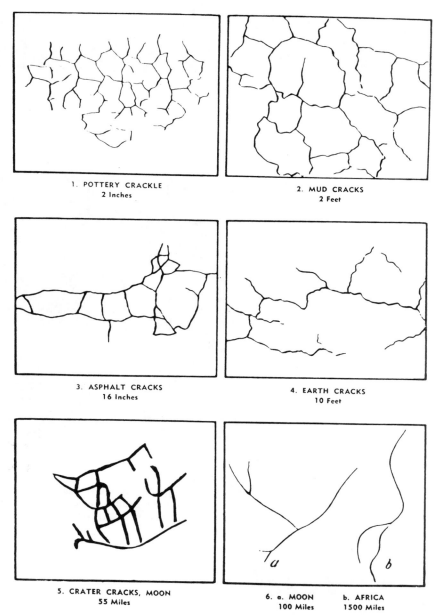

1. POTTERY CRACKLE
2 Inches

2. MUD CRACKS
2 Feet

3. ASPHALT CRACKS
16 Inches

4. EARTH CRACKS
10 Feet

5. CRATER CRACKS, MOON
55 Miles

6. a. MOON   b. AFRICA
100 Miles   1500 Miles

In nature it is unusual to find more than three cracks radiating from a point. In these examples of natural cracks and fissures you can find a few cases of four cracks radiating from a point, but 3-point intersections predominate.

(From *Mars and Its Mystery*, 1906, by Edward S. Morse, Little, Brown, and Co., Boston)

 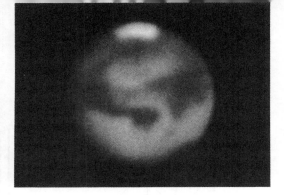

RED   INFRARED

Mars photographed in red and infrared light. If maria (dark markings) are due to green vegetation containing chlorophyll, they should appear dark in red light and bright in infrared light. Since they appear about the same in both, this test is negative for chlorophyll on Mars.

Circles illustrate the small field of view obtained in a large telescope. The large circle shows area of sky taken in by 100-inch telescope at Newtonian focus; next circle at Cassegrain focus; and smallest circle at coudé focus. Only a very small portion of the sky can be seen at one time.

(GRIFFITH OBSERVATORY)

Phobos and Deimos, taken by sixty-inch telescope on Mount Wilson, on Sept. 9, 1956. Mars is huge central image, greatly overexposed. Satellites have been located in their orbits from diagram in *American Ephemeris* for 1956. (MOUNT WILSON AND PALOMAR OBSERVATORIES)

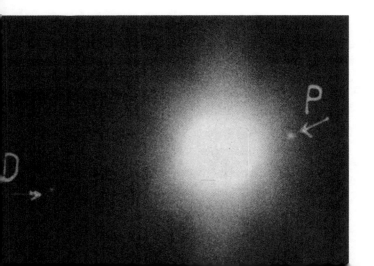 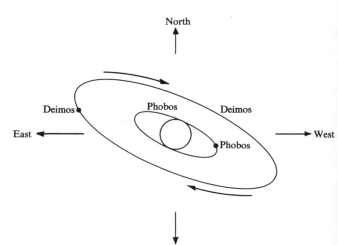

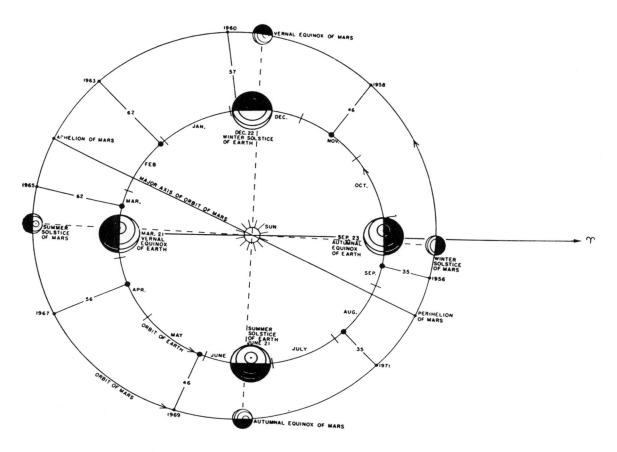

The axes of Mars and Earth are both tilted by about 24° from the vertical to their orbits, but they are tilted in different directions. The northern end of the axis of Earth points to within one degree (twice the apparent diameter of the full moon) of the star at the end of the handle of the Little Dipper. This is the North Star, or Polaris. The axis of Mars is directed toward a point in the northern sky about 45° from Polaris. The nearest bright star to this point is Alpha Cygni, which would be the pole star of Mars.

The beginnings of the four seasonal positions in the orbit of Mars occur very close to those for Earth. They are not, of course, the *same* seasons. If Mars were at opposition on the dates when the seasons began on Earth, the correspondence would be as follows:

Date	Approximate distance of Mars (Miles)	Beginning of season in northern hemisphere of Earth	Beginning of Martian season	
			Northern hemisphere	Southern hemisphere
March 21	61,000,000	Spring	Summer	Winter
June 21	41,000,000	Summer	Autumn	Spring
Sept. 23	35,000,000	Autumn	Winter	Summer
Dec. 22	51,000,000	Winter	Spring	Autumn

The axis of rotation of Earth has a conical motion caused by the attraction of the sun and moon on Earth's equatorial bulge. As a result, the position of the north celestial pole in the heavens is always changing.

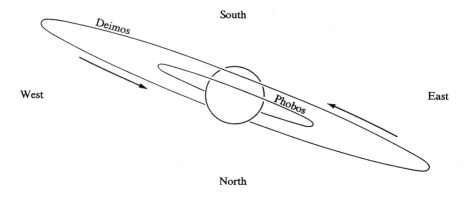

Orbits of Phobos and Deimos

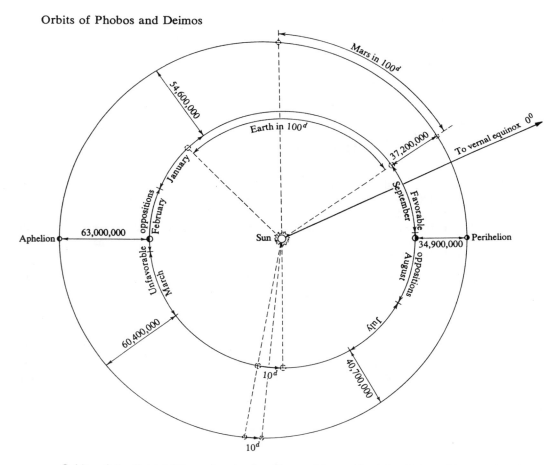

Orbits of Earth and Mars, showing positions of favorable (close) oppositions and unfavorable (distant) oppositions.

Relative motion of Mars and Earth in 10 days and 100 days. These distances would vary slightly, since the motion of the planets depends upon their distance from the sun.

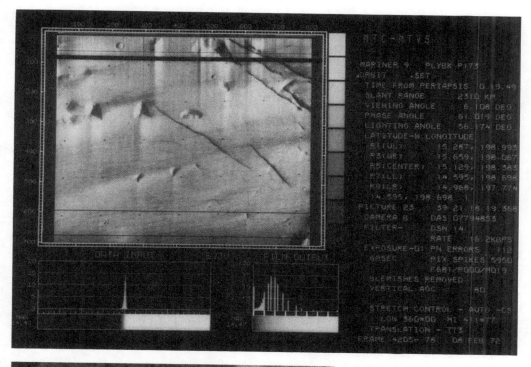

Above: Elysium pyramids (Mariner frame 4205–78): the first indication of a lost civilization on Mars. A set of two large and two small pyramids on the Elysium Plain at center left. *NASA photo.*

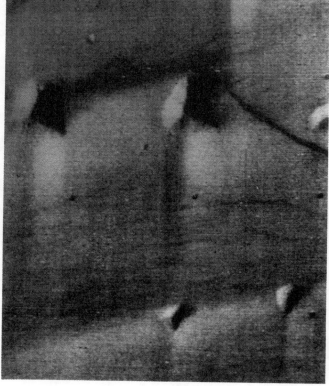

A magnification of Mariner frame 4205–78 showing the four Elysium pyramids. *NASA photo.*

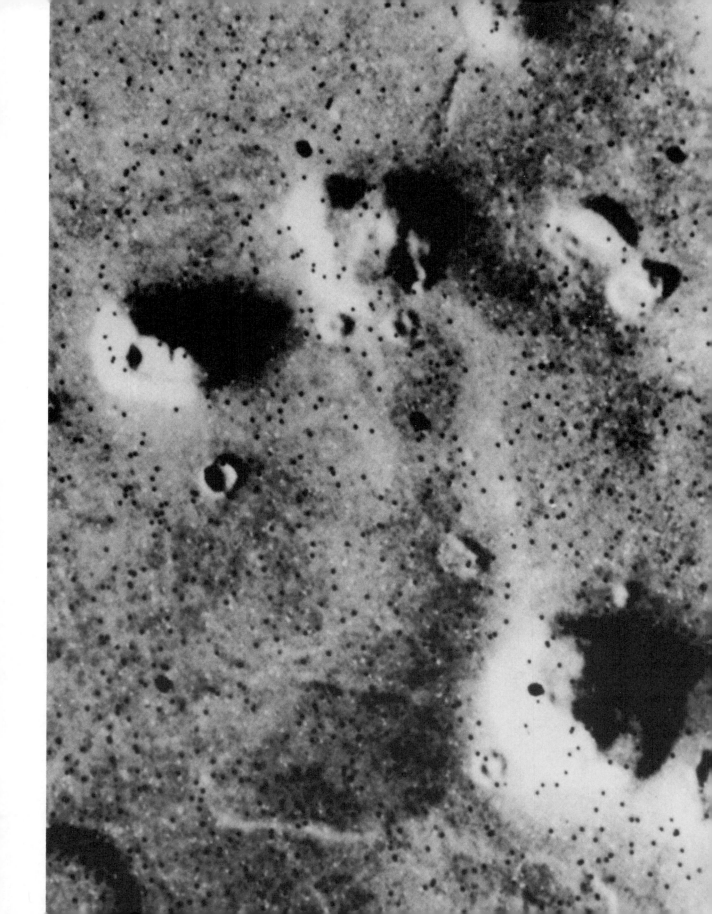

Chapter 6

The Pyramids of Mars

In order to reach the Mountains of Mars, stand at the foot of their awesome pyramids, and to reap its benefits of their energies, one must ascend the genetic ladder of one's forebears.

—Edgar Rice Burroughs
The Chessmen of Mars

In the search for knowledge on Mars, various unmanned missions in the 1960s and 1970s were sent to the Red Planet. The most important of these expeditions was undoubtedly the NASA Viking Mission of 1976. Controlled by NASA engineers at the Jet Propulsion Laboratory back on Earth, two identical Viking spacecraft were launched on a ten-month journey through 440 million miles of space to finally orbit around the red planet. Each of the Vikings was an automated self-powered laboratory capable of splitting up into an orbiter circling the planet, and a lander that could soft-land on the alien world.

While the orbiters were able to explore and comprehensively photograph Mars from the sky, the landers conducted soil and other experiments in preselected areas. As the latter experiments were admitted by NASA scientists to be designed to prove the absence of life in any form on Mars, their results may be discounted as being negatively biased from the start and thus probably worthless. Still, more than 50,000 pictures were taken of the surface of the planet by the Viking orbiters. Now, some 17 years later, many have still to be viewed, let alone analyzed. Some may never see the light of day due to time and staffing cost constraints.

DISCOVERING THE FACE ON MARS

The now well-publicized finding of a "face" on Mars is a fascinating story in itself. The research of several private investigators, some with former NASA connections, have down

189

the years provided the most compelling evidence that suggests either a former civilization or some sort of way station activity that has left a legacy of intriguing monument-type features scattered on the enigmatic planet.

According to Australian science writer Brian Crowley, prior to 1976, the year of the Viking Mission, Dr. James J. Hurtak of the Academy for Future Science, California, published a series of articles highlighting NASA photographs from the previous Mariner 9 expedition of 1971 that showed distinct pyramid-shaped 'mountains' in the Elysium quadrangle region that defied rational explanation as natural formations. Almost prophetically, Hurtak even postulated that if there were pyramids on Mars, somewhere we may even find a Sphinx!

Then came Viking, and thousands more pictures; and the first published work to center on the enigmatic 'Face on Mars', a massive face-like object (imagine Ayers Rock with a face carved on it), was by an obscure Vienna-based Austrian computer scientist, Walter Hain, whose 1979 book in the German language has recently been published in English under the title *We, From Mars* (available from the author c/- Mars Findings, PO Box 1218, Vienna 1070, Austria). Hain's conclusions, like those of Hurtak, were for the most part ignored by establishment scientists who, it seems, simply did not want to believe the possibility of former life on Mars.

The first comprehensive scientific appraisal of the unusual Mars surface features was done by two former NASA contractors, computer scientist Vincent DiPietro and Gregory Molenaar, whose monograph entitled *Unusual Mars Surface Features* was first published in 1982 (now running into several editions and available from Mars Research, PO Box 284, Glenn Dale, Maryland, USA).

DiPietro and Molenaar, initially intrigued by the already-known image of the Mars face, developed their unique Starburst Pixel Interleaving Technique (SPIT) to enhance NASA pictures that showed strange features. With new additions to their investigative team in the forms of plasma physicist Dr. John Brandenburg and Dr. Mark J. Carlotto of The Analytic Science Corporation, their more recent research has thrown up the possibility of at least one other face-like monument staring out into space from the dusty plains of Mars.

Since 1986, a number of books on the subject have been published, including *The Martian Enigmas* by Mark Carlotto and *The Monuments of Mars* by Richard Hoagland of the Mars Investigation Group, who has done more than anyone to publicize the Mars findings, including a recent compelling video presentation to a large group of NASA scientists.

Briefly described, the originally discovered Mars Face feature, with its peculiar Egyptian-style headdress, is a huge mountain-like object in the Cydonia region approximately 1.6 miles (2.5 km) from crown to chin, 1.2 miles (2 km) wide and, judging by the shadow length in one of the frames, between about 1,650 feet (500 meters) and 2,600 feet (800 meters) high. Color enhancement techniques used by the DiPietro/Molenaar team have indicated an eyeball feature in the visible eye socket, while recent enhancements by Carlotto clearly show the presence of sculptured teeth in the mouth area.

Says Brian Crowley, "What goes firmly against any argument that the Face on Mars may be merely a rock formation sculptured to look human-like through water and/or wind erosion is the fact that it represents a full face form, with symmetrically placed features. Any study of simulacra (faces and figures in nature) as related to mountains, hills and rocks on our own planet, reveals that such instances of natural face-like rock sculpture almost invariably present their human facial image in profile."[30]

The initial Face on Mars photographs elicited a wide range of responses relating to the nature of the image, the first being, naturally, a comparison with the Egyptian Sphinx/pyramid configuration at Giza. Hoagland equates the resultant image with the Egyptian god Horus, whose hieroglyph can be translated as 'face'. One of the titles of Horus was 'Lord of the Horizon' and any sighting of the Cydonia object from a viewable distance on the surface of the planet might easily see this description translated into sculptured reality.

Says Brian Crowley about the face, "Another commentator sees the image of the Hindu monkey god Hanuman in the face, while the Zulu author and 'keeper of the tales', Credo Vuzamazulu Mutwa, who sees the features as distinctly Negroid, has insisted to the writer that he considers the Face on Mars a vindication of the old African legends that claim that the Bantu people originally came from the red planet (there are, indeed, both African and Celtic legends that claim descent of certain Earth races from pregnant women who escaped some great holocaust on Mars many tens of thousands of years ago)."

PYRAMIDS AND INCA CITIES?

Even more interesting to many researchers are the angulared constructions about 7 miles (11 km) southwest of the Cydonia Face. This cluster of angled constructions of various sizes suggesting pyramids, one of which appears to be either still under construction (when abandoned?) or partially destroyed.

The Face of Cydonia and its attendant pyramids are not the only out-of-place objects scattered on the dusty plains of Mars. A Mariner 9 picture features a strange series of cubical and rectangular cells ranging from three to five miles in length and forming a pattern which has its closest comparison in early Inca mountain city remains found in northern Peru and Bolivia, as photographed from the sky. Geologists remain baffled by this unusual box-like patterning.

The Mariner 9 frames of the Elysium quadrangle highlights several sets of tetrahedron pyramidal structures which are far too unique to be immediately written off as natural formations. Some of these 'artifacts' are enormous—ten times the height and a thousand times the volume of the Great Pyramid of Giza. Image enhancement reveals some of these massive Martian pyramids reaching more than a half mile into the sky.

Says Brian Crowley, "Another Mars pyramid teeters miraculously on the lip of a huge crater. There is no known explanation for how it might have got there. Other strange anomalies include what looks for all the world like a giant airport (or spaceport) with a central hub and wheel-like extensions, just like a modern airport, and giant wormhole-type features that seem to come straight out of the novel *Dune*.. These are linear effects that lead right up to the crater lip pyramid. There are also pockets of what could be underground tunnels—perhaps an underground network that collapsed due to crater impact."[30]

A SECOND FACE IS DISCOVERED

Ongoing DePietro/Molenaar research that there is evidence for at least one, and possibly two more Faces on Mars that demand closer scrutiny. The most convincing of these finds in a region of Mars known as Utopia, exhibits most of the features of the Cydonia Face, including twin eye cavities and an Egyptian-style headdress (or is it a space helmet?). It also shows two peculiar features that also, on close examination, appear to mark the Cydonia Face, i.e., notches on the cheeks and an indentation above the right eye. However, unlike its apparently well-preserved Cydonia counterpart, the Utopia face appears as if it may have been damaged at some stage (although clearer resolution may disprove this)—much like the Egyptian Sphinx has been defaced back on Earth. It was remade once and later had its nose shot off by a canon.

While sceptics among the scientific community remain unconvinced that either of the two mentioned Faces on Mars could be genuine artifacts, DiPietro/Molenaar's ongoing research indicates the possibility of even a third Face on Mars, although the photographic evidence for this is not anywhere near as convincing as that for Face One and Face Two.

PYRAMIDAL STRUCTURES OF MARS

An early article on Martian pyramids appeared in the journal *Icarus* in 1974. Written by Mack Gipson Jr. and Victor K. Ablordeppey, the brief article entitled **Pyramidal Structures of Mars** described in two paragraphs the Elysium Pyramids:

"Triangular and polygonal pyramid like structures have been observed on the martian surface. Located in the east central portion of Elysium Quadrangle (MC-15), these features are visible on the Mariner photographs, B frames MTVS 4205-3 DAS 07794853 and MTVS 4296-24 DAS 12985882. The structures cast triangular and polygonal shadows. Steep-sided volcanic cones and impact craters occur only a few kilometers away. The mean diameter of the triangular pyramidal structures at the base is approximately 3.0 km, and the mean diameter of the polygonal structures is approximately 6.0 km.

The observed Martian structures tend to line up suggesting joint or fault control. However, they do not appear to be controlled by the visible faults. The structures appear to be either wind-faceted volcanic cones and blocks or solidified

193

blocks which have been rotated in semi-consolidated lava." (*Icarus*, 22:197-204, 1974.)[5]

Another brief news-snippet on strange parallel ridges was published in *Science News* in 1978. The startling headline to the one paragraph news brief read **Strange Hillocks and Ridges on Mars.** The text in entirety read:

"No one knows what chain of events led to the strange appearance of this northwestward extension of the flanks of the huge volcano Arsia Mons in the Tharsis uplands. Countless hillocks, mostly 100 to 500 meters across, cover the flank's edge, which is surrounded by parallel ridges that run for hundreds of kilometers, undisturbed by craters, flow features or even variations in surface brightness. One hypothesis is that the hillocks were formed by a huge landslide, perhaps assisted by gravity since the surrounding plains slope downward about 0.5 o to the northwest. (Ashflow deposits are deemed unlikely, due to the lack of signs that any of the material was blasted into place from vents in the volcano.) The ridges may be folds or "reverse faults" caused by the drag of the landslide over the underlying terrain, which would transmit an outward pressure perhaps capable of passing beneath surface features." (Anonymous; *Science News*, 113:43, 1978.)△

ILLUSTRATIONS FOR PHOTOS STARTING ON PAGE 195:

Page 195: A 3-D tour of the Face on Mars. Sixteen synthetic views of the Face. This matrix suggests that the Face is not a two-dimensional optical illusion but retains a three-dimensional face-like appearance though a wide range of angles of view. Courtesy of Dr. Mark Carlotto.

Page 196: Perspective View of the Face on Mars. Dr. Mark Carlotto's computer-processed, synthetic view from the southwest, 50 degrees from the zenith, showing the Face at upper right, the City at lower left, and part of the five-sided "D&M Pyramid" at lower right. Note the apparent "staircases" in the center slopes of the largest pyramid, as well as some of the smaller pyramids.

Page 197: A Perspective View of Pyramid Cluster. A synthetic perspective view from the northeast, 70 degrees from the zenith, showing the Face on Mars at lower left, the "City" at upper right and part of the five-sided "D&M Pyramid" at upper left. Courtesy of Dr. Mark Carlotto.

Page 198: The Strange "Bowl." The "Bowl" and adjacent structures in the Cydonia region of Mars, to the west of the Face-City complex, from Viking frame 70A10. These objects, each about 2 km wide, appear to display a variety of "architectural" forms. The Bowl itself seems to lack many of the typical characteristics of natural impact craters, and is set into a somewhat rectilinear, platform-like mesa. Courtesy of Dr. Mark Carlotto.

Page 199: The Curious "Cliff" and Crater Pyramid. The "Cliff" in the Cydonia region of Mars, from Viking frame 35A73. The structure, about 3 km long, is situated on the pedestal of a large crater yet displays no evidence of impact damage. Its structure and texture differ markedly from that of its surroundings. Areas immediately adjacent to the Cliff display evidence of possible excavation. The Cliff appears to be directly aligned with other key objects in the "Cydonia Complex," including the possible pyramid on the rim of the nearby crater. Courtesy of Dr. Mark Carlotto.

Page 200: A Synthetic view of the "Runway." A computer processed photo by Dr. Mark Carlotto of the "Runway," about 5 km long and nestled in a shallow basin-like depression. It appears to consist of a straight row of cones or mounds suggestive of a linear particle accelerator or mass-driver. A similar depression nearby encloses three smooth mounds forming a rough "bow-tie" shape. the blemish at the Runway's mid-point is a remnant of a camera registration mark. The objects are located about 140 degrees east of Cydonia, on the slopes of the volcano Hecates Tholus. Courtesy of Dr. Mark Carlotto.

Page 201: A Close-up of the Face On Mars. The Egyptian-style headress is clearly seen around the Face. Even evidence of teeth can be seen.

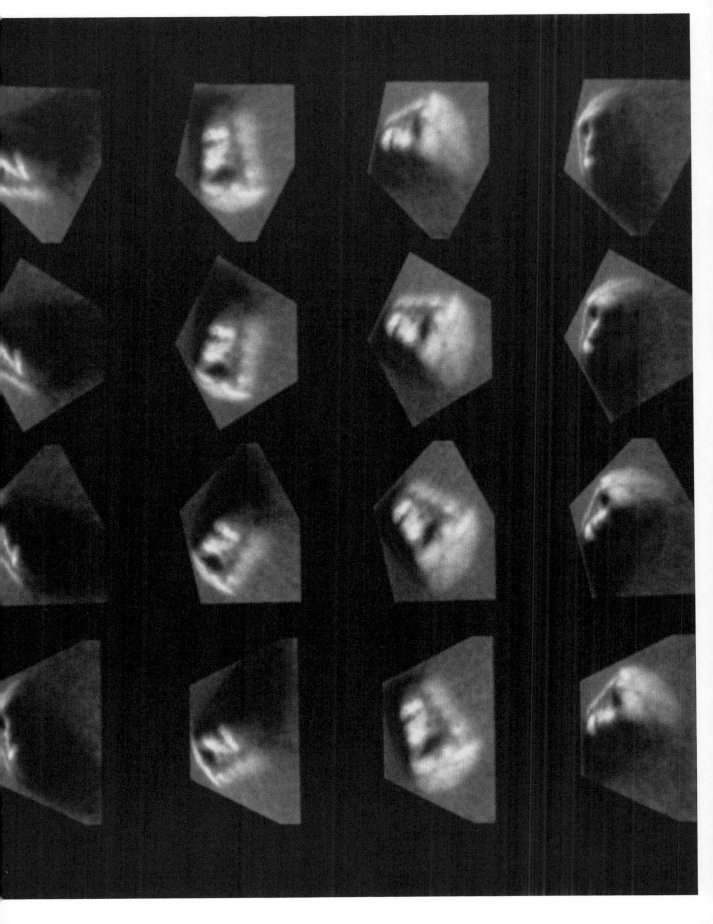

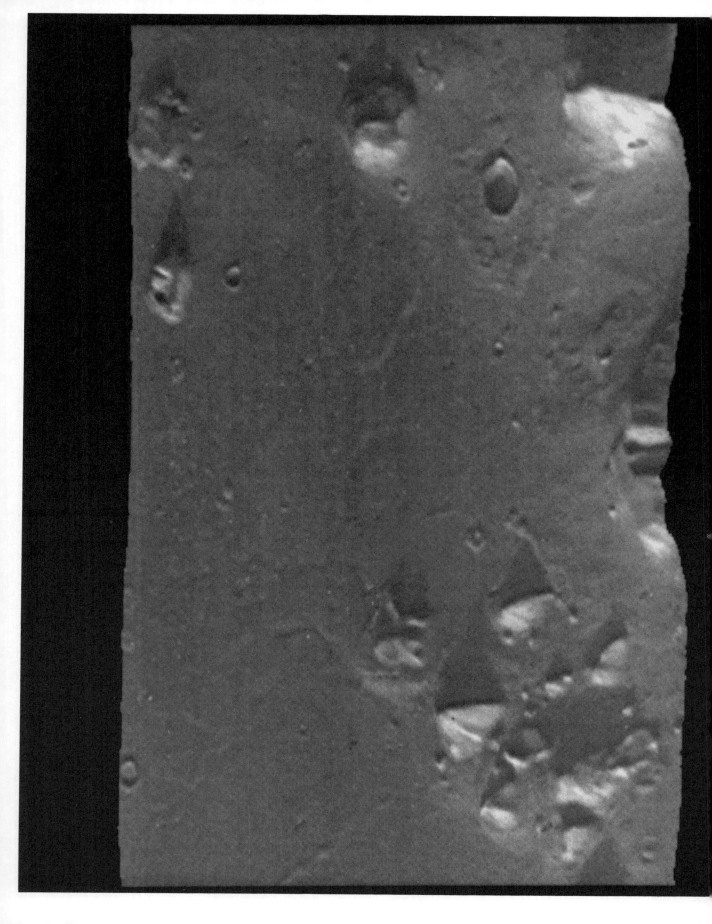

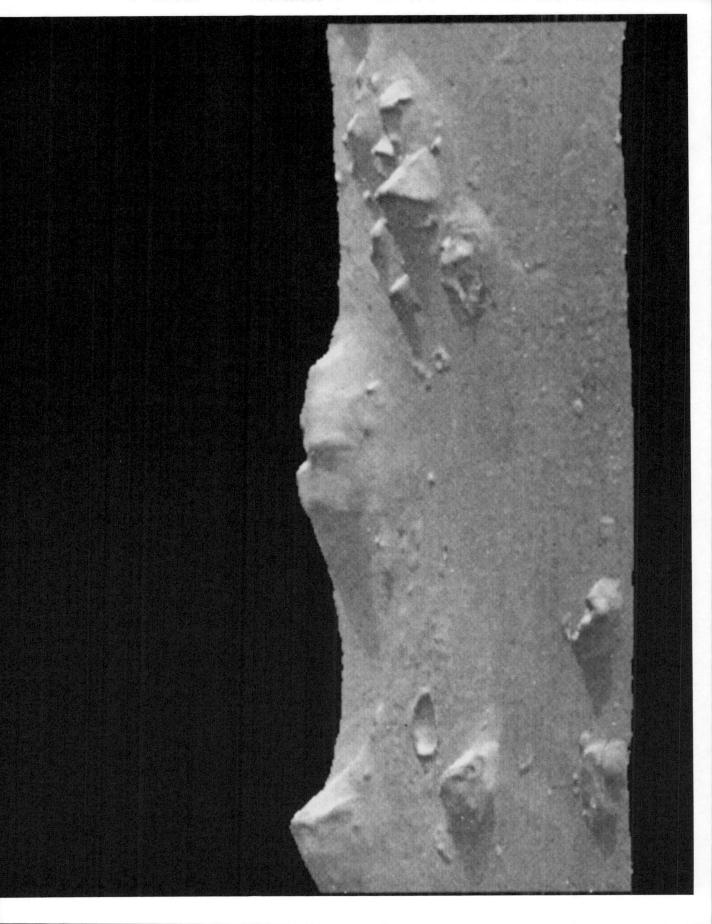

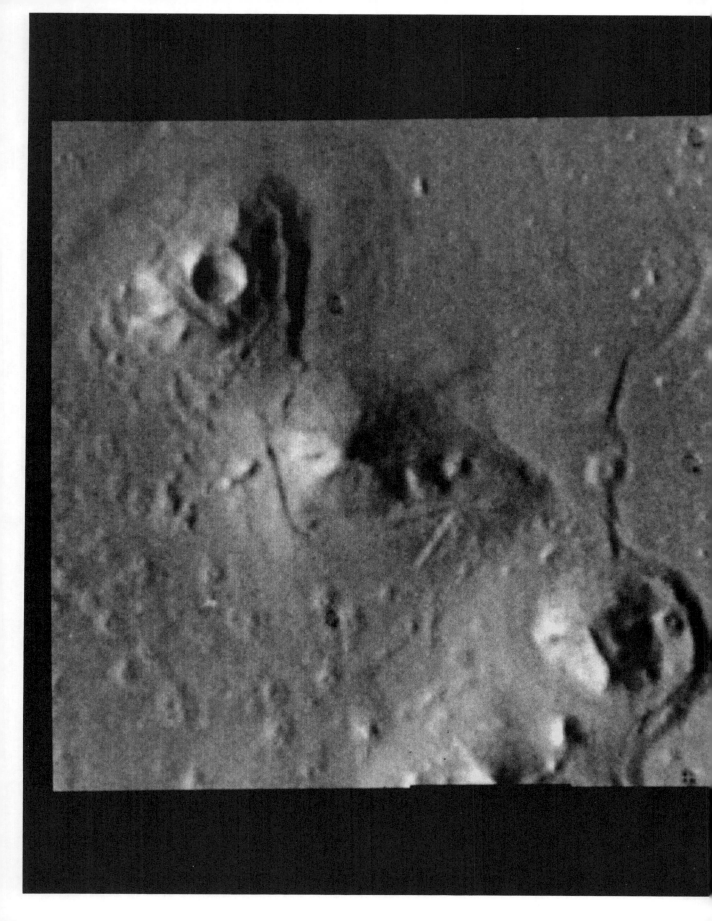

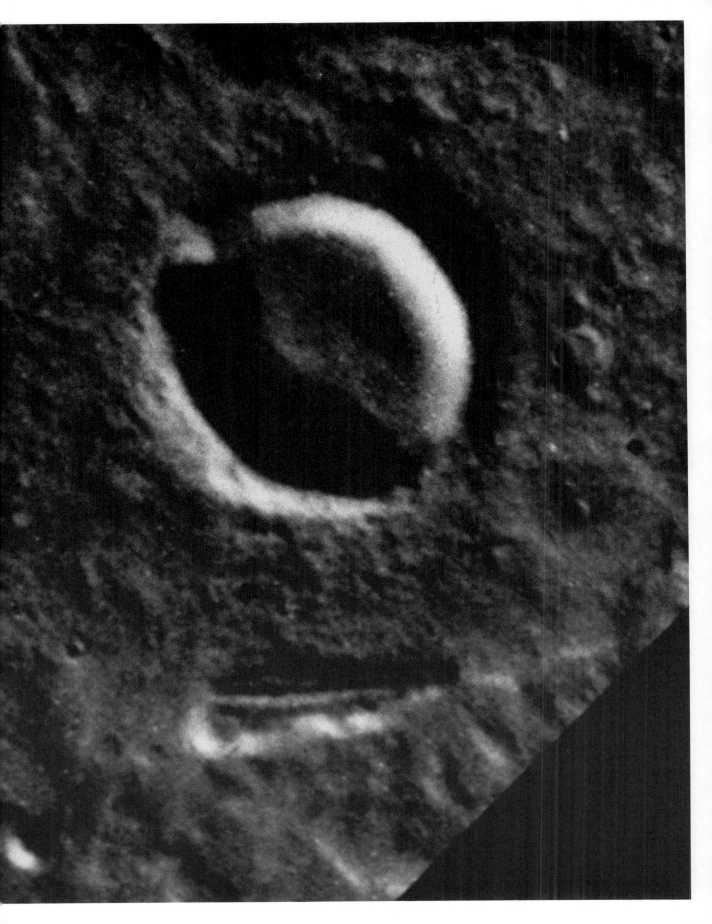

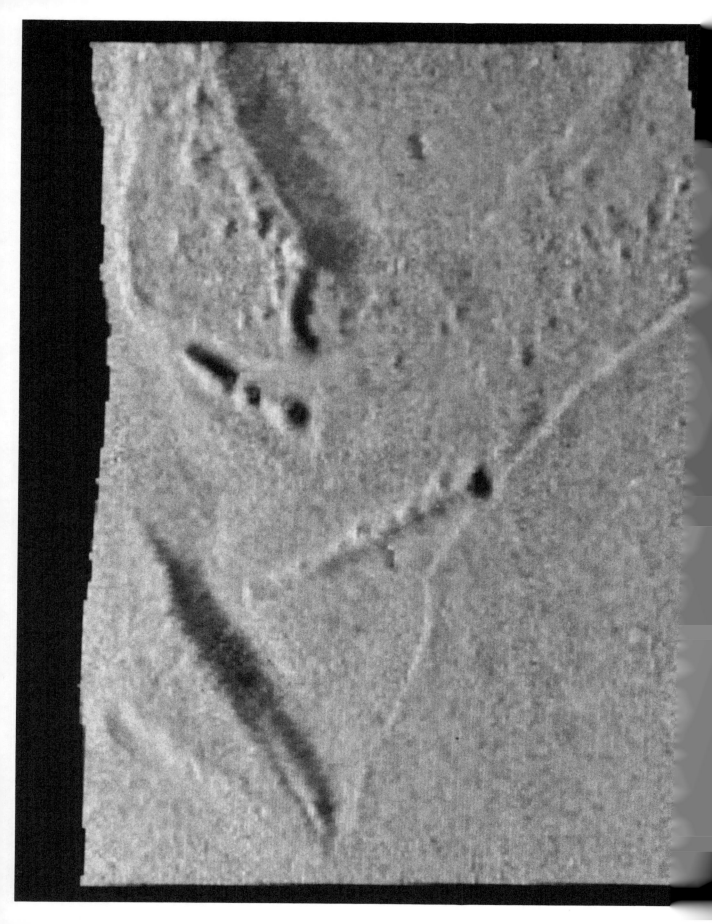

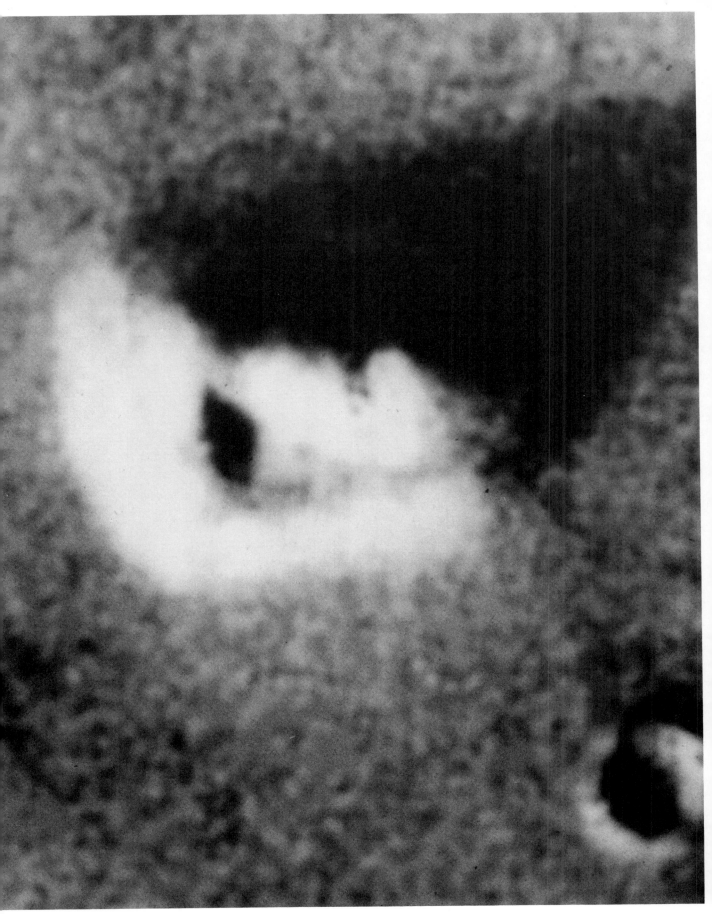

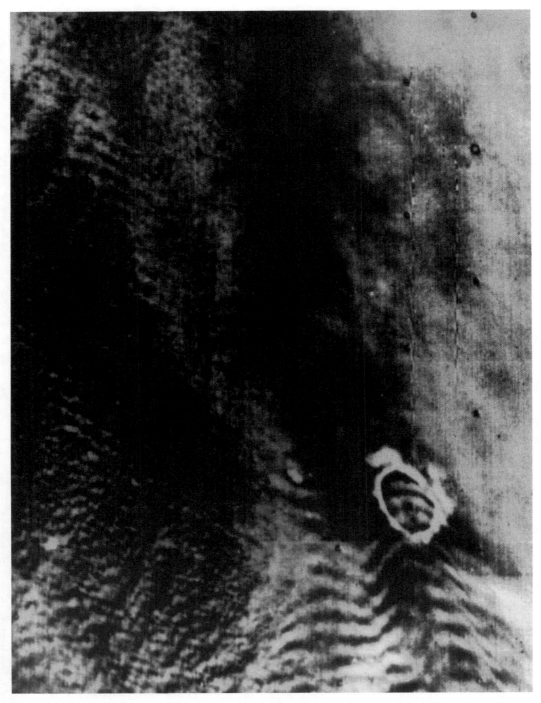

Clouds formations over Mars with a frost-rimmed crater top about 56 miles (90km) in diameter poking through. Taken by Mariner 9.

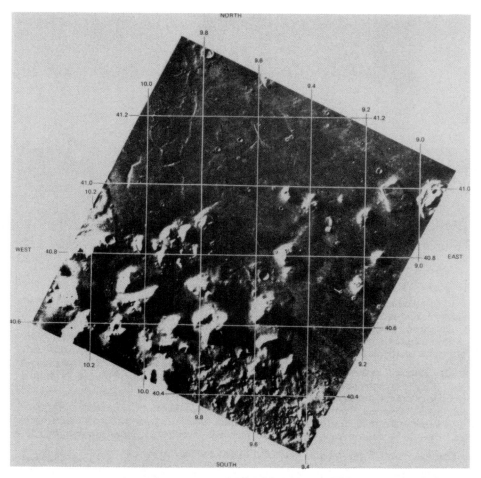

Avinsky's independent modelling, in clay, of "the City." Note that *all* morphologies are modelled as "pyramids"—including "the Fort." This is another clue to the authenticity of the Soviet claim; better images reveal the Fort is anything *but* "pyramidal!"

Frame 70A13, processed by SRI International, showing "Face" (a) and
D & M pyramid (b). Note buttressing at corners of the D & M pyramid.
This does not show up in NASA raw version.

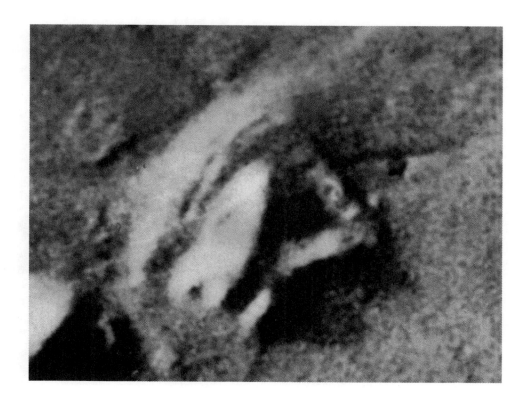

The "Fortress," located at the northeast corner of the "City." It appears
to have three straight walls and an enclosed, interior space. Its long wall
points precisely at the "head" of the "D & M Pyramid." Photo courtesy
of Dr. Mark J. Carlotto, The Analytic Sciences Corporation.

The "Runway" complex, located at an elevation of about 3 miles on the slopes of a massive volcano, Hecates Tholus, in the Utopia region. Pointer indicates the main "Runway" feature, apparently a ruler-straight three-mile long rank of cones or pyramids. Both the "Runway" and its nearby "bow-tie"-shaped companion feature appear to be set into unique, shallow "basins." Photo courtesy of National Space Science Data Center.

The "Mound," or "Tholus," located about 10 miles south of the "Cliff." Its proportions and its surrounding "moat," or peripheral ditch, are characteristic of similar prehistoric structures on Earth. The "Cliff," the D & M Pyramid" and the "Tholus" form a right triangle. Note the similarity of the curious broad grooves on the "Tholus" and its "satellite" mesa. Photo courtesy of National Space Science Data Center.

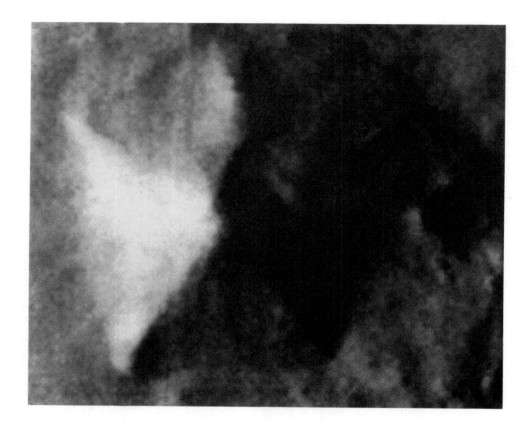

The "D & M Pyramid," whose proportions approximate those of a human figure with outstretched arms. Note apparent extensive damage to right side and bottom surfaces, and resulting debris flow around base, giving the impression of a shortened right "leg." Possible cause of apparent damage is explosive penetration: note "bottomless" hole at right, and apparent domed uplift just right of center. Photo courtesy of Dr. Mark J. Carlotto, The Analytic Sciences Corporation.

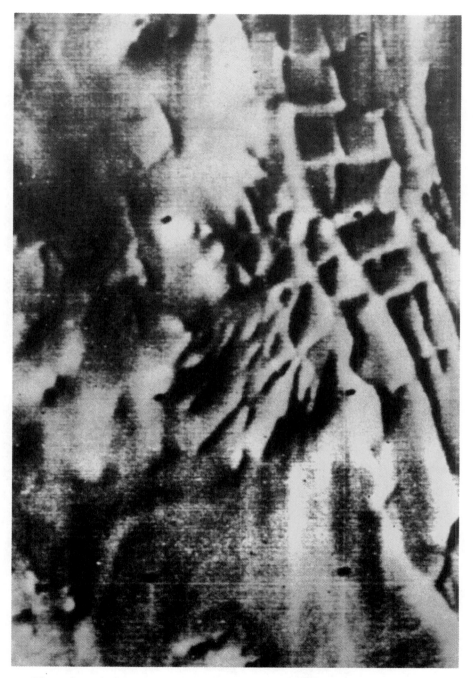

The enigmatic 'Inca City' honeycomb area in the south polar region of Mars. *NASA photo.*

The 'Dome Pyramid' (*at center top*) in the Cydonia region (Viking frame 35A72) which looks like a collapsed pyramid, or a pyramid under construction. *NASA photo*.

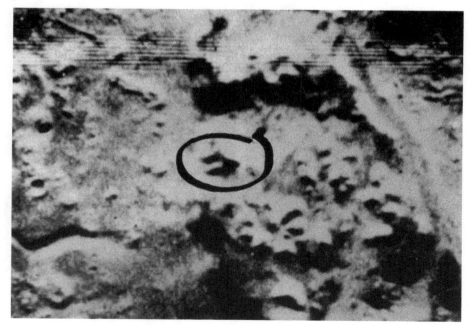

Magnification showing parallel walls and sun angles of the 'Gate Pyramid' (ringed) (Viking frame 072A04), which looks uncannily like the funerary temple ruins at Dendera in Egypt. *NASA photo*.

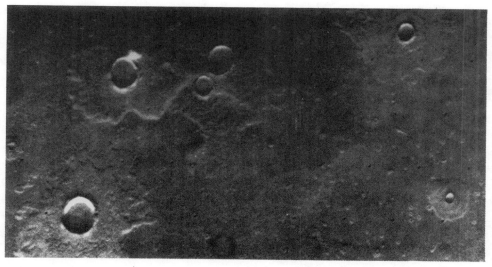

The 'Crater Pyramid' (Viking frame 043A04): a pyramidal construction on the lip of a crater (*at top left*) in a region of smooth surfaces and pedestal craters. *NASA photo*.

Magnification of the 'Crater Pyramid'. Note the sun shadow showing the pyramid shape. *NASA photo*.

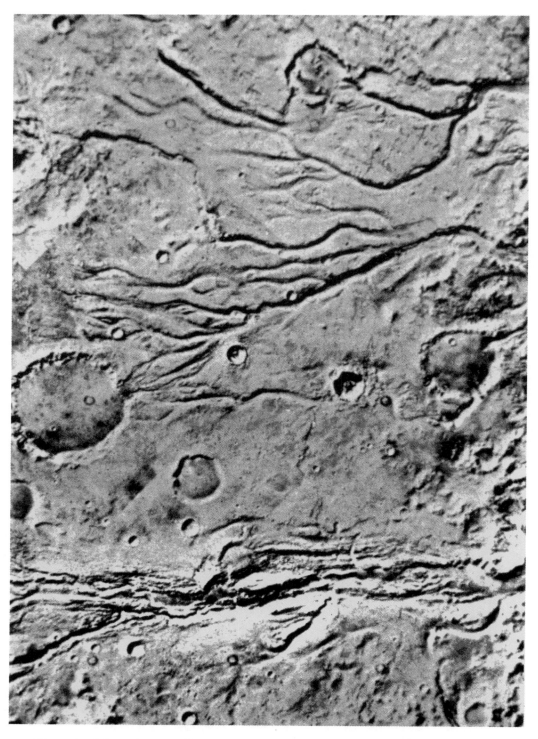

Channels of rivers that once flowed with water on Mars; this is west of Viking 1 landing site. *NASA photo*.

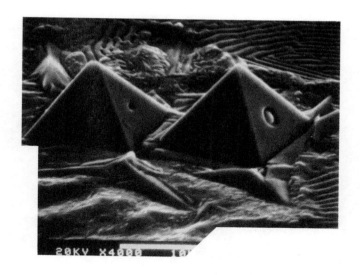

Metallurgy. This S.E.M. image magnified 4000x is of the inner surface shrinkage cavity formed on solidification of a nickel-tin eutectic

alloy sphere levitated in microgravity aboard the space shuttle. To capture the fine detail, Polaroid Type 55 black and white instant film was used.

Note the pyramidal structure of this metal alloy used in a Polaroid advertisement.

Phobos Complex? This image, rotated to the right by 90 degrees, shows severaal anomalies. In the center, a linear ramp or bridge appears to connect two parts of the hill. Other linear structures appear to run diagonally in the upper right side of the image. A 'waterfall' appearance and other anomalies such as a building or vehicle appear on the on the side of the crater in the upper left.

Chapter 7

The Moons of Mars

At most, terrestrial men fancied that there might be other men upon Mars, perhaps inferior to themselves and ready to welcome a missionary enterprise.

—H.G. Wells
The War of the Worlds

Phobos, one of two moons of Mars, has itself always been considered a rather mysterious object, as has its smaller twin, Deimos. Iosef Shklovskii, noted member of the Soviet Academy of Science and co-writer with Dr. Carl Sagan of *Intelligent Life in the Universe*, once calculated from the estimated density of the Martian atmosphere and the peculiar "acceleration" of Phobos that the satellite must be hollow. Could Phobos be a hollowed-out space station of huge proportions?

In July 1988 the Russians launched two probes in the direction of Mars, Phobos I and Phobos II, with the primary intention of investigating the planet's mysterious moon. Phobos I was unfortunately lost en route; Phobos II was also ultimately lost in most intriguing circumstances, but not before it had beamed back certain images and information from the planet Mars itself.

According to author Walter Hain in his book *We From Mars* (1979, 1992, published in Austria) Phobos I and II were launched from Earth in July 1988, to reach Mars in January of 1989. According to Hain, an Austrian who monitored Soviet space missions closely, the Phobos I "failed" two months after launch while en route to Mars. Phobos II, however arrived safely at Mars and was injected into Mars orbit on January 29, 1989.

According to Hain, there was no other word from the Soviet space program until February 24, 1989, when the Associated Press reported that Phobos II was approaching the Martian moon Phobos. The report also included the first of several photographs taken by the space probe of the Martian moon. Phobos II then swung into an elliptical orbit around Mars taking various measurements of the magnetic field and atmosphere of the planet. Afterward, the orbit was modified so as to bring the craft within close proximity to moon of Phobos.

ØØØ

It had been intended that Phobos II would come within 50 meters (165 feet) of the moon and then deploy a "buoy" and anchor. This package of instruments was then to study the atmosphere and relationship between Mars and its mysterious moon.

On March 28, 1989, the Soviet mission control center acknowledged sudden communication "problems" with the spacecraft; and Tass, the official Soviet news agency, reported that "Phobos 2 failed to communicate with Earth as scheduled after completing an operation yesterday around the Martian moon Phobos. Scientists at mission control have been unable to establish stable radio contact."[52]

According to author Zechariah Sitchin in his book *Genesis Revisted* (Avon Books)[52] three months later the Soviet authorities released the taped television transmission that Phobos 2 had sent just before "failing."

However, the last photograph, taken just seconds before the spacecraft fell silent, was not released to the public and they were told so. The television sequence focused on the anomalies of a network of straight lines in the area of the Martian equator. Some of the lines were short, some longer, some thin, some wide enough to look like rectangular shapes "embossed" in the Martian surface. Arranged in rows parallel to each other, the pattern covered an area of some 600 square kilometers (more than 230 square miles). The "anomaly" appeared to be far from a natural phenomenon.

Zechariah Sitchin says that the television clip was accompanied by a live comment by Dr. John Becklake of England's Science Museum. Becklake described the phenomenon as very puzzling because the pattern seen on the surface of Mars was photographed not with the spacecraft's optical camera but with its infrared camera—a camera that takes pictures of objects using the heat they radiate and not by the play of light and shadow on them. In other words, the pattern of parallel lines and rectangles covering an area of almost 250 square miles was a source of heat radiation.

While it is possible that natural sources such of heat radiation such as a geyser or a concentration of radioactive minerals under the surface might create such a perfect geometric pattern, it seems more likely that that the object is not so easily explained. When viewed repeatedly, the pattern definitely looks artificial; but what it was, the scientist said, "I certainly don't know."[52]

⌀⌀⌀

A SHADOW ACROSS THE SURFACE OF MARS

According to Boris Bolitsky, science correspondent for Radio Moscow, just before contact was lost with Phobos 2, several unusual images were radioed back to Earth, described by the Russian as "quite remarkable features." A report taken from *New Scientist* of 8 April 1989, describes the following: "The features are either on the Martian surface or in the lower atmosphere. The features are between 20 and 25 kilometers wide and do not resemble any known geological formation. They are spindle-shaped and are proving to be intriguing and puzzling."

Walter Hain in *We From Mars* says that the Soviet newspaper ISVESTIA reported on the 16th April 1989, "Three days before the accident, the star sensor of the Phobos II probe registered in its field of observation an unknown object of considerable dimensions." A heat-sensitive TV instrument known as Thermoscan registered puzzlng stripes on the Martian surface which the Soviet report claimed were caused by the shadow of the martian moon Phobos which had been projected on to the surface of Mars by sunlight.

According to author Zechariah Sitchin in his book *Genesis Revisted* (Avon Books)[52] Dr. John Becklake of England's Science Museum explained on British national television "As the last picture was halfway through, they [the Soviets] saw something which should not be there." Dr. Becklake went on to state that the Soviets "have not yet released this last picture, and we won't speculate on what it shows."[52]

✐✐✐

Many researchers speculate that the Soviet probe was shot out of orbit around Mars because it was getting too close to the moon Phobos. Was the space probe shot out of space for "seeing too much"? What does the last secret frame show?

This "highly secret" photo was later given to the western press by Colonel Dr. Marina Popovich, a Russian astronaut and pilot, who has long been interested in UFOs. At a UFO conference in 1991, Popovich gave to certain investigators some interesting information that she "smuggled" out of the Soviet Union. Part of the information was what has been called "the first ever leaked account of an alien mothership in the solar system."

The last transmission from Phobos 2 was a photograph of a huge cylindrical spaceship—a huge, approximately 20 km long, 1.5 km diameter cigar-shaped "mothership," that was photographed on March 25, 1989, either coming from, going to, or parked next to, the Martian moon Phobos. After that last frame was radio-transmitted back to Earth, the probe mysteriously disappeared. According to the Russians, it was destroyed—possibly knocked-out with an energy pulse beam!

Australian science writer Brian Crowley says that because of the convex catseye shadow which, because of the overhead solar inclination, prevented shadow-casting by Martian surface features, implies a shadow thrown on the surface by something in orbit—beyond the orbit of Phobos 2 itself. The object is in fact a huge tubular object. One needs little imagination to postulate a giant, hovering cigar-shaped mother craft similar to those documented down the years by UFO investigators.[51]

ØØØ

INFRARED PHOTOS OF AN UNDERGROUND CITY

A well known photo of a space-base on Mars is the Mariner 9 frame 4209-75. The frame is an image of the Martian surface that shows clearly defined rectangular areas. These are interconnected with a latticework of perfectly straight channels, much resembling a city block. There were no corresponding surface features taken by regular cameras. It is located in the equatorial area (at longitude 186.4) and has been described as unusual indentations with radial arms protruding from a central hub caused (according to NASA scientists) by the melting and collapse of permafrost layers. The design of the features brings to mind the structure of a modern airport with a circular hub from which the long structures from which the airplane gates radiate.

Popular theory suggests the heat signature of what may be a set of underground caverns and channels that are too geometrically regular to have been formed naturally. Dr. John Becklake of the London Science Museum says "the city-like pattern is 60 kilometers wide and could easily be mistaken for an aerial view of Los Angeles."[51]

Could there be an underground base on the small Martian moonlet? Could the Martian moon Phobos be an engineered asteroid? One form of artificial moon is a hunk of rock from space (commonly called an asteroid) that is super-heated and then—as a glass-blower blows a glass ball—the moon inflated while molten-hot and then later allowed to cool into a hollow sphere. This artificial sphere could then be moved into orbit around a planet that wanted to be studied. A planet like Mars!.

Is someone or something inhabiting Mars and its satellites? Perhaps we could find a Star Wars type cocktail bar complete with entertainers and mercenaries. Or perhaps an Alternative 3 scenario where a small advance base on Mars has been created by the Earth's elite. Only time will tell as to just who or what is occupying Mars and its satellites.∆

ØØØ

CHAIN CRATERS ON PHOBOS

In an interesting article in the January, 1977, issue of *Astronomy*, entitled *Chain Craters on Phobos,* the anonymous author discusses the strange grooves and craters on Phobos:

"Viking has discovered another mystery in the most unexpected place—on one of the two small Martian moons. Mariner 9's mapping of both Phobos (12 x 14 x 17 miles, or 20 x 23 x 28 kilometers) and Deimos (6 x 7 x 10 miles, or 10 x 12 x 16 kilometers) showed many craters and left most investigators with the impression that they were merely rocky chunks that bore the scars of meteorite impacts. There was a puzzling feature on Phobos that a few analysts noticed but, without better data, could say little about.

"At the limit of resolution were a few small crater pits that seemed to align in one or two chains. This was unusual, because crater chains on the moon are traditionally explained as volcanic pits—small eruption sites strung along fracture lines. Yet Phobos apparently is too small to generate heat and conventional volcanic activity.

"Viking's high resolution photos have revealed that the crater chains are real and part of an extensive system of parallel grooves, a few hundred yards wide. There may be a tendency for the grooves to lie parallel to the direction of the satellite's orbital motion, although there appear to be several swarms with somewhat different orientations. Scientists are at a loss to explain them. Theories being discussed include: grooves left by much smaller satellite debris also orbiting Mars (though the grooves seem to follow contours of Phobos' surface too closely for this to be tenable); fractures radiating from an impact crater not yet recognized (perhaps on the side of Phobos still poorly photographed), or fractures created in the body of the Martian satellite when it was part of a hypothetical larger body that spawned both Martian moons, perhaps during a catastrophic impact." (Anonymous; *Astronomy*, 5:55, January 1977.)△

¤ ¤ ¤

In the latest effort to photograph Mars and its moons, the NASA Mars Observer was launched from Cape Canaveral Air Force base in Florida in late 1992 on a 337-day voyage to Mars. The Mars Observer initially was expected to arrive at Mars by August 19, 1993, and enter a long elliptical orbit over the poles. In mid-November 1993 it was to begin its two-year mapping of the surface of Mars. Then suddenly it was announced that NASA had lost contact with the spacecraft.

America and the world mourned the loss of a valuable scientific tool for understanding Mars. Taxpayers wondered if there was a better way to spend their money than on expensive spaceprobes that didn't work. Was it worth it to make scientific exploratory trips to Mars and was there anything to see there anyway? With the reported loss of the Mars Observer space probe, no new information about Mars would be released to the public. Sadly, a new dark age of scientific information on Mars had begun.*¤*

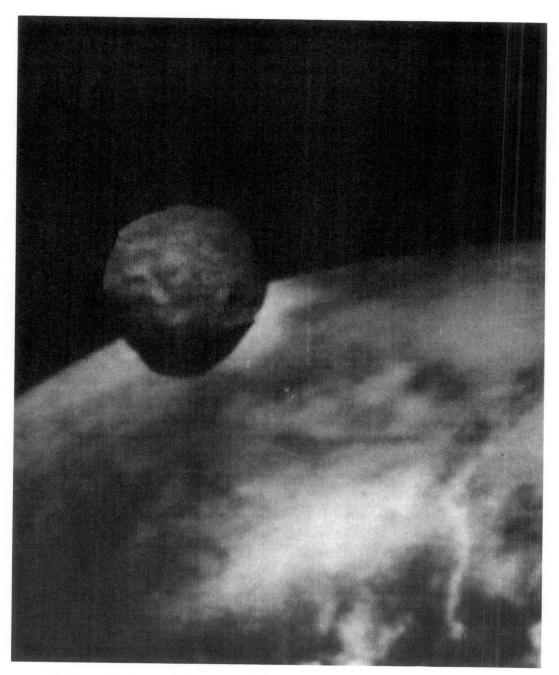

A dramatic view of Phobos with Mars in the background.

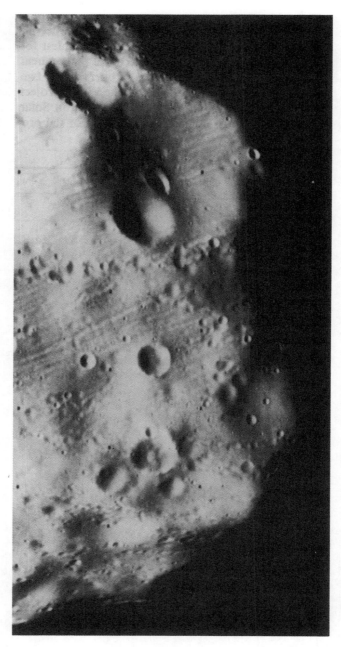

Close-up view of Phobos, showing the grooved and
cratered surface. Viking Orbiter photo 39B84.

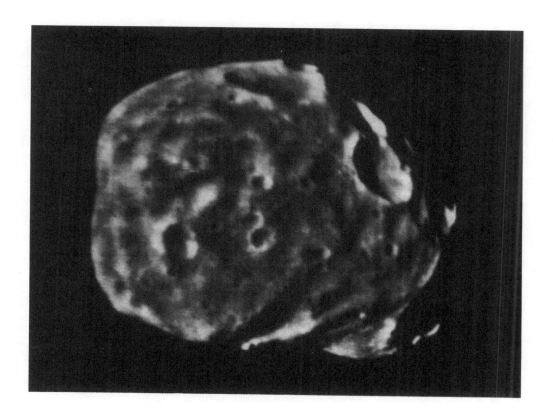

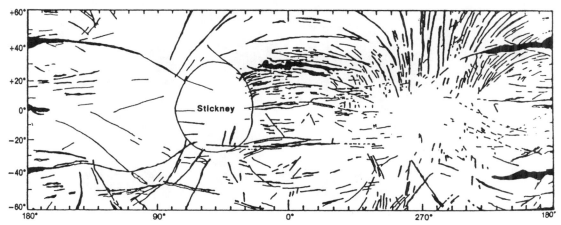

Top: Phobos, photographed from the Russian space-craft Phobos 2 on 21 February 1989 from a range of 273 miles (440 km). **Bottom:** A map of the "grooves."

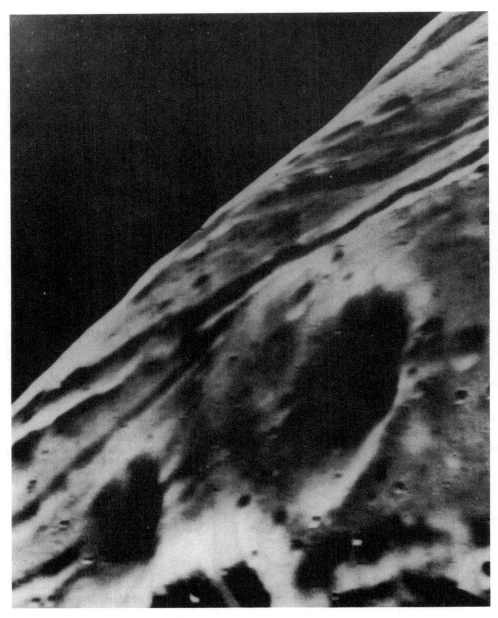

Close-up of the Martian satellite Phobos showing peculiar regolithic markings and pock-mark cratering. *NASA photo*.

A new NASA photo of an anomalous structure on the Moon
released by Richard Hoagland in his latest video, *Hoagland's
Mars III: The Moon-Mars Connection.* In this video Hoagland
shows NASA Lunar Orbiter frame III-84M. It shows what
Hoagland says is a huge mile and a half high ruined skyscraper
on the Moon. "The Shard" as they call it is located just
southwest of the *Sinus Medii* central region of the Moon. The
geometric "star" at the top left of the photo is a camera
registration mark. Hoagland comments that there is no
geological explanation for this structure, particularly the swollen
middle-section of the towering object.

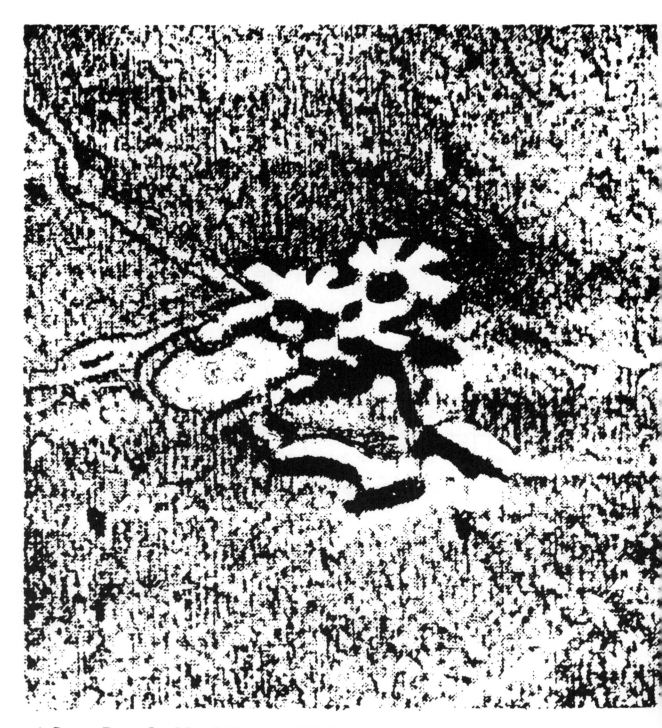

A Space Base On Mars? Blow-up of NASA photo No. 75-H-604 of the Martian surface by Mariner 9. The feature, said to be just beneath the surface of Mars, covers an area of 3.6 to 4.2 miles. Note the "bays," similar to a modern airport, and other artificial-looking features. Enhancement from *Genesis Revisted* by Zechariah Sitchin. ©Zechariah Sitchin.

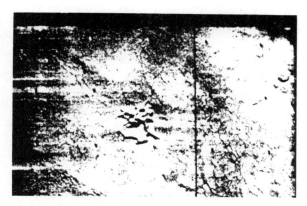

Above and page opposite: NASA photo No. 75-H-604 of the Martian surface by Mariner 9. The feature, said to be just beneath the surface of Mars, covers an area of 3.6 to 4.2 miles. Opposite: A blow-up of NASA frame 75-H-604. Note the "bays" similar to a modern airport and other artificial features. A space base like this on Mars may well have shot out-of-orbit the Soviet Phobos II space probe.

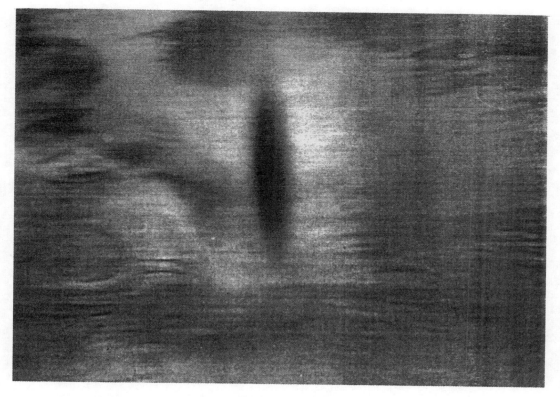

One of the last photos taken by the Soviet Phobos II space probe. It shows a shadow of a long, elipse-shaped object being cast on to the surface of Mars. Could it be the shadow of a long cigar-shaped object rather than the shadow of a Martian moon? This is apparently the shadow of the tubular craft in the photo on the next page.

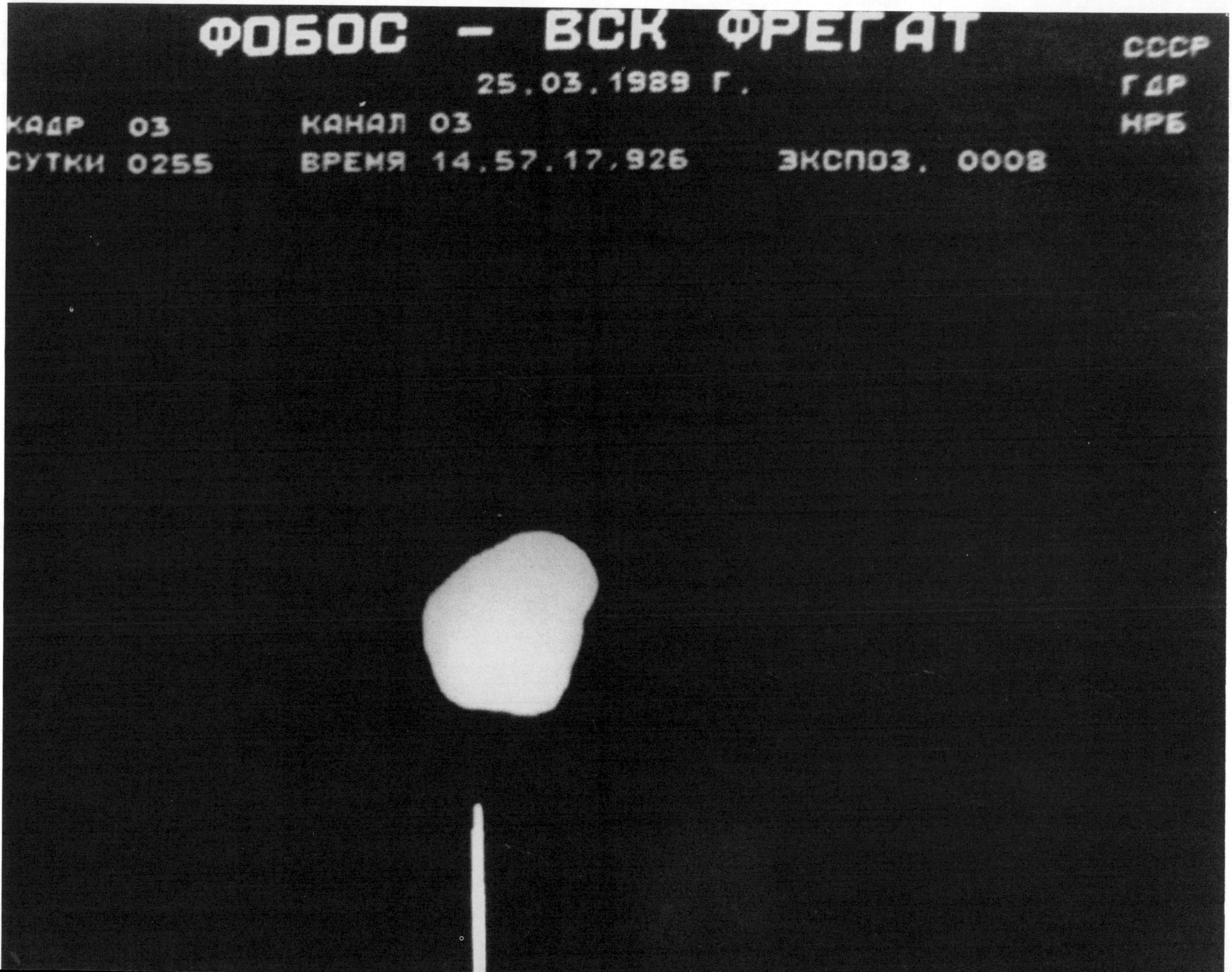

ФОБОС — ВСК ФРЕГАТ

25.03.1989 Г.

КАДР 03   КАНАЛ 03   ЭКСПОЗ. 0008
СУТКИ 0255   ВРЕМЯ 14.57.17,926

СССР
ГДР
НРБ

A city of the future on Mars

From a 1961 book on Mars.

With the nuclear-power plant furnishing the energy for the city, the buildings are designed to make use of sunlight as much as possible. They will contain their own atmosphere and are connected with each other by airtight passages, since outside travel calls for space suits. Nuclear energy will extract oxygen from the oxides on Mars at small cost.

Gravity on the surface of Mars is one-third the gravity on the surface of Earth, which accounts for the extreme lightness of the bridge construction as shown in the picture.

BY COURTESY OF GENERAL MILLS, INC., AND SWIFT-CHAPLIN PRODUCTIONS, INC.

Opposite:

The Last Photo of Phobos. The photo given by Dr. Marina Popovich as the final transmission of the Russian probe Phobos 2 before it was "shot out of orbit." The photo apparently shows the Martian moon Phobos with a long, cigar-shaped craft either coming from or going to the moon.

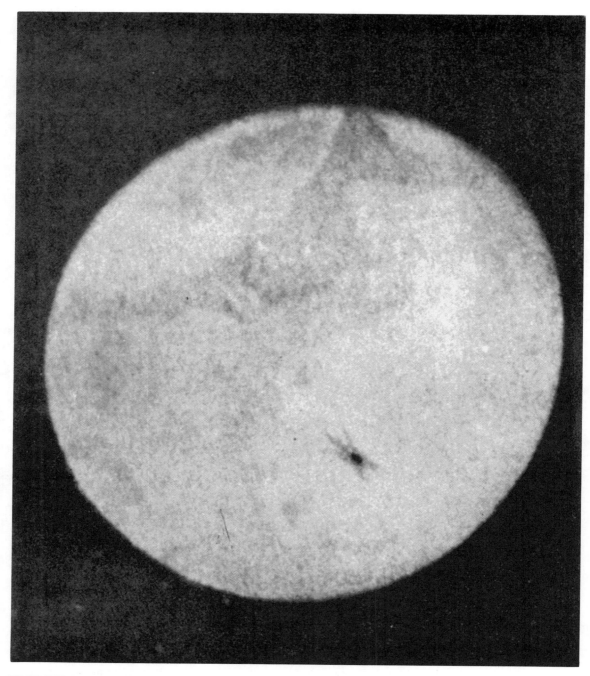

THE FIRST PHOTOGRAPH EVER TAKEN OF A UFO
(Published in *L'Astronomie* of 1885 p. 349)

On 12 August 1883 a M. Bonilla was making observations and photographs of the Sun from the Observatory of Zacatecas, Mexico. He noted large numbers of small objects transiting from the sun's disk, one of which paused, long enough to be photographed before rejoining its companions. He had time to telegraph the Observatories of Mexico City and of Puebla and to receive a reply while the celestial procession continued. Word came back that the objects appeared to them some distance from the sun. Because of this parallax, Bonilla placed the bodies 'relatively near the earth'. Notice the peculiar ray-like projections.

Chapter 8

Mysteries of Venus & Mercury

This night we are going to take you far away from your own Earth, we are going to take you to the planet you call Venus. Take you there just to show you that there are civilizations beyond anything that you know on Earth, take you so that your days of life upon Earth may be brightened by the knowledge of what is, and what can be.

—T. Lobsang Rampa
My Trip To Venus
(1957)

SPACE PROBES TO VENUS

On June 2 and 7, 1983, two of the Soviet Union's mighty PROTON rockets lifted off from the Tyuratam Space Center in the Kazakhstan Republic. Aboard those boosters were a new breed of VENERA probe for the planet Venus.

Designated VENERA 15 and 16, the probes were meant not for landing yet more spherical craft on the Venerean surface but to radar map the planet in detail from orbit.

The Soviet probes' imaging parameters were a vast improvement over the United States PIONEER VENUS Orbiter, which could reveal objects no smaller than 75 kilometers (45 miles) in diameter. And while the

VENERAs' resolution was comparable to that of similar observations made by the 300-meter (1,000-foot) Arecibo radio telescope on the island of Puerto

Rico, the orbiters would be examining the northern pole of Venus. This region was unobtainable by either Arecibo or PIONEER VENUS and appeared to contain a number of potentially interesting geological features worthy of investigation.

On October 10, 1983, after an interplanetary journey of 330 million kilometers (198 million miles) and two mid-course corrections, VENERA 15 fired its braking rockets over Venus to place itself in a polar orbit 1,000 by 65,000 kilometers (600 by 39,000 miles) around the planet, completing one revolution every twenty-four hours. VENERA16 followed suit four days later. The twin probes thus became Venus' first polar-circling spacecraft.

VENERA 15 and 16 revealed that Venus has a surface geology more complex than shown by PIONEER VENUS in the late 1970s. Numerous hills, mountains, ridges, valleys, and plains spread across the landscape, many of them apparently formed by lava from erupting volcanoes in the last one billion years. In planetary terms this makes the Venerean surface rather young. Hundreds of craters were detected as well, the largest of which had to have been created by meteorites (planetoids would be a better term here) at least fourteen kilometers (8.4 miles) across, due to Venus' very dense atmosphere.

There were some disagreements between U.S. and Soviet scientists on the origins of certain surface features. For example, the probes' owners declared that the 96-kilometer (57.6-mile) wide crater at the summit of 10,800-meter (35,640-foot) high Maxwell Montes, the tallest mountain on the planet, was the result of a meteorite impact. American scientists, on the other hand, felt the crater was proof that Maxwell was a huge volcano sitting on the northern "continent" of Ishtar Terra.

In any event, the U.S. decided to wait on making verdicts about Venus until the arrival of their own radar probe, scheduled for later in the decade. Originally named the Venus Orbiting Imaging Radar (VOIR), its initial design was scaled back and the craft was redesignated the Venus Radar Mapper (VRM). Eventually the machine would be called MAGELLAN, after the Portuguese navigator Ferdinand Magellan (circa 1480-1521). This vehicle would map the entire planet in even finer detail than the VENERAs. For the time, however, the Soviet probes maintained that distinction.

Radar imaging was not the only ability of the VENERAs. Bolted next to the POLYUS V radar antenna were the Omega altimeter and the Fourier infrared spectrometer, the latter for measuring the world's temperatures. The majority of the areas covered registered about five hundred degrees Celsius (932 degrees Fahrenheit), but a few locations were two hundred degrees hotter, possibly indicating current volcanic activity. The probes also found that the clouds over the poles were five to eight kilometers (three to 4.8 miles) lower than at the equator. In contrast, the polar air above sixty kilometers (thirty-six miles) altitude was five to twenty degrees warmer than the equatorial atmosphere at similar heights.

When the main mapping mission ended in July of 1984, there were plans for at least one of the VENERAs to radar image the surface at more southerly latitudes. Unfortunately this idea did not come to pass, as the orbiters may not have possessed enough attitude-control gas to perform the operation.

VENERA 15 and 16 ceased transmission in March of 1985, leaving the *Soviet Institute of Radiotechnology and Electronics* with six hundred kilometers (360 miles) of radar data tape to sort into an atlas of twenty-seven maps of the northern hemisphere of Venus.

VENUS BY BALLOON

For years the thick atmosphere of Venus had been a tempting target to scientists who wished to explore the planet's mantle of air with balloon-borne instruments. Professor Jacques Blamont of the

French space agency Centre National d'Etudes Spatiales (CNES) had proposed such an idea as far back as 1967, only to have a joint French-Soviet balloon mission canceled in 1982. Nevertheless, late in the year 1984, such dreams would eventually come true.

When two PROTON rockets were sent skyward on December 15 and 21, the Soviet Union provided Western observers with the first clear, full views of the booster which had been launching every Soviet Venus probe since 1975. This was but one of many firsts for the complex mission.

The unmanned probes launched into space that December were named VEGA 1 and 2, a contraction of the words VENERA and GALLEI—Gallei being the Russian word for Halley. Not only did the spacecraft have more than one mission to perform, they also had more than one celestial objective to explore, namely the comet Halley.

This famous periodic traveler was making its latest return to the inner regions of the solar system since its last visit in 1910. Since it was widely believed that comets are the icy remains from the formation of the solar system five billion years ago, scientists around the world gave high priority to exploring one of the few such bodies which actually come close to Earth.

Most comets linger in the cold and dark outer fringes of the solar system. Some, like Halley, are perturbed by various forces and fall in towards the Sun, where they circle for millennia spewing out ice and debris for millions of kilometers from the warmth of each solar encounter.

The Soviet Union, along with the European Space Agency (ESA) and Japan's Institute of Space and Astronautical Science (ISAS), did not wish to miss out on this first opportunity in human history to make a close examination of Halley. The ESA would be using the cylindrical GIOTTO probe to make a dangerously close photographic flyby of the comet, while Japan's first deep space craft—SAKIGAKE

236

(Pioneer) and SUISEI (Comet) - would view Halley from a much safer distance.

Scientists in the United States also desired to study the comet from the vantage of a space probe, at one time envisioning a vessel powered by solar sails or ion engines. However, government budget cuts to NASA canceled the American efforts. The U.S. would have to make do primarily with Earth-based observations and the sharing of data from other nations, though an instrument named the Dust Counter and Mass Analyzer (DUCMA), designed by Chicago University Professor John Simpson, was added on the Soviet mission in May of 1984.

The Soviets' answer to Halley were the VEGAs. Instead of building an entirely new craft for the mission, the Soviets decided to modify their VENERA bus design to encounter the comet while performing an advanced Venus mission along the way. As VEGA 1 and 2 reached Venus, the buses would drop off one lander/balloon each and use the mass of the shrouded planet to swing them towards comet Halley, much as the U.S. probe MARINER 10 used Venus to flyby Mercury eleven years earlier. The Soviet craft would then head on to Halley, helping to pinpoint the location of the comet's erupting nucleus for the GIOTTO probe to dive in only 605 kilometers (363 miles) away in March of 1986.

As planned, the two VEGAs arrived at Venus in June of 1985. VEGA1 released its payload first on the ninth day of the month, the lander making a two-day descent towards the planet. The craft touched the upper atmosphere on the morning of June 11. Sixty-one kilometers (36.6 miles) above the Venerean surface a small container was released by the lander, which produced a parachute at 55 kilometers (33 miles) altitude. Thus the first balloon probe ever to explore Venus had successfully arrived.

One kilometer after the opening of the parachute, helium gas was pumped into the Teflon-coated plastic balloon, inflating it to a diameter of 3.54

meters (11.68 feet). Dangling on a tether thirteen meters (42.9 feet) below was the instrument package, properly known as an aerostat. The top part of the 6.9-kilogram (15.18-pound) aerostat consisted of a cone which served as an antenna and tether attachment point to the balloon. Beneath it was the transmitter, electronics, and instruments. Connected at the bottom was a nephelometer for measuring cloud particles. The aerostat was painted with a special white finish to keep at bay the corroding mist of sulfuric acid which permeated the planet's atmosphere.

The VEGA 1 balloon was dropped into the night side of Venus just north of the equator. Scientists were concerned that the gas bag would burst in the heat of daylight, so they placed it in the darkened hemisphere to give the craft as much time as possible to return data. This action necessitated that the landers come down in the dark as well, effectively removing the camera systems used on previous missions. The author wonders, though, if they could have used floodlights similar to the ones attached to VENERA 9 and 10 in 1975, when Soviet scientists had thought the planet's surface was enshrouded in a perpetual twilight due to the permanently thick cloud cover.

The first balloon transmitted for 46.5 hours right into the day hemisphere before its lithium batteries failed, covering 11,600 kilometers (6,960 miles). The threat of bursting in the day heat did not materialize. The VEGA 1 balloon was stationed at a 54-kilometer (32.4-mile) altitude after dropping ballast at fifty kilometers (thirty miles), for this was considered the most active of the three main cloud layers reported by PIONEER VENUS in 1978. Indeed the balloon was pushed across the planet at speeds up to 250 kilometers (150 miles) per hour. Strong vertical winds bobbed the craft up and down two to three hundred meters (660 to 990 feet) through most of the journey. The layer's air temperature averaged forty degrees Celsius (104 degrees Fahrenheit) and pressure was a mere 0.5

Earth atmosphere. The nephelometer could find no clear regions in the surrounding clouds.

Early in the first balloon's flight, the VEGA 1 lander was already headed towards the Venerean surface. Both landers were equipped with a soil drill and analyzer similar to the ones carried on VENERA 13 and 14 in 1982. However, VEGA 1 would become unable to report the composition of the ground at its landing site in Rusalka Planitia, the Mermaid Plain north of Aphrodite Terra. While still ten to fifteen minutes away from landing, a timer malfunction caused the drill to accidentally begin its programmed activity sixteen kilometers (9.6 miles) above the surface.

There was neither any way to shut off the instrument before touchdown nor reactivate it after landing. This was unfortunate not only for the general loss of data but also for the fact that most of Venus was covered with such smooth low-level lava plains and had never before been directly examined. Nevertheless, the surface temperature and pressure was calculated at 468 degrees Celsius (874.4 degrees Fahrenheit) and 95 Earth atmospheres respectively during the lander's 56 minutes of ground transmissions. A large amount of background infrared radiation was also recorded at the site.

As had been done when the drills and cameras on VENERA 11 and 12 had failed in December of 1978, the Soviets focused on the data returned during the lander's plunge through the atmosphere. The French-Soviet Malachite mass spectrometer detected sulfur, chlorine, and possibly phosphorus. It is the sulfur—possibly from active volcanoes - which gives the Venerean clouds their yellowish color. The Sigma 3 gas chromatograph found that every cubic meter of air between an altitude of 48 and 63 kilometers (28.8 and 37.8 miles contained one milligram (0.015 grain) of sulfuric acid.

The VEGA 1 data on the overall structure of the cloud decks appeared to be at odds with the information from PIONEER VENUS. The case was made even stronger by the fact that VEGA 2's result nearly matched its twin. The VEGAs found only two main cloud layers instead of the three reported by the U.S. probes. The layers were three to five kilometers (1.8 to 3 miles) thick at altitudes of 50 and 58 kilometers (30 and 34.8 miles). The clouds persisted like a thin fog until clearing at an altitude of 35 kilometers (21 miles), much lower than the PV readings. One possibility for the discrepancies may have been radical structural changes in the Venerean air

over the last seven years.

When the lander and balloon finally went silent, the last functioning part of the VEGA 1 mission, the flyby bus, sailed on for a 708 million-kilometer (424.8 million-mile) journey around the Sun to become the first probe to meet comet Halley. On March 6, 1986, the bus made a 8,890-kilometer (5,334-mile) pass at the dark and icy visitor before traveling on in interplanetary space. The Soviets had accomplished their first mission to two celestial bodies with one space vessel.

On June 13, VEGA 2 released its lander/balloon payload for a two-day fall towards Venus. Like its duplicate, the VEGA 2 balloon radioed information back to the twenty antennae tracking it on Earth for 46.5 hours before battery failure on the morning side of the planet. During its 11,100-kilometer (6,660-mile) flight over Venus, the second balloon entered in a rather still environment which became less so twenty hours into the mission.

After 33 hours mission time the air became even more turbulent for a further eight hours. When the balloon passed over a five- kilometer (three-mile) mountain on the "continent" of Aphrodite Terra, a powerful down-draft pulled the craft 2.5 kilometers (1.5 miles) towards the surface.

Temperature sensors on the VEGA 2 balloon reported that the air layer it was moving through was consistently 6.5 degrees Celsius (43.7 degrees Fahrenheit) cooler than the area explored by the VEGA 1 balloon. This was corroborated by the VEGA

2 lander as it passed through the balloon's level. No positive indications of lightning were made by either balloon, and the second aerostat's nephelometer failed to function.

The VEGA 2 lander touched down on the northern edge of Aphrodite Terra's western arm on the fifteenth of June, 1,500 kilometers (900 miles) southeast of VEGA 1. The lander's resting place was smoother than thought, indicating either a very ancient and worn surface or a relatively young one covered in fresh lava. The soil drill was in working order and reported a rock type known as anorthosite-troctolite, rare on Earth but present in Luna's highlands. This rock is rich in aluminum and silicon but lacking in iron and magnesium. A high degree of sulfur was also present in the soil. The air around VEGA 2 measured 463 degrees Celsius (865.4 degrees Fahrenheit) and 91 Earth atmospheres, essentially a typical day (or night) on Venus.

"Hey, Buddy! Want to buy a Space Probe?"

During the late 1980s a drastic political and economic change was taking over the Soviet Union. President Mikhail Gorbachev began to "open up" his nation to the benefits of increased cooperation with the rest of the nations, particularly those in the West. While the culture became less oppressive than in the past, the economy was taking a very rough ride as it also underwent the effects of a "free market".

These effects hit everywhere, including the space program. Missions at all levels were cut back. The Soviets began making almost desperate attempts to cooperate with other space-faring nations either to keep their remaining programs alive or just to make money.

In early 1992 it was reported that the Soviets were offering for sale several fully-equipped VENERAs they had in storage for the price of 1.6 million dollars each, an incredibly low price for any planetary probe. No nation took them up on the bargain. Meanwhile the United States was gearing up for new Venus missions of their own.

MAGELLAN and GALILEO

The U.S. reactivated their long-dormant planetary exploration with the launch of the Space Shuttle ATLANTIS on May 4, 1989. Aboard the Shuttle was the MAGELLAN spacecraft, a combination of spare parts from other U.S. probes designed to make the most detailed and complete radar-mapping of Venus in history. When MAGELLAN reached the second world in August of 1990, it would be able to map almost the entire planet down to a resolution of 108 meters (360 feet), surpassing the abilities of VENERA 15 and 16.

In the interim another American probe was launched from a Space Shuttle which would make a quick flyby of Venus on its way to orbit the giant planet Jupiter in 1995. On October 18, 1989, the Shuttle ATLANTIS released its second unmanned planetary probe into space, named GALILEO after the famous Italian astronomer who discovered the probe's primary target's major moons in 1610.

In the absence of a powerful enough booster to send GALILEO on a direct flight to the Jovian planet, the probe was sent around Venus and Earth several times to build up enough speed to reach Jupiter. As a result, Venus became GALILEO's first planetary goal in February of 1990. The probe radioed back images of the planet's swirling clouds and further indications of lightning in that violent atmosphere.

EVIDENCE OF OCEANS ON EARLY VENUS

In mid-1993, NASA released findings by the Pioneer Venus Orbiter spacecraft that provided strong new evidence that planet Venus once had three and a half times more water as thought earlier

—enough water to cover the entire surface between 25 and 75 feet deep (762 and 2286 centimeters).

These findings also give new support for the presence of lightning on Venus and discoveries about the ionosphere and top of the atmosphere of Venus. Considered Earth's twin planet, Venus today is very dry and searing hot.

Pioneer entered Venus' atmosphere on Oct. 8, 1992, and burned up soon after, ending 14 years of exploration.

"Many of us have long thought that early in its history Venus had temperate conditions and oceans like Earth's," said Dr. Thomas Donahue, University of Michigan, head of the Pioneer Venus science steering group.

"Findings that Venus was once fairly wet does not prove that major oceans existed, but make their existence far more likely," he said. "The new Pioneer data provides evidence that large amounts of water were definitely there," said Donahue.

"Most scientists think Venus' early oceans vaporized and 'blew off' 3 billion years ago in a runaway greenhouse effect when the cool early sun increased its luminosity and heated the planet very hot," he said. "The oceans evaporated. Solar ultraviolet radiation split the water molecules into hydrogen and oxygen, and the hydrogen was lost to space.

"Pioneer Venus Probe and Orbiter data showed early in the mission," Donahue said, "that on Venus heavy abundant relative to ordinary hydrogen than on Earth and everywhere else we've looked in the solar system—Mars, Comet Halley, meteorites, Jupiter and Saturn." Venus' remarkable hydrogen/deuterium ratio has since been confirmed by independent measurements.

According to NASA, abundant deuterium is taken as clear evidence that Venus once had 150 times as much water in its atmosphere as today. This is because the water's ordinary hydrogen has escaped. But most of the water's heavy hydrogen (deuterium

- twice as heavy as hydrogen) stayed behind because of its weight.

When the Orbiter made its final descent to unexplored regions only 80 miles (129 kilometers) above Venus' surface, it found evidence for 3.5 times as much water as previously suggested by the deuterium ratio.

"We found a new and important easy-escape mechanism, which accelerates hydrogen and deuterium away from the planet," he said. "This means that much more hydrogen had to escape to build up the present high deuterium concentration. A lot more hydrogen lost means a lot more water early on," he said. "This also rules out theories of a dry-from-the-beginning Venus, whose present meager supply of water comes from an occasional comet impact."

The data also show that at Pioneer's lowest altitude 80 miles (129 kilometers) "whistler" radio signals, believed generated by Venus' lightning, were the strongest ever detected. Pioneer has long measured such "lightning" signals. They are the same as the radio signals used in most lightning studies on Earth.

In its final orbits, Pioneer penetrated 7 miles (11 kilometers) below the peak of Venus' ionosphere, which tends to block these radio signals. Here also, the magnetic fields which channel the signals were the strongest ever seen on Venus' night side.

"These results are best explained by a strong and persistent source of lightning in the Venus atmosphere," said Robert Strangeway of UCLA, Pioneer electric field investigator.

Some scientists continue to doubt Venus lightning. They say only optical sightings can prove lightning. A Russian spacecraft has reported visible-light sightings of lightning. Four Russian spacecraft and the U.S. Galileo craft also have observed radio signals believed from lightning.

Over 3 months, Pioneer provided data from 80 to 210 miles (129 to 336 kilometers) altitude. It found the beginning of Venus' real, mixed atmosphere (transition from oxygen to carbon dioxide) at 80 miles (129 kilometers). Below 85 miles (136 kilometers), it identified various waves and a 4-day oscillation of Venus' atmosphere top. The neutral atmosphere above 185 miles (296 kilometers) was more than 10 times denser and 2120 F (1,000 degrees Celsius) hotter than thought.

MARKINGS ON MERCURY AND VENUS

Wesley, W. H.; *Knowledge*, 4:228, 1907

In 1896 Professor Lowell published in the Monthly Notices (vol. lvii., p. 148) a series of drawings of Mercury, showing extremely curious markings on the planet, which he speaks of as much more distinct than the Martian canals, and, in fact, quite easy to see. They appear to have been observed when the planet's surface was not more than half illuminated, and the drawings show them as linear in character, though otherwise they bear little resemblance to the canals of Mars. I give as an example Professor Lowell's drawing of September 23, 1896, in which the markings appear mostly as stripes projecting from the terminator or running parallel with it. There is also a slight shading off of the cusps.

Professor Lowell promised further communications on this planet, but I cannot find any later observations, his work having been recently mostly devoted to Mars.

He also published in the same number of the Monthly Notices some drawings of Venus, showing a number of singular markings like the spokes of a wheel, but in 1902 he wrote in the Astronomische Nachrichten (No. 3, 823) that he had found reason to believe that these markings were due to an optical illusion. I do not know whether he still considers the markings on Mercury as objective, but those which he drew in 1896 do not seem to me at all like the canals of Mars, and, as far as I know, they have not been confirmed by other observers.

THE MARKINGS ON VENUS

Douglass, A. E.; *Royal Astronomical Society, Monthly Notices,* 58:382-385, 1898.

The reading public has been recently addressed on the subject of the markings on Venus in various attempts to show that the discoveries made at this observatory are unworthy of credit. No matter how futile such criticism must prove to be in the long run, some persons will be influenced by it if we do not from time to time make some rejoinder, or give out some statement which will show our continued activity in this line of work, our undiminished confidence in the results obtained, and our answering attitude towards adverse opinion.

In the last six years many thousands of hours have been spent by us at telescopes of 13, 18, and 24 inches aperture and their smaller finders, when the seeing was sufficiently good for profitable work on the finest known planetary detail. Expressed in standard terms, the seeing was practically always such that in a 6-inch aperture the spurious disc of the interference pattern was well defined, and a very large part of the time the rings of the same pattern were unbroken. I consider that any astronomer who cannot say the same for the seeing during his hours of work, and whose hours of work do not reach a commendable number, has no right to criticize our results; for he lacks the experience by which alone he becomes capable of judging.

Under proper conditions of air and aperture the markings on Venus are absolutely certain. Under proper conditions they are to me about as easy or difficult to see as the irregularities on the terminator of the Moon when it is near the first quarter, viewed by the naked eye. I have on a few occasions seen a large projection perfectly distinct. So it is with

Venus. At the best seeing the markings are visible at the first glance.

To say that no markings save M. Antoniadi's symmetrical shadings of atmospheric contrast exist, or that the detail seen here is due to pressure on our objective, or to defective densities in the eye-piece, or to our own eyes, or to the imaginings of our brains; or, most ridiculous of all, to our looking all day at some map and then seeing it on the planet, is to offer suggestions too absurd to be taken seriously.

We use the telescope in both positions, normal and reversed: that shows that the markings are not in the lens. We use different eye-pieces and twist them in varying position angles: that shows that the markings are not there. We sit in different positions, so the markings cannot be in our eyes; and different persons in perfect independence find the same detail, so it is not a mental phenomenon.

The first reason why other observers have not seen these markings is bad atmosphere. When I began observing the third satellite of Jupiter, for days, even weeks, I drew nothing but hazy indefinite markings or belts, such things as M. Antoniadi describes as appearing to him on Venus. But one night after making several drawings of that character the seeing suddenly became superb, the curtain rose as it were, and I saw sharp distinct black lines about which uncertainty was impossible. The very same thing happened on the fourth satellite four days later. I had been drawing the same indefinable shadings, when one night the seeing improved, the curtain again rose, and I perceived sharp definite lines. After once thoroughly understanding the character of the object sought, I could see them and profitably study them under conditions of seeing formerly prohibitory.

The experience on Venus has been similar. On the day succeeding my first good view, I spent nearly the whole afternoon without catching a single certain glimpse. Suddenly the seeing improved for an instant, and I saw the same markings unmistakably. If it had not been for that glimpse, I would have gone away perfectly ready to believe that no markings existed. I am not surprised that other astronomers doubt them.

The second reason why some other observers have not seen them has been the fault of using too large an aperture. Six years ago I discovered "air waves," and over four years ago I explained theoretically why reducing the aperture is often beneficial. All this has been published in full elsewhere (Am. Met. Jour. 1895 and Pop. Ast. 1897). I decided long since that in planetary work the greatest efficiency is obtained with the smallest aperture which supplies the required illumination. There is a limit to this, however. An inch and a half lens shows the markings on Venus nicely, but they are not so well defined as in a lens of three inches, which in our atmosphere is a very satisfactory size to us. When the seeing is very bad an aperture of less than three inches will become necessary.

A third cause of failure is the effect of heating of the lens and tube by the Sun's rays. For this reason I have found it sometimes advantageous to use the small finder, which is far within the dome and well shaded.

A fourth cause comes from the air within the dome being colder than that without. This is likely to harm the seeing. If the interior is warmer than the exterior, it will certainly harm the seeing. In fact my latest experiments show that any dome at all is harmful. A sunshade surrounding the tube would be better both night and day.

A fifth cause of failure, and by no means the least important, is the lack of continuity of observations and the lack of a first good view. By the first I mean fair or good observations made many days in succession. For instance if the seeing is only fair it requires the work of several nights in succession, without intervals, to identify with certainty the longitude presented by a satellite of Jupiter. By a "first good view" I mean the necessity of one first-class observation before one understands what is sought. After that view the observer can obtain valuable results under conditions in which formerly he failed completely from ignorance of what he was after. It is the same in observing the Gegenschein. I have taught many persons to observe it, and I find that teaching consists in getting them to see it well once. After that they can be trusted to pick it out with very small liability to error. This, of course, is most true in atmospheres unclouded by smoke and unlighted by electricity.

No matter how difficult to obtain, a just hearing is our right. No one is entitled to cry out against us until he can show that his atmosphere is approximately as good as the one through which Mr. Lowell discovered these markings. Let our dubious friends, who attempt to show what we as well as they are deluded, devote a portion of their valuable time to work at the telescope under better atmospheric conditions, and no one will misunderstand the silence which will follow.

LIFE ON VENUS

Was there ever life on Venus? Many mystics have claimed contact with space travellers from Venus. Could human-type life ever be able to stand on the surface of Venus? According to current scientific belief, at present the lead-melting temperatures and crushing air pressure would be threatening to any Earth life not protected in something even tougher than a VENERA lander. Plans have been looked into changing the environment of Venus itself into something more like Earth's. However, it should be noted that any such undertaking will require the removal of much of the thick carbon dioxide atmosphere, a major reduction in surface heat, and the ability to speed up the planet's rotation rate to something a bit faster than once every 243 Earth days. Such a project may take centuries if not millennia.

Note the rayed craters on Mercury in this mosaic photo of Mariner 10 images.

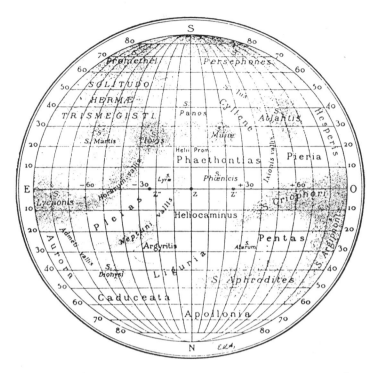

Antoniadi's early map of Mercury, drawn from a 33-inch Meudon refractor telescope. Note the interesting, "mystical" names given to regions of the planet.

Unusual surface markings seen on Mercury by Percival Lowell.

MERCURY

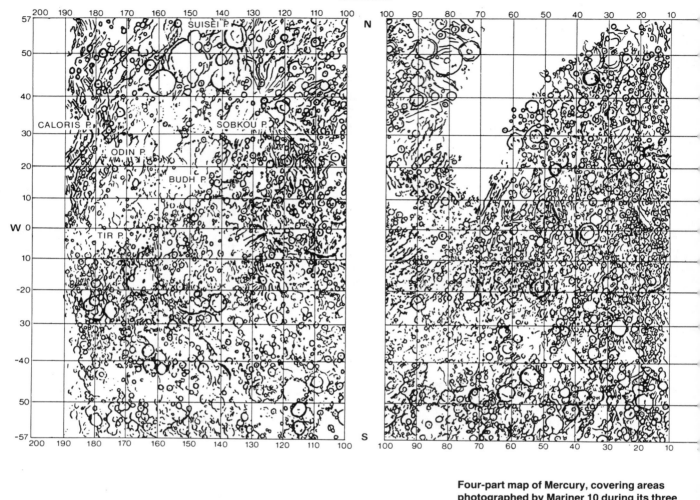

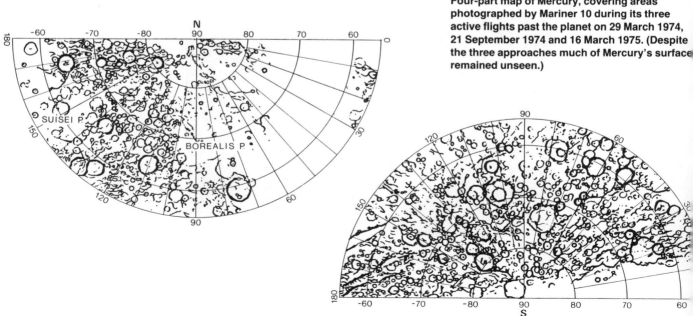

Four-part map of Mercury, covering areas photographed by Mariner 10 during its three active flights past the planet on 29 March 1974, 21 September 1974 and 16 March 1975. (Despite the three approaches much of Mercury's surface remained unseen.)

Craters on Mercury with central pyramid peaks. At least in superficial appearance, Mercury looks much like our Moon.

A rayed crater on Mercury. Do George Leonard's theories on the origin of the rays on the Moon also hold for Mercury and the moons of the outer planets?

Mercury's Caloris Basin can be clearly seen in this enhanced Mariner 10 photo. A 1,300 km (800 mile) diameter ring of mountains up to 2 km (6,500 ft) high rims the outer edge of the basin. Note the many pyramidical peaks and triangular shadows cast by them.

Oblique view of a 98 km diameter crater in the Shakespeare region of Mercury, showing the terraced areas of the crater rim and well developed central "pyramids." Note the double triangular shadows cast by the central structures.

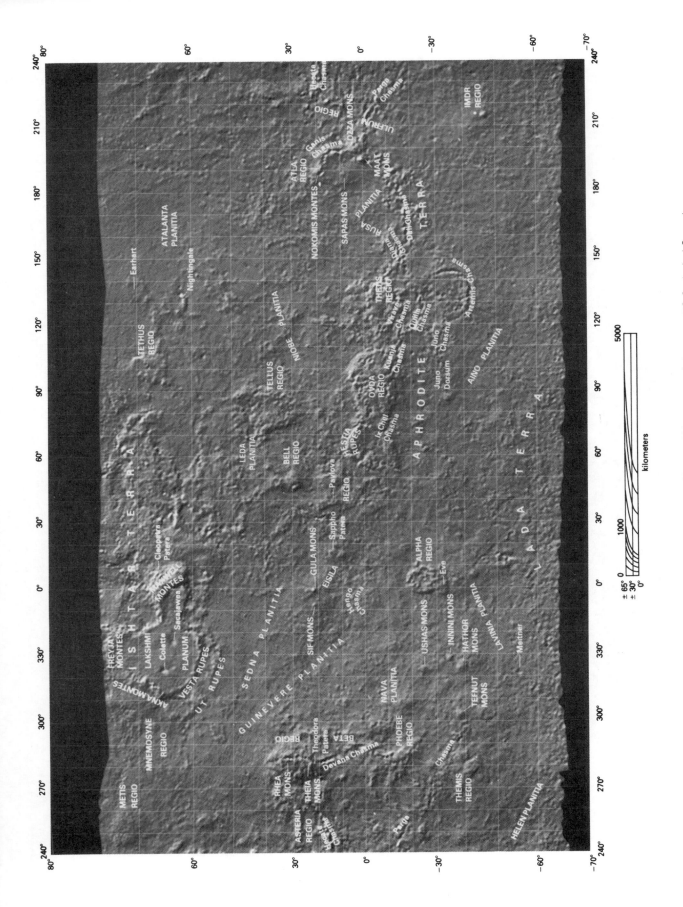

Shaded relief map of Venus based on altimetric data from the Pioneer Venus orbiting spacecraft (courtesy US Geological Survey).

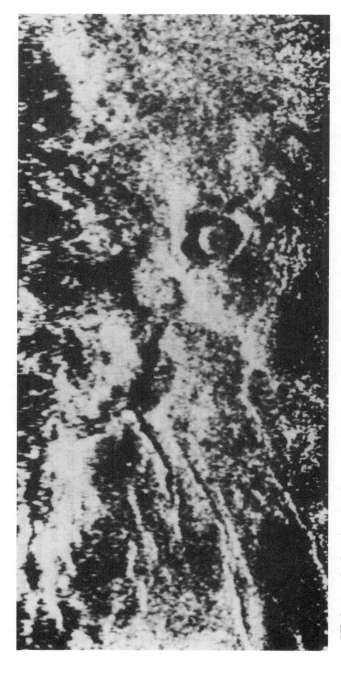

High-resolution image from the Venera 15 mission to Venus showing the area thought to be Metis Regio at about 72°N. The circular dome-shaped feature on the right has a summit depression and an inner "hill." One of the more curious formations on Venus. Image is about 140 by 300 km.

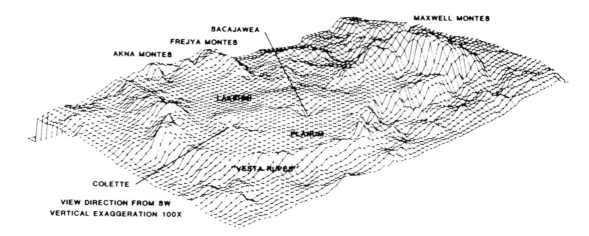

(a) Ishtar Terra

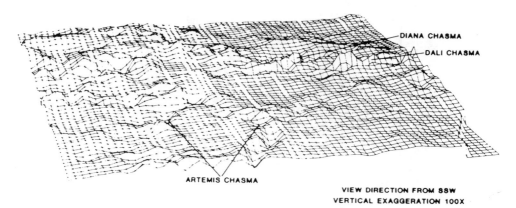

(b) Rift valleys within Aphrodite Terra

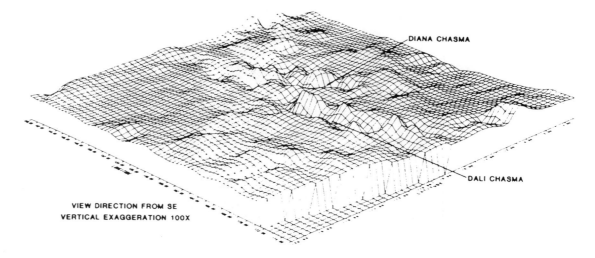

(c) Rift valleys of the Aphrodite region

Diagrams to illustrate the terrains on Venus

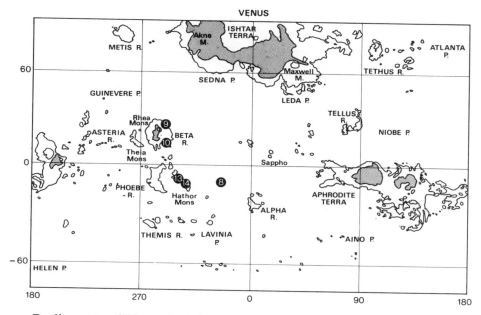

Radio map of Venus' surface, showing major features together with landing sites of the Russian Venus probes (Veneras).

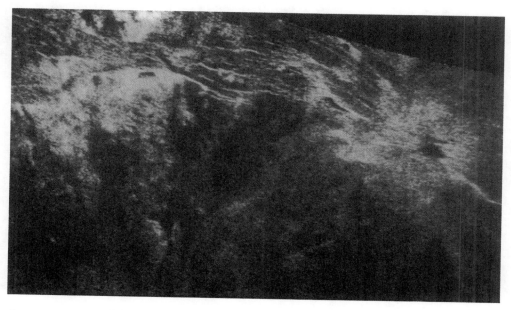

A ray crater on Venus taken from Venera 15 (November 1983). Ray craters on the Moon have been the source of much speculation—does the same hold for Venus, Mercury and other bodies?

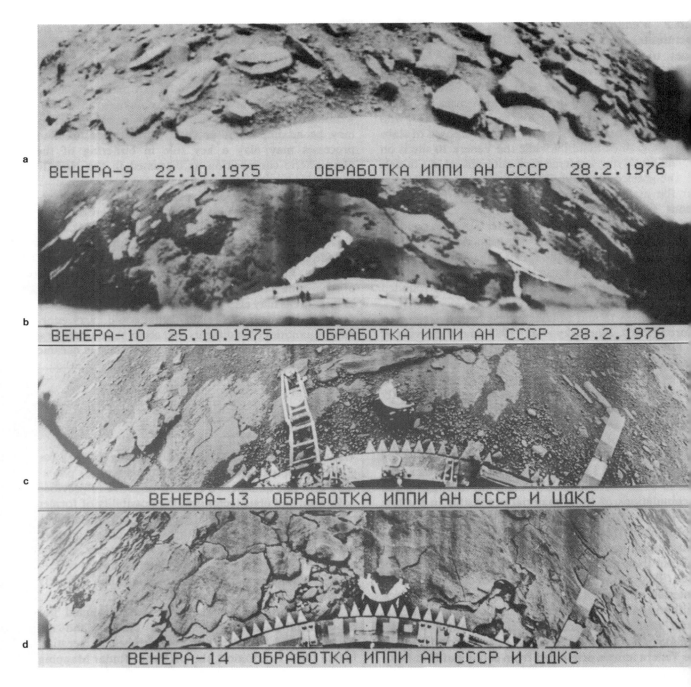

ВЕНЕРА-9   22.10.1975   ОБРАБОТКА ИППИ АН СССР   28.2.1976

ВЕНЕРА-10   25.10.1975   ОБРАБОТКА ИППИ АН СССР   28.2.1976

ВЕНЕРА-13   ОБРАБОТКА ИППИ АН СССР И ЦДКС

ВЕНЕРА-14   ОБРАБОТКА ИППИ АН СССР И ЦДКС

Venera images: (a) Venera 9, (b) Venera 10, (c) Venera 13 and (d) Venera 14

Chapter 9

Mysteries of the Outer Planets

Dr. Shlovskii's stimulating theory [that a moon of Mars is hollow] appeals to me because some ten years ago I made an identical suggestion concerning the innermost moon of Jupiter. In a story called 'Jupiter V' I pointed out certain peculiarities of this satellite and developed the idea that it was a giant spacecraft which, ages ago, had entered the solar system and then been 'parked' in orbit round Jupiter while its occupants went off in more conveniently sized vehicles to colonize the planets.
—Arthur C. Clarke
Voices From the Sky
(1965, Harper & Row)

More Ancient Space Bases on the Outer Moon's?

If theories that there is space-faring life in our Solar System (other than our current civilization) is correct, that could there be life on the moons of the outer planets? If there are space-bases on Mars, its moon Phobos, and on our Moon, then is it logical to assume that other moons in the solar system are also being mined and are used as space-bases? What better view of Jupiter, Saturn, Uranus or Neptune than from one of the moons?

Furthermore, what if many, or all, of the outer moons are artificial? Are they, as if possible with our Moon, and the moons of Mars, actually hollow? Is it possible that the ray craters are the entrances to underground installations or the hollow interiors of these moons?

The outer planets and their moons remain a mystery. While NASA gives us photos and data on these far-away objects, their often preconcluded observations may only be masking the real data.

For instance, an unusual photo of Umbriel, the darkest of the Uranian satellites shows a bright ring at the top of the photo which is the southern pole. Is this a photo of a hollow moon? Other moons, such as Calisto, seem to be lit from the inside.

Many of the outer moons have one, and usually only one, large "umbilical" crater. These distintive and unusual craters are often huge in comparison with the size of the moon, yet are said to be "impact craters."

Are these large craters from some incredible impact with the moon, or are they the result of the formation of the moon, in an inflation effort that creates a hollow satellite, much as a glass blower blows a glass ball? In this theory, an asteroid or similar object, is super-heated into a molten blob or rock and then "inflated" like a glass ball.

The result is a spherical, cratered and "grooved" artificial satellite, as many of the outer moons appear to be.

The small, rocky Saturnian satellite of Hyperion, is a similar satellite to Phobos. The Saturnian satellite of Mimas has a huge "umbillical crater" named Herschel.

The Saturnian satellite Tethys also has the huge crater Odysseus. Voyager image 147J1+000 shows a layered plains area near Lerna Regio on Io. Layered plains are considered to consist of lava flows with interleaved pyroclastic materials derived from volcanic plumes. Bright, wispy zone at the base of the scarp (arrow) is thought to be sulfur dioxide frost, perhaps generated by geyser activity, or perhaps steam from an underground facility?

The Uranian satellite Oberon has a heavily cratered surface and "rays." So does the Uranian satellite Titania.

Voyager images of Dione shows bright, wispy streaks crossing the moon. The trailing hemisphere of Dione shows a heavily cratered terrain and the parallel groups of cloudy wisps. Is Dione, and other outer moons the result of planet (or moon) terra-forming?

Is it possible that the moons of many of the outer planets could well have water, a breathable atmosphere, and a hospitable climate?

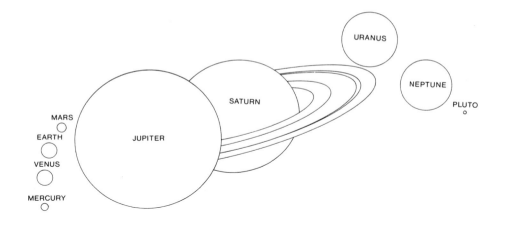

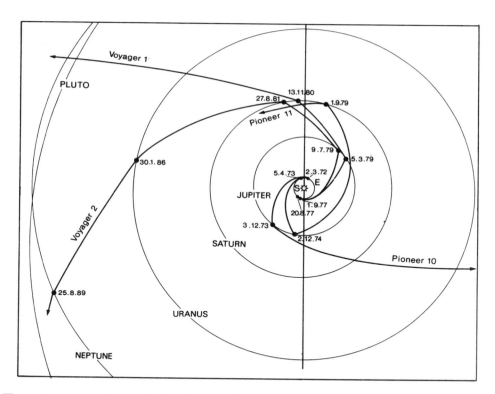

Top: A comparison of the planets. **Bottom:** The paths of Voyager 1 and 2, Pioneer 10 and 11, with encounter dates (E=Earth, S=Sun). Pluto was not encountered by any of the spacecraft, but its orbit is included for completeness and because between 1979 and 1999 it actually comes within the orbit of Neptune.

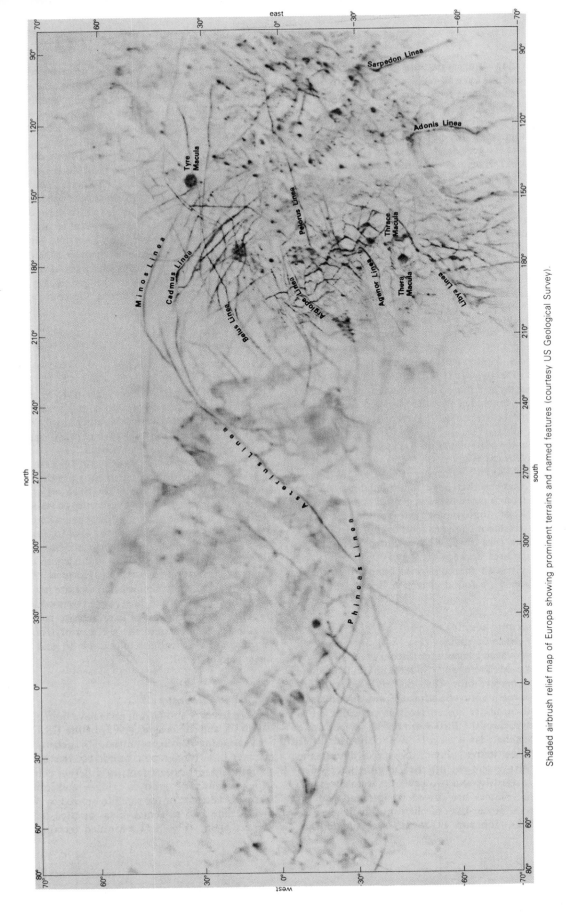

Shaded airbrush relief map of Europa showing prominent terrains and named features (courtesy US Geological Survey).

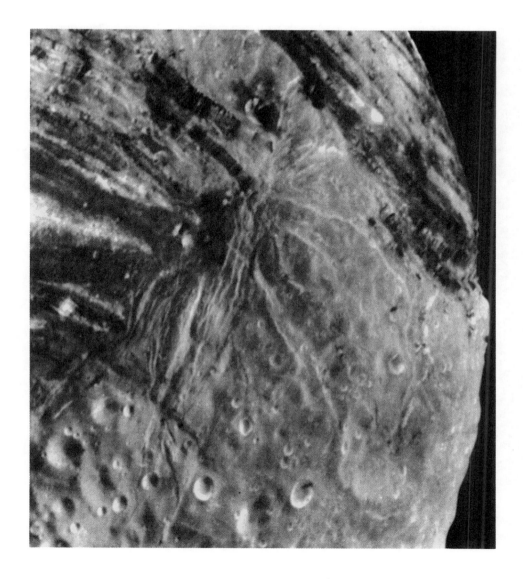

Voyager 2 high resolution photo of Uranus' satellite Miranda. Note "rays" and curious lines intersecting at right angles.

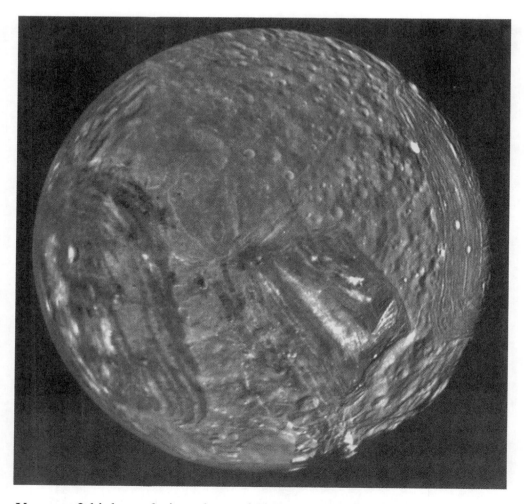

Voyager 2 high resolution photo of Uranus' satellite Miranda, south polar view. Note "rays" and grooves.

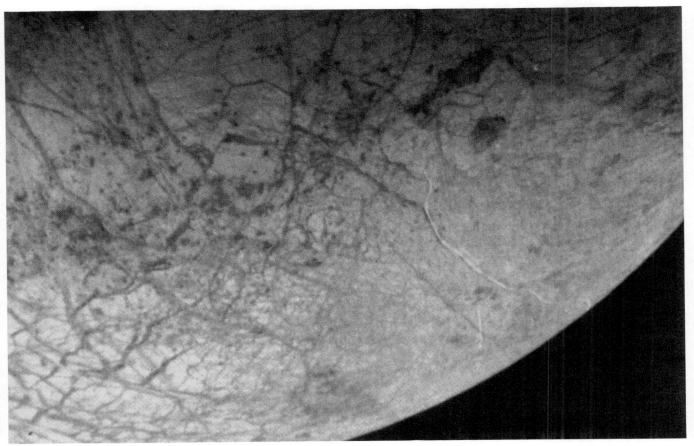

Top: The Jovian satellite Ganymede, from Voyager 1, on 5 March 1979, from 155,500 miles (250,000 km). Resolution on this picture is down to to 12.8 miles (4.5 km). **Bottom:** The Jovian satellite Europa from Voyager 2, on 9 July 1979, from 150,000 miles (241,000 km). The surface is strikingly different from other satellites of the outer planets. Note the rays on Ganymede.

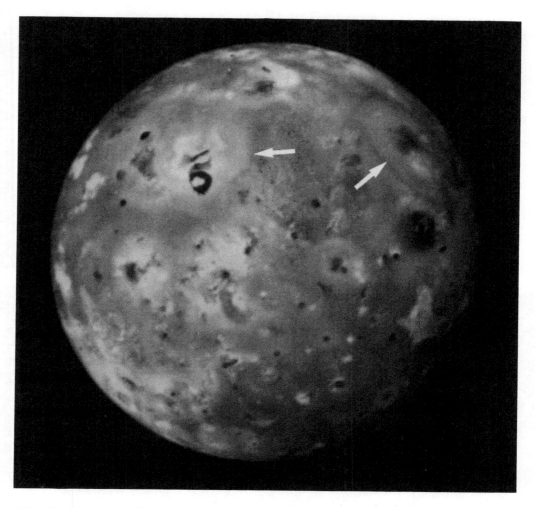

The Jovian moon Io taken by Voyager 1 showing dark spots. The left arrow points to an unusual circular dark feature, thought to be a volcanic vent, but could it be a "lake" on the moon? The right arrow points to another circular dark area, also thought to be a volcanic vent. (Voyager 1: 42J1+000)

Voyager image of the trailing hemisphere of Dione showing bright, wispy streaks crossing the moon. Note rays in the south polar region. (Voyager 1: 1182S1-001)

Voyager image of the trailing hemisphere of Dione showing the heavily cratered terrain and the parallel groups of cloudy wisps. Is Dione, and other outer moons the result of planet (or moon) terra-forming? (Voyager 1: 6251+000)

Voyager image of leading hemisphere of Dione showing troughs and trough networks in the northern hemisphere.

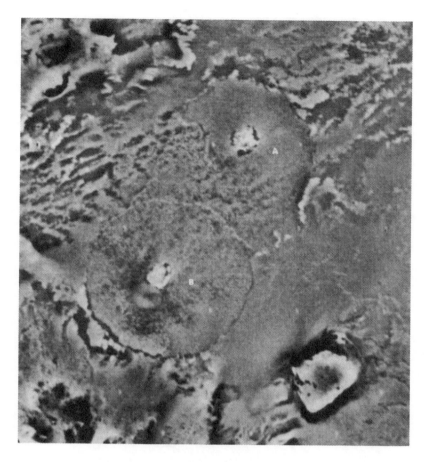

A Voyager 1 image of two unusual volcanic constructs, Apis Tholus (A) and Inachu Tholus (B) on Io. These disc-shaped cones are thought to be volcanoes. The moons of many of the outer planets could well have water, a breathable atmosphere, and a hospitable climate. (Voyager 1: 71J1+000)

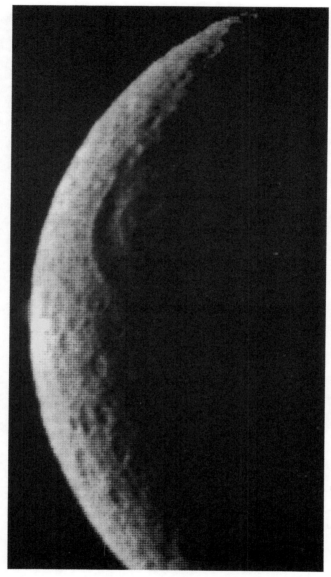

A multi-ringed basin about 450 km across found on the Saturnian satellite Rhea. Note the large crater-basin. (Voyager 1: 1152S1+009)

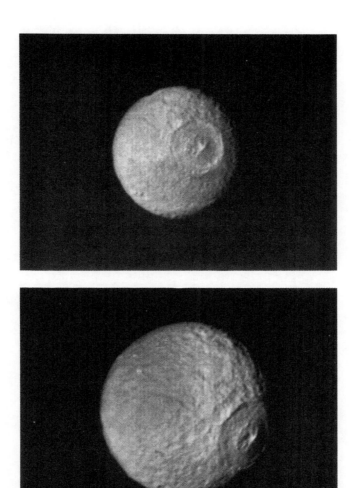

Two views of the Saturnian satellite Tethys showing the huge crater Odysseus. Note that many of the outer moons have one, and one only large "umbilical" crater. Are these large craters from some incredible impact with the moon, or are they the result of the formation of the moon, in an inflation effort that creates a hollow satellite, much as a glass blower blows a glass ball?

Voyager image of the Saturnian satellite of Mimas showing the huge crater named Herschel. Note that many of the outer moons have one, and one only large "umbilical" crater. Are these large craters from some incredible impact with the moon, or are they the result of the formation of the moon, in an inflation effort that creates a hollow satellite, much as a glass blower blows a glass ball?

Top: The Saturnian satellite Enceladus, from Voyager 2, on 25 August 1981, from 74,000 miles (119,000 km). Resolution on this picture is down to to 1.2 miles (2 km). **Bottom:** The Saturnian satellite Dione photographed from Voyager 1, showing the cratered landscape; the most prominent craters are Dido and Aeneas.

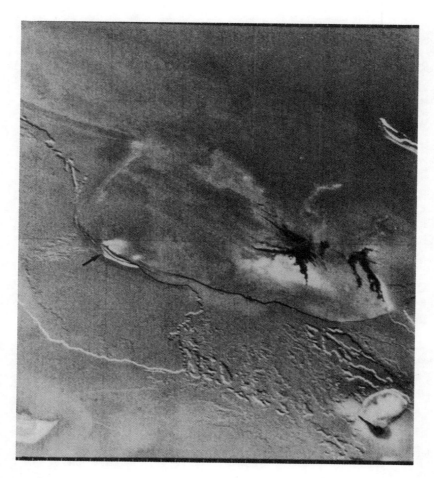

Voyager image showing layered plains near Lerna Regio, Io. Layered plains are considered to consist of lava flows with interleaved pyroclastic materials derived from volcanic plumes. Bright, wispy zone at the base of the scarp (arrow) is thought to be sulfur dioxide frost, perhaps generated by geyser activity, or perhaps steam from an underground facility? Area shown is 880 km wide. (Voyager 1: 147J1+000)

Voyager views of the small, rocky Saturnian satellite of Hyperion, showing its irregular shape and large crater-related scarps. A similar satellite to Phobos. (Voyager 2: JPL P-23932)

View of the Uranian satellite Oberon, showing its heavily cratered surface and "rays." (Voyager 2: JPL P-29501)

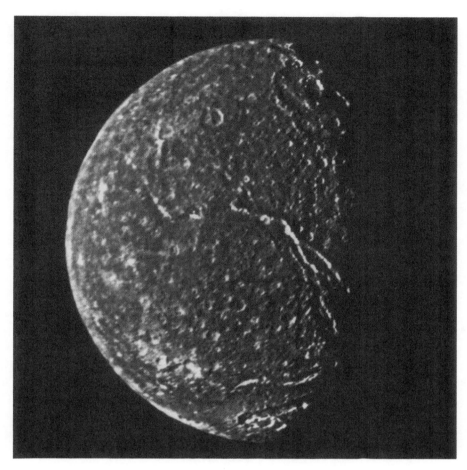

View of the Uranian satellite Titania, showing craters and multi-ring basins
(upper right). Notice the curious "rays." (Voyager 2: JPL P-29522)

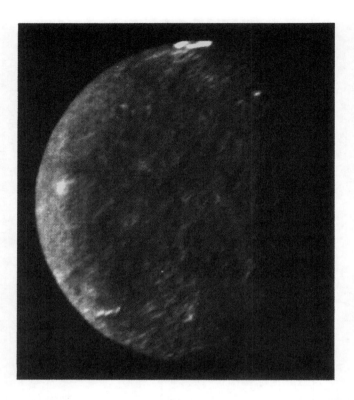

An unusual photo of Umbriel, the darkest of the Uranian
satellites. It is about 1200 km in diameter and the bright ring at
the top of the photo is the southern pole. Is this moon hollow
or is this a frost deposit? (Voyager 2: JPL P-29521)

Mosaic of high-resolution (1.2 km/pixel) images of the Uranian moon Ariel, showing the fractured surface and white streaks on the lower craters. (Voyager 2: JPL P-29520)

The Detroit News

MICHIGAN'S LARGEST NEWSPAPER

Friday

January 16, 1981

15¢

with geysers of water shooting skyward from many manholes,

more stranded people and to prevent

Continued on Page 2A

auto maker in late 1979.

Continued on Page 4A

Lesson from history

10th planet? Pluto's orbit says 'yes'

By HUGH McCANN
News Staff Writer

If new evidence from the U.S. Naval Observatory of a 10th planet in the solar system is accurate, it could prove that the Sumerians, an ancient eastern Mediterranean civilization, were far ahead of modern man in astronomy.

Astronomer Thomas Van Flandern told a meeting of the American Astronomical Society in Albuquerque this week that irregularities in the orbit of Pluto, the farthest known planet from the sun, indicates that the solar system contains a 10th planet.

Pluto was the last planet discovered, in 1930. Since then, astronomers have been searching unsuccessfully for planets farther out. Indeed, Pluto had unknowingly been photographed but remained unrecognized for a long time because it was so difficult to see. Presumably, any other new planets would be easy to miss visually.

Sumerian tablet in East Berlin shows a solar system with sun, moon and 10 planets.

planet is four times the size of Pluto and 1.5 times its distance from the sun.

Van Flandern's announcement comes as no surprise to Zecharia Sitchin, whose book, *The 12th Planet*, came out three years ago.

CHICAGO SUN-TIMES, FRIDAY, DECEMBER 30, 1983
PAGE 5

Heavenly body poses a cosmic riddle to astronomers

By Thomas O'Toole
Washington Post

WASHINGTON—A heavenly body that could be anything from a newly formed galaxy to a planetlike addition to this solar system has been found in the direction of the constellation Orion by an orbiting telescope.

The mysterious in this object

what it is," said Gerry Neugebauer, chief scientist on the project for California's Jet Propulsion Laboratory and director of the Palomar Observatory for the California Institute of Technology.

The most fascinating explanation of this mystery body, which is so cold it casts no light and has never been seen

Houck of Cornell University's Center for Radio Physics and Space Research and a member of the tracking team. "If it is that close, I don't know how the world's planetary scientists would even begin to classify it."

Whatever it is

Then, what is it? What if it is as large as Jupiter and so close to the sun it would be part of the solar system? Conceivably, it could be the 10th planet astronomers have searched for in vain. It also might have

... to become a star some age but not hot enough

... omer and Houck hope the mystery is a distant galaxy either so ... have not begun to ... that its

---

THE DETROIT NEWS — Friday, Dec. 28, 1983

'Mystery' body found in space

Washington Post News Service

WASHINGTON — A mysterious heavenly body has been found in the direction of the constellation Orion by an orbiting telescope called the Infrared Astronomical Observatory.

It is possibly as large as the giant planet Jupiter and possibly so close to Earth that it would be part of this solar system.

So mysterious is the object that astronomers do not know if it is a planet, a giant comet, a "protostar" that never got hot enough to become a star, a distant galaxy so young that it is still in the process of forming its first stars, or a galaxy so shrouded in dust that none of the light cast by its stars ever gets through.

PHILADELPHIA INQUIRER, DEC. 30, 1983

At solar system's edge, giant object is mystery

By Thomas O'Toole
Washington Post Service

WASHINGTON — A heavenly body possibly as large as the giant planet Jupiter and possibly so close to Earth that it would be part of this solar system has been found in the direction of the constellation Orion by an orbiting telescope called the Infrared Astronomical Observatory (IRAS).

So mysterious is the object that astronomers do not know if it is a planet, a giant comet, a "protostar" that never got hot enough to become a star, a distant galaxy so young that it is still in the process of forming its first stars or a galaxy so shrouded in dust that none of the light cast by its stars ever gets through.

"All I can tell you is that we don't know what it is," said Gerry Neugebauer

in the heavens. The second observation took place six months after the first and suggested that, during that time, the body had not moved from its spot in the sky, near the western edge of the constellation Orion.

"This suggests it's not a comet cause a comet would not be on as the one we've observed a comet would probably have moved Houck said

Whatever it is, Houck said mystery body is so cold that its temperature is no more than 40 above absolute zero, whil degrees Fahrenheit below

When IRAS scientists first mystery body and calcu could be as close as 50 there was some specu might be moving tow

"It's not

Giant object mystifies astronomers

By Thomas O'Toole

WASHINGTON — A heavenly body possibly as large as the giant planet Jupiter and possibly so close to Earth that it would be part of this solar system has been found in the direction of the constellation Orion by an orbiting telescope called the Infrared Astronomical Observatory (IRAS).

So mysterious is the object that astronomers do not know if it is a planet, a giant comet, a "protostar" that never got hot enough to become a star, a distant galaxy so young that it is still in the process of forming its first stars or a gala dust that no

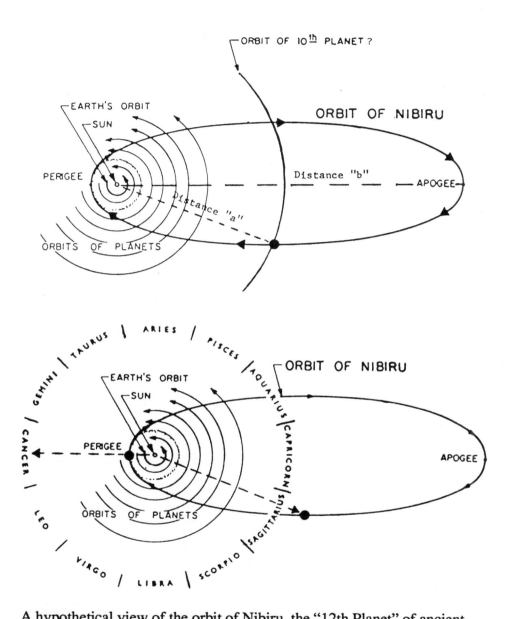

A hypothetical view of the orbit of Nibiru, the "12th Planet" of ancient Sumerian texts as theorized by Zecharia Sitchin.

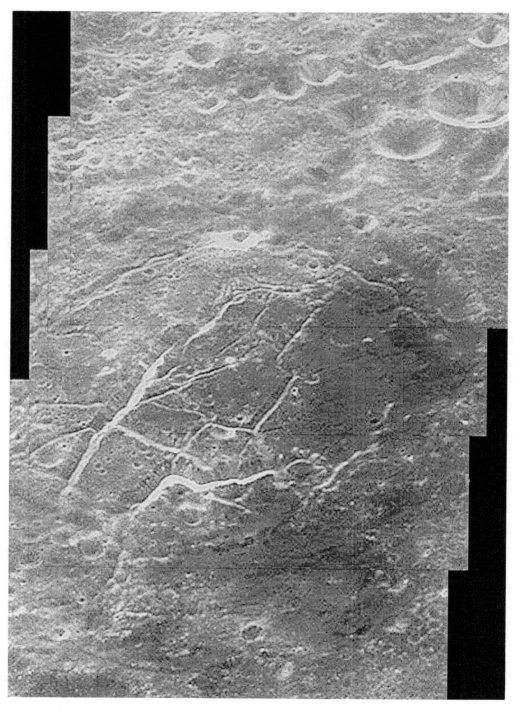

This is amosaic of images from Clementine. The area is approximately 37 degrees South Latitude, 193 degrees West Longitude (167 degrees East Longitude). Right in the middle of the farside of the moon. Are these long, deep groves simply faults within the huge crater? What could cause such deep grooves?

NASA TECHNICAL
MEMORANDUM

NASA TM X-58007
March 1967

PRELIMINARY INVESTIGATION OF A LUNAR "ROLLING STONE"

By J. M. Eggleston, A. W. Patteson, J. E. Throop,
W. H. Arant, and D. L. Spooner
Manned Spacecraft Center
Houston, Texas

NATIONAL AERONAUTICS AND SPACE ADMINISTRATION

PRELIMINARY INVESTIGATION OF A LUNAR "ROLLING STONE"

By J. M. Eggleston, A. W. Patteson, J. E. Throop,
W. H. Arant, and D. L. Spooner
Manned Spacecraft Center

INTRODUCTION

During the analysis of Lunar Orbiter II photography at the Manned Spacecraft Center, Houston, Texas, several large boulders were noted which appeared to have moved or rolled down the interior walls of lunar craters. The boulder or "rolling stone" discussed in this paper was identified as a large, near-spherical object located at or near the bottom of a slope with a clearly defined track down that slope. This paper presents a preliminary investigation on one of the rolling stones. The boulder studied in this investigation is within the crater Sabine D at 23° 39' E longitude and 01° 20' N latitude in the southwestern area of Mare Tranquillitatis. The area, shown in figure 1, was photographed by Lunar Orbiter II as primary site six.

INVESTIGATION

A preliminary investigation was conducted to determine some of the physical characteristics of the rolling stone and the surrounding lunar terrain. The area where the boulder is located is one of the better potential lunar module landing sites. Thus, any information derived from this investigation will be helpful in the selection of lunar module landing sites.

The size and shape of the crater Sabine D were determined by measurements made on Lunar Orbiter II medium-resolution photography (fig. 2). Stereoscopic measurements were taken of the path to determine the depth of the crater. The profile constructed from the measurements is shown in figure 3. The crater was determined to be approximately 2700 meters in diameter and approximately 550 meters deep. The average slope of the crater wall along the path of the boulder is approximately 31°. The boulder came to rest at a point where the angle of the slope becomes about 13° and appears to be resting in a small crater.

The dimensions of the boulder and the track down the crater wall were measured on Lunar Orbiter II high-resolution photography. A portion of frame number 79 showing the crater Sabine D, the boulder, and the track is shown in figure 4. The measurements were taken directly from the photography and confirmed by microdensitometer measurements made with a Joyce-Loebl scanning microdensitometer. The isodensity map from the microdensitometer scans of the high-resolution negative photograph is shown in figure 5. Using the methods indicated, the boulder was determined to be approximately 9 meters in diameter. The track was found to average approximately 5 meters in width and was nearly uniform in width throughout its length. In addition, the boulder was determined to be nearly spherical in shape, a characteristic not observed on rocks nearby or on the crater rim.

The isodensity pattern of the illuminated portion of the boulder as presented in figure 5 has a greater area of density fall-off at the sunward edge of the boulder that can be explained by the combined effects of the frequency response of the photographic system and the size of the scanning aperture used on the microdensitometer. The isodensity pattern of this rock (and one other investigated thus far) shows a definite symmetry in the light reflection pattern with brightest points near the center of the illuminated area. The normally used lunar photometric function would predict that the brightest points should be at the sunward edge of the boulder with a continuing light fall-off as the shadow area is approached. (Such a pattern was observed on one of the other rolling stones.) Further consideration of the isodensity patterns of the two rocks indicates that the observed patterns can best be explained by the assumption of a convex glossy (specular) surface on the rock. The assumption of a retroreflecting or a diffuse reflectance characteristic would require a concave rock surface in the vicinity of the brightest area. It would therefore appear that the boulder analyzed for this paper is unusual in that it does not reflect light in the same way as most lunar material. One explanation for this characteristic could be the compressing or rubbing effect due to its movement down the crater wall.

The physical dimensions of the boulder and the track were used in a graphic determination of the depth of the track, and the depth was found to be approximately 0.75 meter (fig. 6). An attempt was made to analyze the shape of the track depression at several positions along the path. However, no clearly defined shape could be consistently obtained. This interpretation of slopes depends on the photometric model used in combination with the isodensitometer measurements. It is believed that the photometric function of the compressed material in the track does not follow that normally measured from the lunar surface (retroreflecting). If this difference in photometric functions is indeed the case, it might explain the difficulty in defining the shape of the track with respect to the adjoining lunar terrain.

These data were used to make some preliminary calculations to determine the approximate range of bearing strengths of the crater wall material. To simplify these calculations, the boulder and the track were considered in a static situation. If the surface area of the spherical segment of the boulder is considered as being flat, that is, the radius → ∞, then the bearing strength so calculated would be conservative. However, the contact of the rolling stone with the surface was transient, and the depression made by the rolling stone is probably less than would be made by a static stone. These two effects should tend to oppose one another.

The volume of a spherical boulder 9 meters in diameter is 382 cubic meters. The mass of the boulder over a density range which would include possible rock types that might be encountered on the lunar surface is shown in figure 7. The graph covers the range of densities from 0 to 3 grams per cubic centimeter. The surface of the spherical segment of the boulder in contact with the lunar surface is 212 000 square centimeters. The ratio of the range of possible masses computed to the area results in a range of possible bearing strengths for the crater wall material. A graph of mass versus bearing strength is shown in figure 8.

The only direct measurement of the bearing strength of the lunar surface was obtained from Surveyor I and from two Russian "soft-landed" Lunik spacecraft. According to reference 1, at the impact point and under the impact conditions of Surveyor I, the lunar surface did create a maximum dynamic resistance of 4×10^5 to 7×10^5 dynes per square centimeter (6 to 10 psi). This statement is taken to mean that the dynamic bearing strength of the surface at the Surveyor I touchdown point is at least equal to or greater than 4×10^5 dynes per square centimeter. Reference 1 also states that the static bearing capacity and other soil properties that would produce such a dynamic effect have not been conclusively determined. However, in reference 2, it was stated that, if the material is homogeneous and similar to that observed at the surface to a depth of 1 foot or 30 centimeters, the preliminary analysis indicates that the soil has a static bearing capacity at the scale of the Surveyor I footpad of about 3×10^5 dynes per square centimeter or 5 pounds per square inch.

The area in which Surveyor I landed and the area in which the rolling stone is located are separated by $60°$ in lunar longitude. However, if the rolling stone interacted with lunar material having a bearing strength similar to that experienced by Surveyor I, then the boulder would have a uniform density between 1.3 and 2.3 grams per cubic centimeter.

CONCLUSIONS

Without knowing the density or mass of the lunar boulder, the bearing strength of the soil on the slopes of the crater cannot be uniquely determined. However, the following was determined:

(1) Large, cohesive, and near-spherical boulders exist on the lunar surface.

(2) At least a few lunar boulders have moved or have been moved recently enough that their tracks have not been obliterated by lunar erosional processes.

(3) One such boulder, whose reflectance properties were analyzed by microdensitometer measurements, appeared to reflect as a Lambert surface.

(4) The wall of a lunar crater (Sabine D) having a slope of about $30°$ appeared to be covered with a compressible material which failed under the pressure of the boulder as it moved down the slope.

Determination of the mass and density of the boulder and of the exact bearing strength of the surface on which the boulder moved will depend upon additional data. Many new and unusual features are to be found on the lunar surface, some of which will be amenable to limited analysis. The rolling stones are examples of such features. As knowledge of the lunar surface increases, it is to be expected that these isolated and limited analyses will more closely fit together.

Manned Spacecraft Center
National Aeronautics and Space Administration
Houston, Texas, March 20, 1967
914-50-89-00-72

REFERENCES

1. Jaffe, L. D., et al.: Surveyor I Mission Report. Part II, Scientific Data and Results. Rept. 32-1-23. Jet Propulsion Lab., Sept. 10, 1966.

2. Surveyor I - A Preliminary Report. NASA SP-126, 1966.

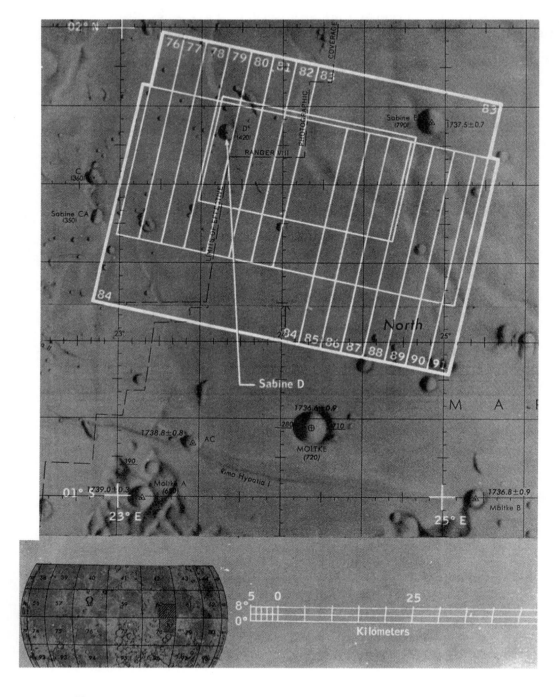

Figure 1. - Location map for Lunar Orbiter II primary site six.

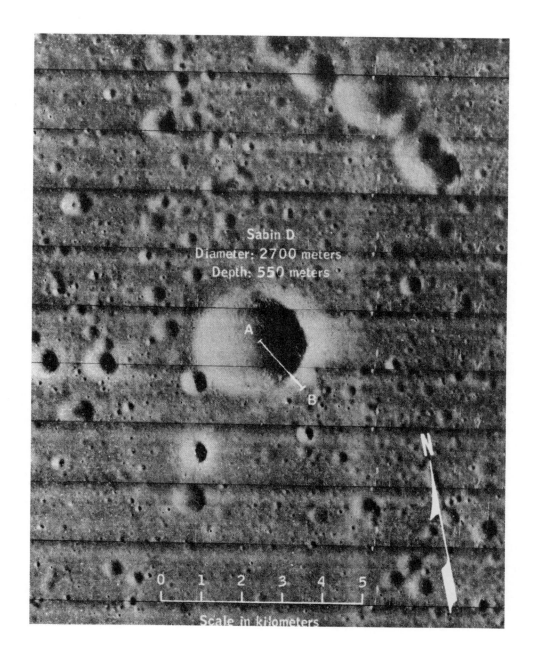

Figure 2. - Medium-resolution Lunar Orbiter II photograph showing crater Sabine D and profile line A-B.

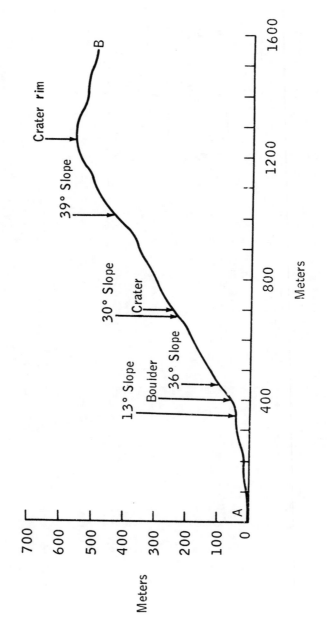

Figure 3. - Profile down wall of crater Sabine D along track of boulder.

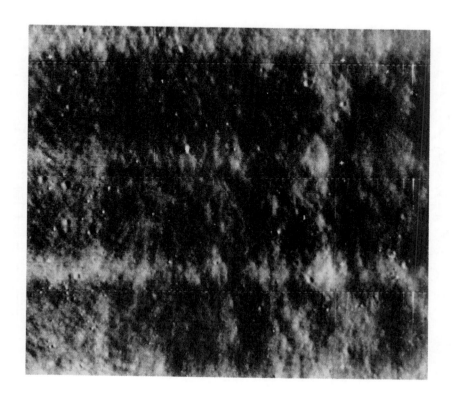

Figure 4. - Portion of photograph of crater Sabine D showing
the boulder and the track.

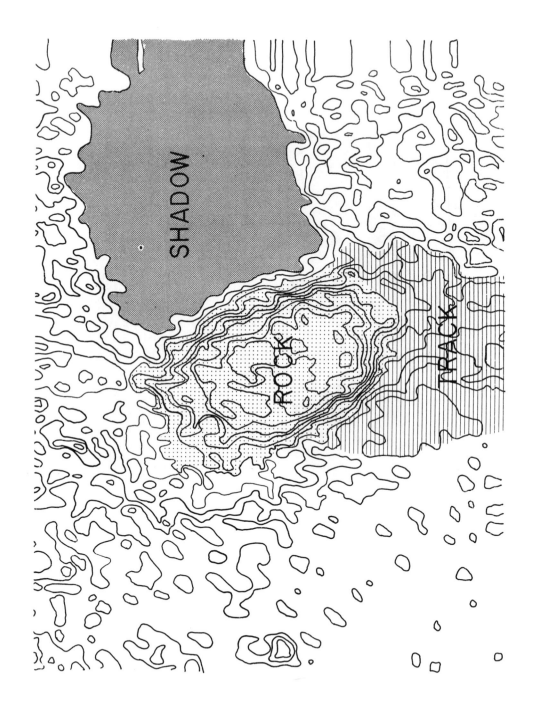

Figure 5. - Isodensity map of boulder, boulder shadow, and track from high-resolution photography.

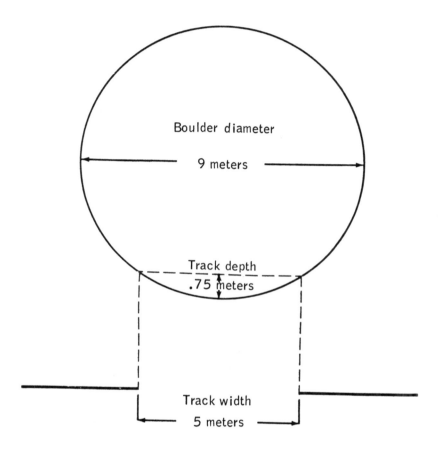

Boulder diameter

9 meters

Track depth

.75 meters

Track width

5 meters

Figure 6. - Graphic determination of track depth.

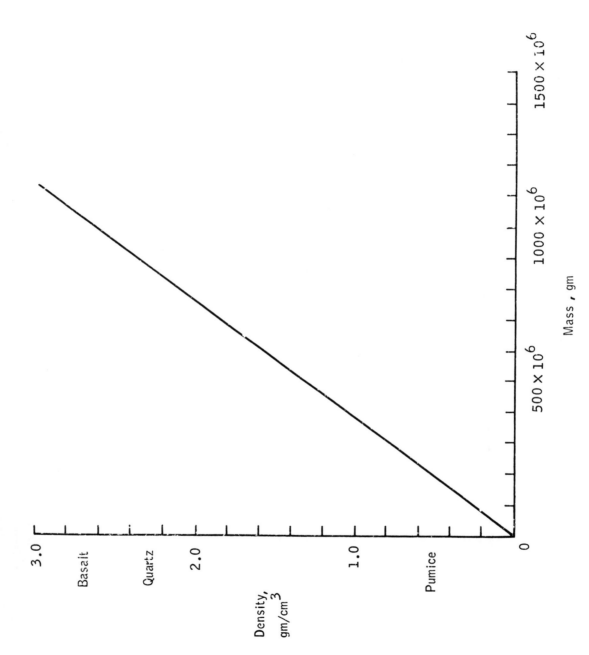

Figure 7. – Density versus mass for a range of possible lunar rock types.

11

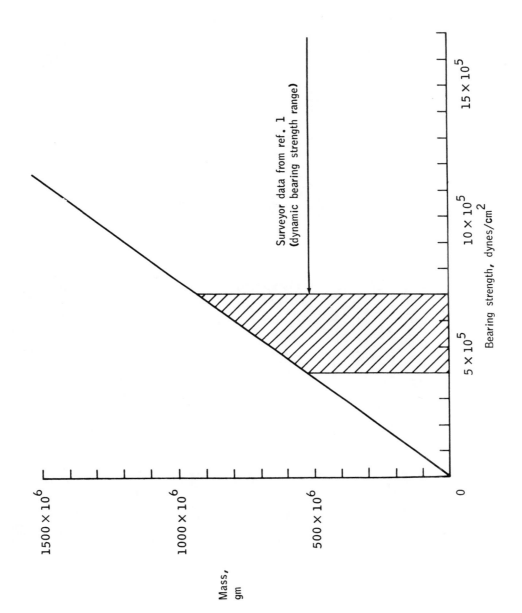

Figure 8. - Mass versus bearing strength.

MSC 8694-68

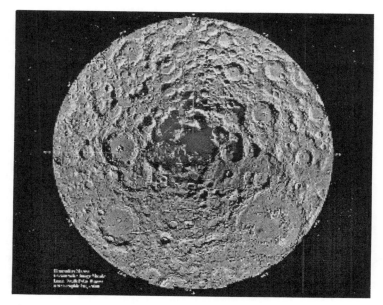

Clementine mosaic showing a large dark area at the South Pole of the Moon that is thought to contain water in the form of ice.

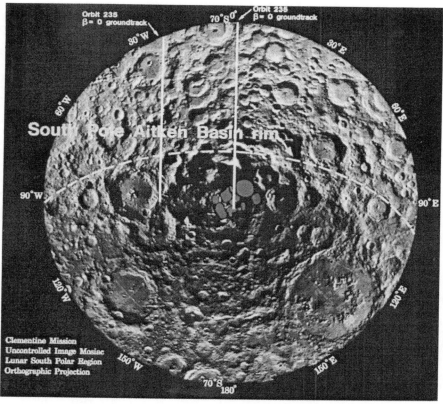

Ice at the Moon's South Pole was recently announced by NASA.

Chapter 11

NASA Reports Water on the Moon

Ice on the Moon

Since the first edition of this book, NASA has discovered—or rather, admitted—that there is indeed water on the Moon. This was reported to be highly probable in the first edition of the book, published in 1994. NASA's discovery was, in fact, made in 1994 but was kept quiet until November 1996 when it was announced that evidence from the Clementine spacecraft suggested the possibility of ice on the surface of the Moon.

Scientists have long speculated that the Moon's surface might contain water, whether or not it was there since the inception of the orb. The Moon is continuously bombarded by meteorites and micrometeorites, most of which contain water ice, and the lunar craters show that many of these were very large objects. Any ice which survived impact would be scattered over the lunar surface. However, the likelihood of finding water ice on the Moon is seriously diminished due to prevailing conditions. As the Moon has no atmosphere, any substance on the lunar surface is exposed directly to vacuum. For water ice, this means it will rapidly turn into vapor and escape into space, as the Moon's low gravity cannot hold gas for any appreciable time. Over the course of a lunar day (approximately 29 Earth days), all regions of the Moon are exposed to sunlight, and the temperature on the Moon in direct sunlight reaches about 395 degrees K (250 degrees above zero F). So any ice exposed to sunlight for even a short period would disappear. The only way for ice to exist on the Moon would be in an area never exposed to the sun. Thus, scientists focussed on searching the lunar landscape for such spots in order to find any traces of water ice.

My Darlin' Clementine

The 1994 Clementine imaging experiment showed that such permanently shadowed areas do exist in the bottom of deep craters near the Moon's south pole. In fact, it appears that approximately 6,000 to 15,000 square kilometers (2,300 to 5,800 square miles) of area around the south pole is permanently shadowed. The permanently shadowed area near the north pole appears on Clementine images to be considerably less. Much of the area around the south pole is within the South Pole-Aitken Basin (the largest impact crater in the solar system, at 2,500 km (1,550 miles) in diameter and 12 km deep at its lowest point). Many smaller craters exist on the floor of this basin. Since they are down in this basin, the floors of many of these craters are never exposed to sunlight. Within these craters the temperatures would never rise above about 100 degrees K (280 degrees below zero F). Any water ice at the bottom of the crater could probably exist for billions of years at these temperatures.

One of the problems in studying a permanently shadowed area is that no pictures can be obtained. The Clementine spacecraft searched for the ice by transmitting an S-band radio signal through its high gain antenna towards a lunar target. The signals were reflected off the Moon and received by a 70 meter Deep Space Network (DSN) antenna on the Earth. Frozen volatiles such as water ice are much more reflective to S-band radio waves than are lunar rocks. Radio waves reflected off ice also have different characteristics from those reflected off silicate rock.

An analysis of the signals returned from Clementine's orbit 234 showed reflection characteristics suggestive of water ice for the permanently shadowed areas near the south pole. The ice was believed to be in the bottom of a crater, along with other frozen volatiles, such as methane. The deposit was estimated to be approximately the size of a small lake, four football fields in surface area and 16 feet deep. This estimate was very uncertain, however, due to the nature of the data.

Reflections from regions which are not permanently shadowed do not show these characteristics. It is possible that other scattering mechanisms could be responsible for this result, but the interpretation of the radio return sand the fact that they are associated only with the permanently shadowed regions seem to indicate that water ice is the most likely possibility.

The Lunar Prospector

The Lunar Prospector, a NASA Discovery mission, was launched into lunar orbit on 6 January 1998 from Cape Canaveral Air Station, aboard an Athena 2 rocket. It was soon announced that data returned by the Lunar Prospector spacecraft indicated that water ice is present at both the north and south lunar poles, in agreement with Clementine results for the south pole. According to NASA *Press Release 98-38* of 5 March 1998:

>...Just two months after the launch of the cylindrical spacecraft, mission scientists have solid evidence of the existence of lunar water ice, including estimates of its volume, location and distribution. "We are elated at the performance of the spacecraft and its scientific payload, as well as the resulting quality and magnitude of information about the

Moon that we already have been able to extract," said Dr. Alan Binder, Lunar Prospector Principal Investigator from the Lunar Research Institute, Gilroy, CA.

The presence of water ice at both lunar poles is strongly indicated by data from the spacecraft's neutron spectrometer instrument, according to mission scientists. Graphs of data ratios from the neutron spectrometer "reveal distinctive 3.4 percent and 2.2 percent dips in the relevant curves over the northern and southern polar regions, respectively," Binder said. "This is the kind of data 'signature' one would expect to find if water ice is present."

However, the Moon's water ice is not concentrated in polar ice sheets, mission scientists cautioned. "While the evidence of water ice is quite strong, the water 'signal' itself is relatively weak," said Dr. William Feldman, co-investigator and spectrometer specialist at the Department of Energy's Los Alamos National Laboratory, NM. "Our data are consistent with the presence of water ice in very low concentrations across a significant number of craters." Using models based on other Lunar Prospector data, Binder and Feldman predict that water ice is confined to the polar regions and exists at only a 0.3 percent to 1 percent mixing ratio in combination with the Moon's rocky soil, or regolith.

How much lunar water ice has been detected? Assuming a water ice depth of about a foot and a half (.5 meters)—the depth to which the neutron spectrometer's signal can penetrate—Binder and Feldman estimate that the data are equivalent to an overall range of 11 million to 330 million tons (10-300 million metric tons) of lunar water ice, depending upon the assumptions of the model used. This quantity is dispersed over 3,600 to 18,000 square miles (10,000-50,000 square kilometers) of water ice- bearing deposits across the northern pole, and an additional 1,800 to 7,200 square miles (5,000-20,000 square kilometers) across the southern polar region. Furthermore, twice as much of the water ice mixture was detected by Lunar Prospector at the Moon's north pole as at the south.

Dr. Jim Arnold of the University of California at San Diego previously has estimated that the most water ice that could conceivably be present on the Moon as a result of meteoritic and cometary impacts and other processes is 11 billion to 110 billion tons. The amount of lunar regolith that could have been "gardened" by all impacts in the past 2 billion years extends to a depth of about 6.5 feet (2 meters), he found. On that basis, Lunar Prospector's estimate of water ice would have to be increased by a factor of up to four, to the range of 44 million to 1.3

billion tons (40 million to 1.2 billion metric tons). In actuality, Binder and Feldman caution that, due to the inadequacy of existing lunar models, their current estimates "could be off by a factor of ten in either direction."

. . . There are various ways to estimate the economic potential of the detected lunar water ice as a supporting resource for future human exploration of the Moon. One way is to estimate the cost of transporting that same volume of water ice from Earth to orbit. Currently, it costs about $10,000 to put one pound of material into orbit. NASA is conducting technology research with the goal of reducing that figure by a factor of 10, to only $1,000 per pound. Using an estimate of 33 million tons from the lower range detected by Lunar Prospector, it would cost $60 trillion to transport this volume of water to space at that rate, with unknown additional cost of transport to the Moon's surface.

From another perspective, a typical person consumes an estimated 100 gallons of water per day for drinking, food preparation, bathing and washing. At that rate, the same estimate of 33 million tons of water (7.2 billion gallons) could support a community of 1,000 two-person households for well over a century on the lunar surface, without recycling.

. . .

NASA's neutron spectrometer experiments measured the speed of neutrons, which are slowed after collisions with hydrogen atoms. A large number of "slow" (or thermal) and "intermediate" (or epithermal) neutrons indicated a higher incidence of collisions with hydrogen atoms. A significant amount of hydrogen indicated the existence of water. Utilizing other techologies, scientists fine-tuned their estimates of the amount of water on the Moon. According to *Press Release 98-158* of September 3, 1998:

. . . The north and south poles of the Moon may contain up to six billion metric tons of water ice, a more than tenfold increase over previous estimates, according to scientists working with data from NASA's Lunar Prospector mission.

Growing evidence now suggests that water ice deposits of relatively high concentration are trapped beneath the soil in the permanently shadowed craters of both lunar polar regions. The researchers believe that alternative explanations, such as concentrations of hydrogen from the solar wind, are unlikely.

. . . In March, mission scientists reported a water signal with a minimum abundance of one percent by weight of water ice in rocky

302

lunar soil (regolith) corresponding to an estimated total of 300 million metric tons of ice at the Moon's poles. "We based those earlier, conscientiously conservative estimates on graphs of neutron spectrometer data, which showed distinctive dips over the lunar polar regions," said Dr. Alan Binder of the Lunar Research Institute, Gilroy, CA, the Lunar Prospector principal investigator. "This indicated significant hydrogen enrichment, a telltale signature of the presence of water ice.

"Subsequent analysis, combined with improved lunar models, shows conclusively that there is hydrogen at the Moon's poles," Binder said. "Though other explanations are possible, we interpret the data to mean that significant quantities of water ice are located in permanently shadowed craters in both lunar polar regions.

"The data do not tell us definitively the form of the water ice," Binder added. "However, if the main source is cometary impacts, as most scientists believe, our expectation is that we have areas at both poles with layers of near-pure water ice." In fact, the new analysis "indicates the presence of discrete, confined, near-pure water ice deposits buried beneath as much as 18 inches (40 centimeters) of dry regolith, with the water signature being 15 percent stronger at the Moon's north pole than at the south."

How much water do scientists believe they have found? "It is difficult to develop a numerical estimate," said Dr. William Feldman, co-investigator and spectrometer specialist at the Department of Energy's Los Alamos National Laboratory, NM. "However, we calculate that each polar region may contain as much as three billion metric tons of water ice."

Feldman noted he had cautioned that earlier estimates "could be off by a factor of ten," due to the inadequacy of existing lunar models. The new estimate is well within reason, he added, since it is still "one to two orders of magnitude less than the amount of water predicted as possibly delivered to, and retained on, the Moon by comets," according to earlier projections by Dr. Jim Arnold of the University of California at San Diego.

. . . Toward the end of the Lunar Prospector's useful life, NASA scientists decided to orchestrate a controlled crash of the craft on July 31, 1999 into a crater near the south pole of the Moon in a long-shot effort to verify the existence of water ice. The chances of producing irrefutable evidence were estimated at less than 10%, and, unforunately, the crash did not produce such evidence. As reported in

Press Release 99-63 dated 13 October 1999:

. . . This lack of physical evidence leaves open the question of whether ancient cometary impacts delivered ice that remains buried in permanently shadowed regions of the Moon, as suggested by the large amounts of hydrogen measured indirectly from lunar orbit by Lunar Prospector during its main mapping mission.

. . . Worldwide observations of the crash were focused primarily on using sensitive spectrometers tuned to look for the ultraviolet emission lines expected from the hydroxyl (OH) molecules that should be a by-product of any icy rock and dust kicked up by the impact of the 354-pound spacecraft.

"There are several possible explanations why we did not detect any water signature, and none of them can really be discounted at this time," said Dr. Ed Barker, assistant director of the university's McDonald Observatory at UT Austin, who coordinated the observing campaign.

These explanations include: * the spacecraft might have missed the target area; * the spacecraft might have hit a rock or dry soil at the target site; * water molecules may have been firmly bound in rocks as hydrated mineral as opposed to existing as free ice crystals, and the crash lacked enough energy to separate water from hydrated minerals; * no water exists in the crater and the hydrogen detected by the Lunar Prospector spacecraft earlier is simply pure hydrogen; * studies of the impact's physical outcome were inadequate; * the parameters used to model the plume that resulted from the impact were inappropriate; * the telescopes used to observe the crash, which have a very small field of view, may not have been pointed correctly; * water and other materials may not have risen above the crater wall or otherwise were directed away from the telescopes' view.

Although the crash did not confirm the existence of water ice on the Moon, "this high-risk, potentially high-payoff experiment did produce several benefits," said Dr. David Goldstein, the aerospace engineer who led the UT Austin team. "We now have experience building a remarkably complex, coordinated observing program with astronomers across the world; we established useful upper limits on the properties of the Moon's natural atmosphere, and we tested a possible means of true 'lunar prospecting' using direct impacts." . . .

The Important Implications of Lunar Ice
The existence of ice on the Moon has obvious value for the furtherance of

pure science: it could represent relatively pristine cometary or asteroid material which has remaind intact for millions or billions of years. The simple fact that the ice is there will help scientists constrain models of impacts on the lunar surface and the effects of meteorite gardening, photo dissociation, and solar wind sputtering on the Moon.

Beyond the scientifically intriguing aspects, deposits of ice on the Moon would have many practical aspects for future manned lunar exploration. Optimistic estimates foresee the ice facilitating a lunar rocket refueling station or even a human colony within the next 50 years. Current space missions are hampered by the exorbitant cost of carrying fuel and food. "It's very interesting in terms of the exploration of the moon," said Joseph Burns, a planetary scientist at Cornell University. "It gives us a means of not having to bring our lunch up there."

The amount of water in current estimates represents a potential bonanza. "Our data are consistent with the presence of water ice across a significant number of craters," said William C. Feldman, co-investigator and spectrometer specialist at the Los Alamos National Laboratory. "There is enough there to support a modest amount of colonization for centuries."

According to NASA, an area the size of a football field would yield enough water to provide for the drinking, food preparation, bathing and washing needs of a crew of six persons; generate 100 megawatts of electrical power for a year; or produce enough propellant to transport two crews of four people each from the Earth to the moon.

If the water can be mined, it will become an enabling factor for establishing permanent or semi-permanent moon bases and, possibly, for setting up a staging area for future manned missions to Mars. The water could be used for domestic purposes, but also broken into its component hydrogen and oxygen to provide breathable air. The two elements could also be recombined as fuel for spacecraft or machinery on the base itself. "This is a tremendous resource for further exploration," said Binder. Indeed, the NASA scientists estimate that the supply of water would reduce the cost of a mission to Mars by about 50 percent.

The discovery of an area on the nearby crater rim which is never subject to darkness further excites NASA scientists. The crater's rim caught in the spotlight could, scientists said, serve as a stage to land vehicles and set up solar panels. These could then heat the surrounding ice into water or separate it into hydrogen and oxygen to be used as rocket propellant. "If you go to this spot, you could use solar panels because the sun would never set," Paul Spudis, one of the scientists who made the discovery, said at a Pentagon news conference. "It may be the most valuable piece of real estate in the solar system."

All the same, some scientists think that it may still be less expensive to ship water into space than to extract it from the lunar soil. But the NASA scientists strongly disagree, pointing out that gold is economically mined at the rate of a few grains per ton. According to Feldman, the water could be extracted simply by heating the soil in a closed chamber, much like a still; energy could be provided by solar panels located above the craters. "It'll be like making moonshine," he quipped. "We have paved the way for future missions."

References

1) Fluxes of fast and epithermal neutrons from Lunar Prospector: Evidence for water ice at the lunar poles, Feldman et al., Science, v. 281, p. 1496, 1998

2) Stability of polar frosts in spherical bowl-shaped craters on the Moon, Mercury, and Mars,Ingersoll et al., Icarus, v. 100, p. 40, 1992

3) The behavior of volatiles on the lunar surface, Watson et al., Journal of Geophysical Research, v. 66, p. 3033, 1961

4) Ice in the lunar polar regions, Arnold, Journal of Geophysical Research, v. 84, p. 5659,1979

5) The Clementine bistatic radar experiment, Nozette et al., Science, v. 274, p. 1495, 1996

NASA Press Release (13 October 1999) - on results of Lunar Prospector crash impact on the Moon NASA Press Release

(3 September 1998) - announcing enhanced estimate of quantity of water on the Moon NASA Press Release

(5 March 1998) - announcing the detection of ice on the Moon

Cornell Press Release (3 June 1999) - radar provides 3-D views of lunar poles

Lunar Prospector Neutron Spectrometer Experiment

Clementine Bistatic Radar Experiment

RUSSIAN DISCOVERIES OF "MARKERS" ON THE MOON!

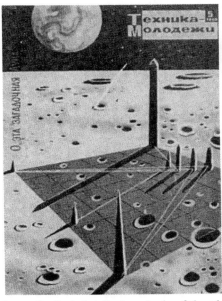

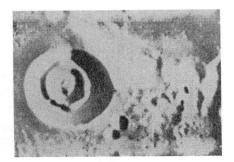

Above, Left: A detailed analysis of the obelisk complex on the Moon (the Blair Cuspids) appeared on the cover of the Russian publication *Technology For Youth*. According to the article, the largest obelisk is 15 stories high. Above, Right: Close-up of one of the so-called Russian "Moon Markers" showing a circular pattern, or "lid" that is on each one.

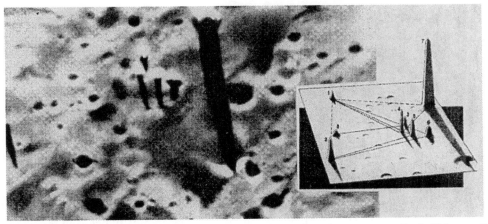

The photo of the Blair Cusbids and the Russian analysis of the seven tall obelisks on the Moon with their long shadows which appeared in the Russian publication *Technology For Youth*.

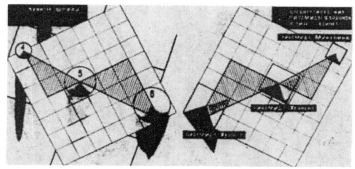

Above: The Russians have claimed to have discovered an alignment of small circular "Moon Markers" that form several straight lines on the Moon, apparently marking out a sort of "runway" pattern on the Moon. Above is the Russian diagram of the "Moon Markers" mapped out on an Egyptian "abaka"—a geometric grid of 49 squares used by the ancient Egyptians to design the alignment of the pyramids. The Russian diagrams showed that the "Moon Markers" showed the identical mathematical design.

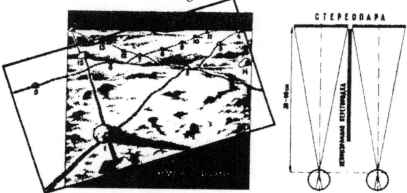

Above: Russian diagrams of the "Moon Markers" showing the "runway" pattern on the Moon.

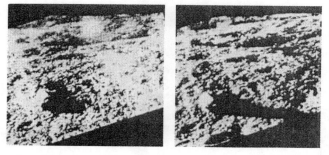

Above: This amazing Russian 3-D view of the "Moon Markers" shows the "runway" pattern on the Moon very clearly. Hold a piece of cardboard vertically between the two photographs and rest your forehead against it. As your left eye sees the left photo and the right eye sees the right photo, a 3-D image appears and you will see the evenly spaced markers stretch into the distance.

Chapter 12

A Brief History of the Moon

PRE-5000 BC—PREHISTORY
The Moon represented the ongoing breeding of the human race. Indo-European myths and the beliefs of natives in many parts of the world recognize the role of the moon in the fertility of all species, as well as with matters of consciousness and life after death. Manas/Mana/Men meant both "moon" and "mind." It also meant "wise-blood." Manna fell to feed us, and we were civilized if we had manners.

4000 BC—ANCIENT INDIA
The Vedas said all souls return to the moon after death. Indian Epics describe aerial ships called Vimanas and even describe trips to the Moon.

2500 BC SUMERIA
The great ziggurat of the moon god at Ur was begun by Ur-Nammu enclosing a much older previous tower (2113 BC) There were men who traced the movements of the moon and the lesser objects in the sky. They were known as "Chaldeans" and were highly regarded throughout the ancient world.

2000 BC—EGYPT
To the Egyptians the Moon was the Mother of the Universe. Up the Nile was a land called Khemennu, "Land of the Moon." The pygmies who lived to the south recall that all people were made on the moon. The local site was "The Mountains of the Moon." Later the earth base of the Moon Goddess was moved to Elephantine. The name may mean God of the Phan-tin-a. That was where Hebrew mercenaries saw Yaweh's giant chariot with its bones of iron and decided he was indeed the God of gods.

1800 BC—SHEBA
To the Shebans, there were beings known as "close kindred" or "mu-karrabin" which we know as "cherubim," a form of angel. They were said to guard the gates of the shrine at Marib. It was dedicated to the moon-goddess. They guarded the gates of Eden and the throne of god. A Cherumbim was also a Chaldean Chariot of the Moon Priestesses.

1600 BC—MINOA
The Agean island of Thera is wiped away in a massive blast, taking with it the dominance of the Minoans and leading to the steady decline of Terrene civilization (1450 BC). "Garlanded white bulls were sacrificed to the lunar cow-goddess in Crete

and Mycenae from a very early date. The highly civilized Minoan culture can be traced to no known source, although ancestral to today's civilization.

800 BC—GREECE

The Pythagoreans viewed the moon as the home of the dead. The cresent of the moon had especial significance. The Greek myths said the star-father Uranus was defeated with a sickle and his genitals cut off. The Greeks tallied "moon" with "power." She ruled the world from Mt Olympus until the coming of the Hellenic gods led by Cronos—the genital mutilator of the sky-father himself. The wearing of a cresent was a sign of respect for the Goddess. It was often stylized as an arc, the vessel of life. The gods were kept alive, it was said, by "sacer" or taboo moon-fluid. It was recognized that women had peak psychic powers at commencement of womanhood, during intercourse and at menopause. Virgin births were highly regarded and were not then accompanied with angst. Visitations by incubi were accepted and indeed sought, even in later Christian churches.

600 AD—PERSIA

The Dioscuri are two golden stars to the Mithraic sun-worshippers. They are The Twins or alpha and beta Gemini. They were said to be born out of the World Egg of Leda and were the gods of the (one and the same) morning and evening stars. Each wore his half of the cap or crown—Castor and Pollux. Pollux means abundant wine, the same wine mentioned in the legends of Noah of the arc—the first biblical patriach to get drunk. He was called the "New-wine sailor," or Deucalion, the ancient flood hero. i.e. Moon-Venus-Wine-Flood-Halfmoon-Water-More Water...

200 BC—ROME

Diana was known to the Romans as the Queen of Heaven, one of her three aspects being the Lunar Virgin. She could reside in groves where sacred kings engaged in mortal combat in her honour, sort of cock-fight cum sacrifice ceremony, with breeding ahead for one and godhood for the other. The Roman Plutarch said: "The effects of the moon are similar to the effects of reason and wisdom, whereas that of the sun appear to be brought about by physical force and violence." Mania was a state of high ecstasy induced in moonlight. According to Plutarch the moon has "the light which makes moist and pregnant, is promotive of the generation of living beings and the fructification of plants." The moon was the top god, a class in itself. Caeserius of Heisterbach said: "The soul is a spiritual substance of spherical nature, like the globe of the moon." The Gospels commanded destruction of all the temples of Diana in the name of their own unique trinity. Nearly all records are destroyed or decay in the following 1000 years. But the old ways are remembered in name. "Dione" or "Diane"—originally of the Danae—became a new Virgin, the Mary-Dione or Madonna.

200 BC—CELT-NORSE

Moon = lune = rune—"The word "rune" itself is derived from the Norse "runar," magic sign, and the Old German "runa" meaning either `to whisper' or `a secret'. The term to `rown', `roon' or `round' in the ear was in common usage in Anglo-Saxon England and signified the whispering of a secret.

800 AD—ARABIA
The Arabian Moon Goddess "Tree of Paradise" was Fatima. The Daughter of the Prophet Mohammed is known as Fatima. "Mary" comes from the same root stock. Te-Mari the sacred palm tree of life. The reflective limestone facing of the pyramids is torn off and Sirus turns from red to white.

1600 AD—RENAISSANCE
The metal of the Moon is silver. Even during the renaissance women were often encouraged to pray to the moon-goddess, who could be assured of fulfilling their wishes. Practioners of arcane arts learned to "draw down the moon." Adept women were said to be able to reverse the flow of time, according to both Virgil and St. Augustine. And to the modern magicians of 1620 no circle of protection was ever drawn without careful regard to the time of the moon.

Modern Moon Events

1740—Telescope specialist James Short watched an object about the size of Mercury or the Moon (!) near to Venus. Similarly transient but reliable sightings occurred in 1672, 1686, 1759, 1823, and 1884.

1783-87—Sir William Herschel observes "volcanoes" on the Moon.

1788—German astronomer J. H. Schroter observes a fifth magnitude point of light for fifteen minutes. It is located to the east of the shadow of the lunar Alps. Later in the lunar day a huge black shadow is seen there. Ash?

1828—Black rains in Clyde Valley, same time on successive days. Ash from a volcano?

1859 March—Dr. Lescarbault observes a black speck crawling across the face of the sun. Velocity suggests it is a new planet.

1862—More black specks crawl across the face of the sun....

1877—Two moons, Phobos and Deimos, appear in orbit around Mars. Impossible that they were not earlier observed.

1879-89—Numerous unusual events seen to occur on the moon.

1880—Crater Aristarchus seen to have a thin bright line of blue light across it.

1903, March 3—Several major observatories watch brilliant flickering light in Aristarchus Crater. Launching?

1903 May—Large dust storm or cloud occurs on Mars. Arrival?

1903 December 17—First a point, then growing to a bright oblique rift in five minutes, is observed on Jupiter.

1911 Oct-Nov—Number of brilliant white spots on Mars near Hesperia. Retaliation?

1912 January 27—"....I was surprised to see the left cusp [of the Moon] showing the presence of an intensely black body about 250 miles long and fifty wide....in shape like a crow poised. Of course dark places are here and there on the lunar surface, but not like this... I cannot but think that a very interesting and curious phenomenon happened." (Dr. F. B. Harris, *Popular Astronomy, June-July 1912*)

1913 January 20—A diamond shaped halo was seen around the moon, three lunar diameters in diameter. It was square in shape, with one corner down towards the horizon. "...it may be very uncommon." noted an officer.

1913, Feb 9—40 to 60 "slow-moving" fireballs passed over Canada and the Atlantic. Total path length 5,500 miles, at near orbital height....A white object independent of the others kept its own pace. The whole performance was very much like that of a fleet of alien craft entering hostile territory. Chant was enchanted.

1913—On Feb. 10—Residents of Toronto saw three groups of dark objects pass high over their city going west to east and then return in broken formation.

1919—A protruding white spot on Jupiter seen over 2 nights in January.

1928 August—Jupiter's south-tropical belt emits a number of dark spots that travelled faster than the rotation rate of the clouds in that zone. Most passed north of the Great Red Spot but a few entered it and disappeared.

1931, June 17—A series of bright flashes seen on the face of the new moon. Launchings?

1931—Sir Francis Chichester saw "a dull grey-white airship... like an oblong pearl..." that vanished and reappeared...

1933, May 2—The SS Transylvania sighted an orange ray projected from the Moon. Duration: 15 minutes.

1956—A huge blazing "X-marks the spot" cross sprang into sight on the surface of the moon. Each arm was two miles long. It was just northwest of the ring plain Fra Mauro near a small dark crater named Parry. (The picture is reproduced in Harvard Observatory's *Sky and Telescope* pp 414 June 1958.)

1958/1961—Soviet astronomer reports detection of carbon and hydrogen near crater Aristarchus on the moon.

1958—Reddish glow from crater Alphonsus.

1963—US Assistant Defence Secretary Arthur Sylvester says that the government has a right to lie and to generate news if a matter of national security was involved.

1963—October 29 and November 27 Lowell Observatory's 24 inch telescope spots ruby red points of light near Aristarchus crater on the moon and soon after same red lights at the rim of the crater. (Lights also spotted there 1821, 1825, 1835, 1866/67, 1880, and 1903)

1967—Surveyor 4 carried by an Atlas Agena was launched to the Moon for JPL. Surveyors could land and then hop from site to site in short flights to precise locations. Surveyor 5 had the same landing weight as #3 & 4 but it did not carry surface samplers!

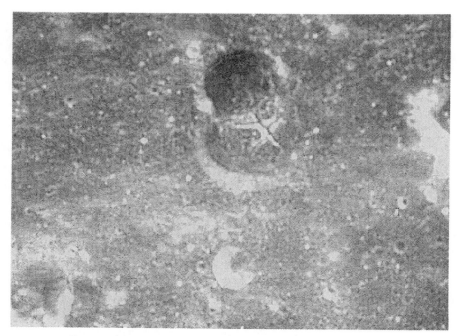

Crater with strange cross-shape on the edge.

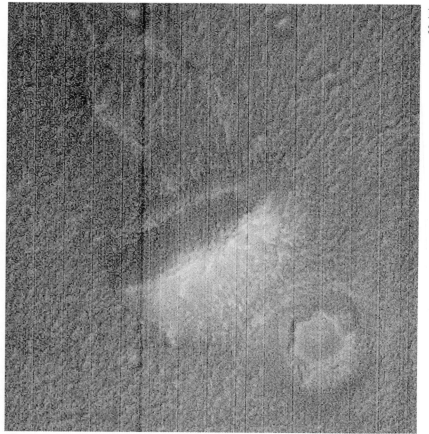

Dome City and Hexagon Spaceport.

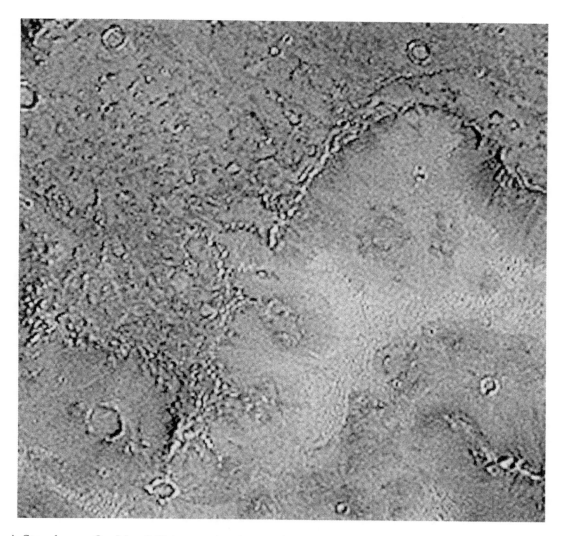

A Stonehenge On Mars? This amazing image shows what appears to be a partial 'stonehenge' arrangement of large upright boulders near a large valley formed by the erosion of water millions of years ago on Mars. This formation is located approximately 6 degrees S latitude, 357.5 W longitude. North is approximately toward the top of the image. This circular area lies on the edge of an ancient river. The natural barrier to the right of the standing formation may have protected the boulders from innundation by the otherwise destructive water that may have been moving to the right from this bend in the ancient river. Note the alignment of the radial feature with the strange complex to the northwest, and also to the dark mark in the shallow area to the southeast. Could this be a landing approach beacon of some type, or an astronomical observatory? One important question to answer is what direction was the ancient North on Mars before the catyclysm? 2X enlargement.

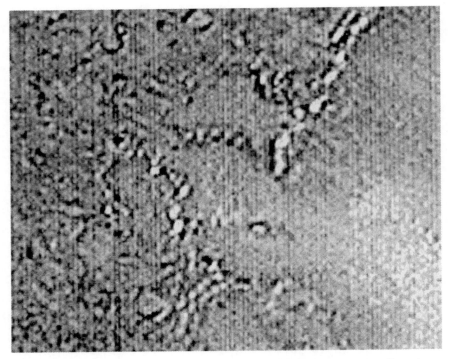

These images show the central area more closely. The linear feature, as well as the unusual complex to the northeast and southwest, can be seen. Other boulders which may have been scattered by a large surge of water are nearby. Then there is the triangular feature at about 8:00. Combination of first image and new full resolution image processed from the raw image (2x) More detail can be seen in the highly anomalous structures in this area.

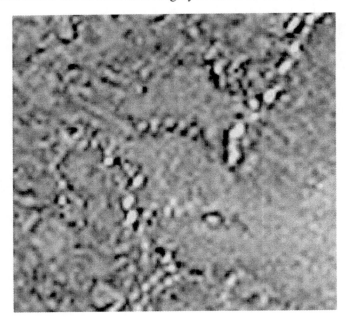

BIBLIOGRAPHY & FOOTNOTES

1. *The Science Book of Space Travel,* Harold Leland Goodwin, 1954, Franklin Watts, NYC.

2. *Exploring the Moon Through Binoculars & Small Telescopes,* Ernest H. Cherrington Jr., 1969, Dover Publications, New York.

3. *Patrick Moore's Armchair Astronomy,* Patrick Moore, 1984, Patrick Stephens Ltd., U.K.

4. *The Science Book of Space Travel,* Harold Goodwin, 1954, Franklin Watts, Inc. NYC.

5. *The Moon and the Planets, A Catalog of Astronomical Anomalies,* compiled by William Corliss, 1985, The Sourcebook Project, Glen Arm, Maryland.

6. *Lore and Lure of Outer Space,* Ernst & Johanna Lehner, 1964, Tudor Publishing Co., New York.

7. *Exploring the Earth and Moon,* Patrick Moore, 1991, Todd Publishing, Ltd., London.

8. *Exploring the Planets,* Brian Jones, 1991, Gallery Books, London.

9. *Moonscapes,* Rosemary Ellen Guiley, 1991, Prentice Hall, New York.

10. *The Moon Observer's Handbook,* Fred W. Price, 1988, Cambridge University Press.

11. *A Portfolio of Lunar Drawings,* Harold Hill, 1991, Cambridge University Press.

12. *Moons, Myths & Man,* H.S. Bellamy, 1936, Faber & Faber, London.

13. *Echoes of the Ancient Skies, The Astronomy of Lost Civilizations,* Dr. E.C. Krupp, 1983, Harper & Row, NYC.

14. *Philip's Guide to Stars & Planets,* Patrick Moore, 1980, 1993, George Philip, London.

15. *The Moon Book,* Bevan M. French, 1977, Penguin Books, New York.

16. *The Moon Puzzle,* N. O. Bergquist, 1954, Grafisk Forlag, Copenhagen.

17. *Dark Matter, Missing Planets & New Comets,* Tom Van Flandern, 1993, North Atlantic Books, Berkeley, California.

18. *Life Beyond Planet Earth?,* Janet & Colin Bord, 1991, Grafton Publishers, London.

19. *Somebody Else Is On the Moon,* George Leonard, 1976, Pocket Books, New York.

20. *Our Mysterious Spaceship Moon,* Don Wilson, 1975, Dell Publishing, New York.

21. *Secrets of Our Spaceship Moon,* Don Wilson, 1979, Dell Publishing, New York.

22. *We Discovered Alien Bases On the Moon,* Fred Steckling, 1981, GAF Publishers, Los Angeles.

23. *The UFO Encyclopedia,* compiled by John Spencer, 1991, Avon Books, New York.

24. *Flights Into Yesterday,* Leo Deuel, 1969, St. Martin's Press, New York.

25. *The Planet Venus,* Garry Hunt & Patrick Moore, 1982, Faber & Faber, London.

26. *Mars,* Robert Richardson & Chesley Bonestell, 1964 Harcourt, Brace & World, Inc. New York.

27. *There Is Life On Mars,* The Earl Nelson, 1955, Citadel Press, New York & London.

28. *Life and the Universe,* The Earl Nelson, 1953, Citadel Press, New York & London.

29. *Flying Saucer From Mars,* Cedric Allingham, 1955, British Book Center, New York.

30. *The Face on Mars: Evidence of a Lost Martian Civilization,* Brian Crowley & James Hurtak, 1986, Sun Publishing, Melbourne.

31. *The Monuments of Mars,* Richard Hoagland, 1987, North Atlantic Books, Berkeley.

32. *The Riddle of the Flying Saucers,* Gerald Heard,1950, Carroll & Nicholson, London.

33. *Flying Saucers Have Landed,* Desmond Leslie & George Adamski, 1953, Neville Spearman, London.

34. *Inside the Spaceships,* George Adamski, 1955, Neville Spearman, London.

35. *My Visit To Venus,* T. Lobsang Rampa, 1956, republished 1988, Saucerian Press/Inner Light, New Brunswick, NJ.

36. *We Are Not The First,* Andrew Tomas, 1971, Souvenir Press, London.

37. *Not Of This World,* Peter Kolosimo, 1970, Souvenir Press, London.

38. *The Sun & Solar System Debris,* compiled by William Corliss, 1986, The Sourcebook Project, Glen Arm, MD.

39. *Mysterious Universe: A Handbook of Astronomical Anomalies,* William Corliss, 1979, The Sourcebook Project, Glen Arm, MD.

40. *Proceedings of the Third Lunar Conference.* 3 Volumes (2918 pages). 1971, M.I.T. Press.

41. *A Guide to the Moon,* Patrick Moore, 1953, W.W. Norton, London.

42. *Our Moon,* H. Percival Wilkins, 1954, Frederick Muller, Ltd. London.

43. *Science Digest,* "Is There a Tunnel on the Moon?" November 1952 (Vol.32), p.70.

44. *Patrick Moore's Armchair Astronomy,* 1984, Thorsons Publishing, London.

45. *Moongate*, William Brian, 1982, Future Science Pub., Portland, Oregon.

46. *From Outer Space To You,* Howard Menger, 1959, Pyramid Books, New York.

47. *Looking For the Aliens,* Peter Hough & Jenny Randles, 1991, Blandford, London.

48. *The Martian Enigmas,* Mark Carlotto, 1991, North Atlantic Books, Berkeley.

49. *The McDaniel Report on Mars,* Stanley V. McDaniel, 1993, North Atlantic Books, Berkeley.

50. *The Facts of Life,* Richard Milton, 1992, Corgi Books, London.

51. *Return To Mars*, Brian Crowley & Anthony Pollock, 1989, Matchbooks, Melbourne, Australia.

52. *Genesis Revisited,* Zecharia Sitchin, 1990, Avon Books, New York.

53. *Casebook on Alternative 3,* Jim Keith, 1994, Illuminet Press, Lilburn, Georgia.

54. *The Case For the Face,* Stanley McDaniel & Monica Paxson, 1997, Adventures Unlimited Press, Kempton, Illinois.

55. *Earthlike Planets: Surfaces of Mercury, Venus, Earth, Moon, Mars,* Bruce Murray, Michael C. Malin, and Ronald Greeley, 1981, W. H. Freeman and Company, San Francisco, California,

56. *Venus Geology, Geochemistry and Geophysics,* Barsukov, V. L., Senior Editor, 1992,University of Arizona Press, Tucson.

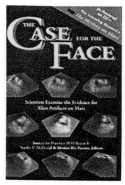

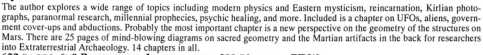

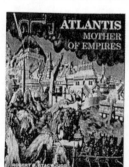

LOST CONTINENTS & THE HOLLOW EARTH

I Remember Lemuria and the Shaver Mystery

by David Hatcher Childress & Richard Shaver

Lost Continents & the Hollow Earth is Childress' thorough examination of the early hollow earth stories of Richard Shaver and the fascination that lost continents and the hollow earth have had for the American public. Shaver's rare 1948 book *I Remember Lemuria* is reprinted in its entirety, and the book is packed with illustrations from Ray Palmer's *Amazing Stories* magazine of the 1940s. Palmer and Shaver told of tunnels running through the earth—tunnels inhabited by the Deros and Teros, humanoids from an ancient spacefaring race that had inhabited the earth, eventually going underground, hundreds of thousands of years ago. Childress discusses the famous hollow earth books and delves deep into whatever reality may be behind the stories of tunnels in the earth. Operation High Jump to Antarctica in 1947 and Admiral Byrd's bizarre statements, tunnel systems in South America and Tibet, the underground world of Agartha, UFOs coming from the South Pole, more.

344 PAGES. 6X9 PAPERBACK. ILLUSTRATED. $16.95. CODE: LCHE

INSIDE THE GEMSTONE FILE

Howard Hughes, Onassis & JFK

by Kenn Thomas & David Hatcher Childress

Steamshovel Press editor Thomas takes on the Gemstone File in this run-up and run-down of the most famous underground document ever circulated. Photocopied and distributed for over 20 years, the Gemstone File is the story of Bruce Roberts, the inventor of the synthetic ruby widely used in laser technology today, and his relationship with the Howard Hughes Company and ultimately with Aristotle Onassis, the Mafia, and the CIA. Hughes kidnapped and held a drugged-up prisoner for 10 years; Onassis and his role in the Kennedy Assassination; how the Mafia ran corporate America in the 1960s; more.

320 PAGES. 6X9 PAPERBACK. ILLUSTRATED. $16.00. CODE: IGF

KUNDALINI TALES

by Richard Sauder, Ph.D.

Underground Bases and Tunnels author Richard Sauder on his personal experiences and provocative research into spontaneous spiritual awakening, out-of-body journeys, encounters with secretive governmental powers, daylight sightings of UFOs, and more. Sauder continues his studies of underground bases with new information on the occult underpinnings of the U.S. space program. The book also contains a breakthrough section that examines actual U.S. patents for devices that manipulate minds and thoughts from a remote distance. Included are chapters on the secret space program and a 130-page appendix of patents and schematic diagrams of secret technology and mind control devices.

296 PAGES. 7X10 PAPERBACK. ILLUSTRATED. BIBLIOGRAPHY. $14.95. CODE: KTAL

LIQUID CONSPIRACY

JFK, LSD, the CIA, Area 51 & UFOs

by George Piccard

Underground author George Piccard on the politics of LSD, mind control, and Kennedy's involvement with Area 51 and UFOs. Reveals JFK's LSD experiences with Mary Pinchot-Meyer. The plot thickens with an ever expanding web of CIA involvement, from underground bases with UFOs seen by JFK and Marilyn Monroe (among others) to a vaster conspiracy that affects every government agency from NASA to the Justice Department. This may have been the reason that Marilyn Monroe and actress-columnist Dorothy Killgallen were both murdered. Focusing on the bizarre side of history, *Liquid Conspiracy* takes the reader on a psychedelic tour de force.

264 PAGES. 6X9 PAPERBACK. ILLUSTRATED. $14.95. CODE: LIQC

ATLANTIS: MOTHER OF EMPIRES

Atlantis Reprint Series

by Robert Stacy-Judd

Robert Stacy-Judd's classic 1939 book on Atlantis. Stacy-Judd was a California architect and an expert on the Mayas and their relationship to Atlantis. Stacy-Judd was an excellent artist and his book is lavishly illustrated. The eighteen comprehensive chapters in the book are: The Mayas and the Lost Atlantis; Conjectures and Opinions; The Atlantean Theory; Cro-Magnon Man; East Is West; And West Is East; The Mormons and the Mayas; Astrology in Two Hemispheres; The Language of Architecture; The American Indian; Pre-Panamanians and Pre-Incas; Columns and City Planning; Comparisons and Mayan Art; The Iberian Link; The Maya Tongue; Quetzalcoatl; Summing Up the Evidence; The Mayas in Yucatan.

340 PAGES. 8X11 PAPERBACK. ILLUSTRATED. INDEX. $19.95. CODE: AMOE

COSMIC MATRIX

Piece for a Jig-Saw, Part Two

by Leonard G. Cramp

Leonard G. Cramp, a British aerospace engineer, wrote his first book *Space Gravity and the Flying Saucer* in 1954. *Cosmic Matrix* is the long-awaited sequel to his 1966 book *UFOs & Anti-Gravity: Piece for a Jig-Saw*. Cramp has had a long history of examining UFO phenomena and has concluded that UFOs use the highest possible aeronautic science to move in the way they do. Cramp examines anti-gravity effects and theorizes that this super-science used by the craft—described in detail in the book—can lift mankind into a new level of technology, transportation and understanding of the universe. The book takes a close look at gravity control, time travel, and the interlocking web of energy between all planets in our solar system with Leonard's unique technical diagrams. A fantastic voyage into the present and future!

364 PAGES. 6X9 PAPERBACK. ILLUSTRATED. BIBLIOGRAPHY. $16.00. CODE: CMX

THE TIME TRAVEL HANDBOOK
A Manual of Practical Teleportation & Time Travel
edited by David Hatcher Childress

In the tradition of *The Anti-Gravity Handbook* and *The Free-Energy Device Handbook*, science and UFO author David Hatcher Childress takes us into the weird world of time travel and teleportation. Not just a whacked-out look at science fiction, this book is an authoritative chronicling of real-life time travel experiments, teleportation devices and more. *The Time Travel Handbook* takes the reader beyond the government experiments and deep into the uncharted territory of early time travellers such as Nikola Tesla and Guglielmo Marconi and their alleged time travel experiments, as well as the Wilson Brothers of EMI and their connection to the Philadelphia Experiment—the U.S. Navy's forays into invisibility, time travel, and teleportation. Childress looks into the claims of time travelling individuals, and investigates the unusual claim that the pyramids on Mars were built in the future and sent back in time. A highly visual, large format book, with patents, photos and schematics. Be the first on your block to build your own time travel device!
316 PAGES. 7X10 PAPERBACK. ILLUSTRATED. $16.95. CODE: TTH.

PATH OF THE POLE
Cataclysmic Pole Shift Geology
by Charles Hapgood

Maps of the Ancient Sea Kings author Hapgood's classic book *Path of the Pole* is back in print! Hapgood researched Antarctica, ancient maps and the geological record to conclude that the Earth's crust has slipped in the inner core many times in the past, changing the position of the pole. *Path of the Pole* discusses the various "pole shifts" in Earth's past, giving evidence for each one, and moves on to possible future pole shifts. Packed with illustrations, this is the sourcebook for many other books on cataclysms and pole shifts such as *5-5-2000: Ice the Ultimate Disaster* by Richard Noone. A planetary alignment on May 5, 2000 is predicted to cause the next pole shift—a date that is less than a year away! With Millennium Madness in full swing, this is sure to be a popular book.
356 PAGES. 6X9 PAPERBACK. ILLUSTRATED. $16.95. CODE: POP.

IN SEARCH OF ADVENTURE
A Wild Travel Anthology
compiled by Bruce Northam & Brad Olsen

An epic collection of 100 travelers' tales—a compendium that celebrates the wild side of contemporary travel writing—relating humorous, revealing, sometimes naughty stories by acclaimed authors. Indeed, a book to heat up the gypsy blood in all of us. Stories by Tim Cahill, Simon Winchester, Marybeth Bond, Robert Young Pelton, David Hatcher Childress, Richard Bangs, Linda Watanabe McFerrin, Jorma Kaukonen, and many more.
459 PAGES. 6X9 PAPERBACK. ILLUSTRATED. $17.95. CODE: ISOA

ECCENTRIC LIVES AND PECULIAR NOTIONS
by John Michell

The first paperback edition of Michell's fascinating study of the lives and beliefs of over 20 eccentric people. Published in hardback by Thames & Hudson in London, *Eccentric Lives and Peculiar Notions* takes us into the bizarre and often humorous lives of such people as Lady Blount, who was sure that the earth is flat; Cyrus Teed, who believed that the earth is a hollow shell with us on the inside; Edward Hine, who believed that the British are the lost Tribes of Israel; and Baron de Guldenstubbe, who was sure that statues wrote him letters. British writer and housewife Nesta Webster devoted her life to exposing international conspiracies, and Father O'Callaghan devoted his to opposing interest on loans. The extraordinary characters in this book were—and in some cases still are—wholehearted enthusiasts for the various causes and outrageous notions they adopted, and John Michell describes their adventures with spirit and compassion. Some of them prospered and lived happily with their obsessions, while others failed dismally. We read of the hapless inventor of a giant battleship made of ice who died alone and neglected, and of the London couple who achieved peace and prosperity by drilling holes in their heads. Other chapters on the Last of the Welsh Druids; Congressman Ignacius Donnelly, the Great Heretic and Atlantis; Shakespearean Decoders and the Baconian Treasure Hunt; Early Ufologists; Jerusalem in Scotland; Bibliomaniacs; more.
248 PAGES. 6X9 PAPERBACK. ILLUSTRATED. $14.95. CODE: ELPN.

THE CHRIST CONSPIRACY
The Greatest Story Ever Sold
by Acharya S.

In this highly controversial and explosive book, archaeologist, historian, mythologist and linguist Acharya S. marshals an enormous amount of startling evidence to demonstrate that Christianity and the story of Jesus Christ were created by members of various secret societies, mystery schools and religions in order to unify the Roman Empire under one state religion. In developing such a fabrication, this multinational cabal drew upon a multitude of myths and rituals that existed long before the Christian era, and reworked them for centuries into the religion passed down to us today. Contrary to popular belief, there was no single man who was at the genesis of Christianity; Jesus was many characters rolled into one. These characters personified the ubiquitous solar myth, and their exploits were well known, as reflected by such popular deities as Mithras, Heracles/Hercules, Dionysos and many others throughout the Roman Empire and beyond. The story of Jesus as portrayed in the Gospels is revealed to be nearly identical in detail to that of the earlier savior-gods Krishna and Horus, who for millennia preceding Christianity held great favor with the people. *The Christ Conspiracy* shows the Jesus character as neither unique nor original, not "divine revelation." Christianity re-interprets the same extremely ancient body of knowledge that revolved around the celestial bodies and natural forces. The result of this myth making has been "The Greatest Story Ever Sold."
256 PAGES. 6X9 PAPERBACK. ILLUSTRATED. $14.95. CODE: CHRC.

24 HOUR CREDIT CARD ORDERS—CALL: 815-253-6390 FAX: 815-253-6300

EMAIL: AUPHQ@FRONTIERNET.NET   HTTP://WWW.ADVENTURESUNLIMITED.CO.NZ

LOST CITIES OF ATLANTIS, ANCIENT EUROPE
& THE MEDITERRANEAN
by David Hatcher Childress

Atlantis! The legendary lost continent comes under the close scrutiny of maverick archaeologist David Hatcher Childress in this sixth book in the internationally popular *Lost Cities* series. Childress takes the reader in search of sunken cities in the Mediterranean; across the Atlas Mountains in search of Atlantean ruins; to remote islands in search of megalithic ruins; to meet living legends and secret societies. From Ireland to Turkey, Morocco to Eastern Europe, and around the remote islands of the Mediterranean and Atlantic, Childress takes the reader on an astonishing quest for mankind's past. Ancient technology, cataclysms, megalithic construction, lost civilizations and devastating wars of the past are all explored in this book. Childress challenges the skeptics and proves that great civilizations not only existed in the past, but the modern world and its problems are reflections of the ancient world of Atlantis.
524 PAGES. 6X9 PAPERBACK. ILLUSTRATED WITH 100S OF MAPS, PHOTOS AND DIAGRAMS. BIBLIOGRAPHY & INDEX. $16.95. CODE: MED

LOST CITIES OF CHINA, CENTRAL INDIA & ASIA
by David Hatcher Childress

Like a real life "Indiana Jones," maverick archaeologist David Childress takes the reader on an incredible adventure across some of the world's oldest and most remote countries in search of lost cities and ancient mysteries. Discover ancient cities in the Gobi Desert; hear fantastic tales of lost continents, vanished civilizations and secret societies bent on ruling the world; visit forgotten monasteries in forbidding snow-capped mountains with strange tunnels to mysterious subterranean cities!
A unique combination of far-out exploration and practical travel advice, it will astound and delight the experienced traveler or the armchair voyager.
429 PAGES. 6X9 PAPERBACK. ILLUSTRATED. FOOTNOTES & BIBLIOGRAPHY. $14.95. CODE: CHI

LOST CITIES OF ANCIENT LEMURIA & THE PACIFIC
by David Hatcher Childress

Was there once a continent in the Pacific? Called Lemuria or Pacifica by geologists, Mu or Pan by the mystics, there is now ample mythological, geological and archaeological evidence to "prove" that an advanced and ancient civilization once lived in the central Pacific. Maverick archaeologist and explorer David Hatcher Childress combs the Indian Ocean, Australia and the Pacific in search of the surprising truth about mankind's past. Contains photos of the underwater city on Pohnpei; explanations on how the statues were levitated around Easter Island in a clockwise vortex movement; tales of disappearing islands; Egyptians in Australia; and more.
379 PAGES. 6X9 PAPERBACK. ILLUSTRATED. FOOTNOTES & BIBLIOGRAPHY. $14.95. CODE: LEM

ANCIENT TONGA
& the Lost City of Mu'a
by David Hatcher Childress

Lost Cities series author Childress takes us to the south sea islands of Tonga, Rarotonga, Samoa and Fiji to investigate the megalithic ruins on these beautiful islands. The great empire of the Polynesians, centered on Tonga and the ancient city of Mu'a, is revealed with old photos, drawings and maps. Chapters in this book are on the Lost City of Mu'a and its many megalithic pyramids, the Ha'amonga Trilithon and ancient Polynesian astronomy, Samoa and the search for the lost land of Havai'iki, Fiji and its wars with Tonga, Rarotonga's megalithic road, and Polynesian cosmology. Material on Egyptians in the Pacific, earth changes, the fortified moat around Mu'a, lost roads, more.
218 PAGES. 6X9 PAPERBACK. ILLUSTRATED. COLOR PHOTOS. BIBLIOGRAPHY. $15.95. CODE: TONG

ANCIENT MICRONESIA
& the Lost City of Nan Madol
by David Hatcher Childress

Micronesia, a vast archipelago of islands west of Hawaii and south of Japan, contains some of the most amazing megalithic ruins in the world. Part of our *Lost Cities* series, this volume explores the incredible conformations on various Micronesian islands, especially the fantastic and little-known ruins of Nan Madol on Pohnpei Island. The huge canal city of Nan Madol contains over 250 million tons of basalt columns over an 11 square-mile area of artificial islands. Much of the huge city is submerged, and underwater structures can be found to an estimated 80 feet. Islanders' legends claim that the basalt rocks, weighing up to 50 tons, were magically levitated into place by the powerful forefathers. Other ruins in Micronesia that are profiled include the Latte Stones of the Marianas, the menhirs of Palau, the megalithic canal city on Kosrae Island, megaliths on Guam, and more.
256 PAGES. 6X9 PAPERBACK. ILLUSTRATED. INCLUDES A COLOR PHOTO SECTION. BIBLIOGRAPHY. $16.95. CODE: AMIC

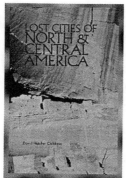

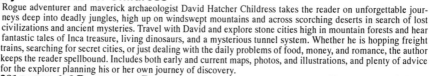
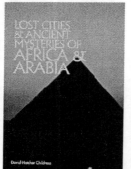

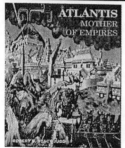

ATLANTIS: MOTHER OF EMPIRES
Atlantis Reprint Series
by Robert Stacy-Judd
Robert Stacy-Judd's classic 1939 book on Atlantis is back in print in this large-format paperback edition. Stacy-Judd was a California architect and an expert on the Mayas and their relationship to Atlantis. He was an excellent artist and his work is lavishly illustrated. The eighteen comprehensive chapters in the book are: The Mayas and the Lost Atlantis; Conjectures and Opinions; The Atlantean Theory; Cro-Magnon Man; East is West; And West is East; The Mormons and the Mayas; Astrology in Two Hemispheres; The Language of Architecture; The American Indian; Pre-Panamanians and Pre-Incas; Columns and City Planning; Comparisons and Mayan Art; The Iberian Link; The Maya Tongue; Quetzalcoatl; Summing Up the Evidence; The Mayas in Yucatan.
340 PAGES. 8X11 PAPERBACK. ILLUSTRATED. INDEX. $19.95. CODE: AMOE

SECRET CITIES OF OLD SOUTH AMERICA
Atlantis Reprint Series
by Harold T. Wilkins
The reprint of Wilkins' classic book, first published in 1952, claiming that South America was Atlantis. Chapters include Mysteries of a Lost World; Atlantis Unveiled; Red Riddles on the Rocks; South America's Amazons Existed!; The Mystery of El Dorado and Gran Payatiti—the Final Refuge of the Incas; Monstrous Beasts of the Unexplored Swamps & Wilds; Weird Denizens of Antediluvian Forests; New Light on Atlantis from the World's Oldest Book; The Mystery of Old Man Noah and the Arks; and more.
438 PAGES. 6X9 PAPERBACK. ILLUSTRATED. BIBLIOGRAPHY & INDEX. $16.95. CODE: SCOS

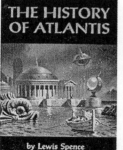

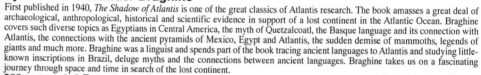

THE SHADOW OF ATLANTIS

ALEXANDER BRAGHINE

THIS 1940 CLASSIC ON ATLANTIS, MEXICO AND ANCIENT EGYPT IS BACK IN PRINT

ATLANTIS REPRINT SERIES

THE SHADOW OF ATLANTIS
The Echoes of Atlantean Civilization Tracked through Space & Time
by Colonel Alexander Braghine
First published in 1940, *The Shadow of Atlantis* is one of the great classics of Atlantis research. The book amasses a great deal of archaeological, anthropological, historical and scientific evidence in support of a lost continent in the Atlantic Ocean. Braghine covers such diverse topics as Egyptians in Central America, the myth of Quetzalcoatl, the Basque language and its connection with Atlantis, the connections with the ancient pyramids of Mexico, Egypt and Atlantis, the sudden demise of mammoths, legends of giants and much more. Braghine was a linguist and spends part of the book tracing ancient languages to Atlantis and studying little-known inscriptions in Brazil, deluge myths and the connections between ancient languages. Braghine takes us on a fascinating journey through space and time in search of the lost continent.
288 PAGES. 6X9 PAPERBACK. ILLUSTRATED. $16.95. CODE: SOA

THE RIDDLE OF THE PACIFIC

JOHN MACMILLAN BROWN

This rare 1924 book is back in print!

RIDDLE OF THE PACIFIC
by John Macmillan Brown
Oxford scholar Brown's classic work on lost civilizations of the Pacific is now back in print! John Macmillan Brown was an historian and New Zealand's premier scientist when he wrote about the origins of the Maoris. After many years of travel thoughout the Pacific studying the people and customs of the south seas islands, he wrote *Riddle of the Pacific* in 1924. The book is packed with rare turn-of-the-century illustrations. Don't miss Brown's classic study of Easter Island, ancient scripts, megalithic roads and cities, more. Brown was an early believer in a lost continent in the Pacific.
460 PAGES. 6X9 PAPERBACK. ILLUSTRATED. $16.95. CODE: ROP

THE HISTORY OF ATLANTIS
by Lewis Spence
Lewis Spence's classic book on Atlantis is now back in print! Spence was a Scottish historian (1874-1955) who is best known for his volumes on world mythology and his five Atlantis books. *The History of Atlantis* (1926) is considered his finest. Spence does his scholarly best in chapters on the Sources of Atlantean History, the Geography of Atlantis, the Races of Atlantis, the Kings of Atlantis, the Religion of Atlantis, the Colonies of Atlantis, more. Sixteen chapters in all.
240 PAGES. 6X9 PAPERBACK. ILLUSTRATED WITH MAPS, PHOTOS & DIAGRAMS. $16.95. CODE: HOA

ATLANTIS IN SPAIN
A Study of the Ancient Sun Kingdoms of Spain
by E.M. Whishaw
First published by Rider & Co. of London in 1928, this classic book is a study of the megaliths of Spain, ancient writing, cyclopean walls, sun worshipping empires, hydraulic engineering, and sunken cities. An extremely rare book, it was out of print for 60 years. Learn about the Biblical Tartessus; an Atlantean city at Niebla; the Temple of Hercules and the Sun Temple of Seville; Libyans and the Copper Age; more. Profusely illustrated with photos, maps and drawings.
284 PAGES. 6X9 PAPERBACK. ILLUSTRATED. TABLES OF ANCIENT SCRIPTS. $15.95. CODE: AIS

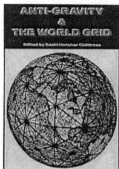

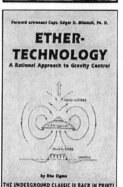

FREE ENERGY SYSTEMS

THE FREE-ENERGY DEVICE HANDBOOK
A Compilation of Patents and Reports
by David Hatcher Childress

A large-format compilation of various patents, papers, descriptions and diagrams concerning free-energy devices and systems. *The Free-Energy Device Handbook* is a visual tool for experimenters and researchers into magnetic motors and other "over-unity" devices. With chapters on the Adams Motor, the Hans Coler Generator, cold fusion, superconductors, "N" machines, space-energy generators, Nikola Tesla, T. Townsend Brown, and the latest in free-energy devices. Packed with photos, technical diagrams, patents and fascinating information, this book belongs on every science shelf. With energy and profit being a major political reason for fighting various wars, free-energy devices, if ever allowed to be mass distributed to consumers, could change the world! Get your copy now before the Department of Energy bans this book!

292 PAGES. 8X10 PAPERBACK. ILLUSTRATED. BIBLIOGRAPHY. $16.95. CODE: FEH

UFOS AND ANTI-GRAVITY
Piece For A Jig-Saw
by Leonard G. Cramp

Leonard G. Cramp's 1966 classic book on flying saucer propulsion and suppressed technology is available again. *UFOS & Anti-Gravity: Piece For A Jig-Saw* is a highly technical look at the UFO phenomena by a trained scientist. Cramp first introduces the idea of 'anti-gravity' and introduces us to the various theories of gravitation. He then examines the technology necessary to build a flying saucer and examines in great detail the technical aspects of such a craft. Cramp's book is a wealth of material and diagrams on flying saucers, anti-gravity, suppressed technology, G-fields and UFOs. Chapters include Crossroads of Aerodymanics, Aerodynamic Saucers, Limitations of Rocketry, Gravitation and the Ether, Gravitational Spaceships, G-Field Lift Effects, The Bi-Field Theory, VTOL and Hovercraft, Analysis of UFO photos, more. "I feel the Air Force has not been giving out all available information on these unidentified flying objects. You cannot disregard so many unimpeachable sources." — John McCormack, Speaker of the U.S. House of Representatives.

388 PAGES. 6X9 PAPERBACK. HEAVILY ILLUSTRATED. $16.95. CODE: UAG

THE HARMONIC CONQUEST OF SPACE
by Captain Bruce Cathie

A new, updated edition with additional material. Chapters include: Mathematics of the World Grid; the Harmonics of Hiroshima and Nagasaki; Harmonic Transmission and Receiving; the Link Between Human Brain Waves; the Cavity Resonance between the Earth; the Ionosphere and Gravity; Edgar Cayce—the Harmonics of the Subconscious; Stonehenge; the Harmonics of the Moon; the Pyramids of Mars; Nikola Tesla's Electric Car; the Robert Adams Pulsed Electric Motor Generator; Harmonic Clues to the Unified Field; and more. Also included are tables showing the harmonic relations between the earth's magnetic field, the speed of light, and anti-gravity/gravity acceleration at different points on the earth's surface. New chapters in this edition on the giant stone spheres of Costa Rica, Atomic Tests and Volcanic Activity, and a chapter on Ayers Rock analysed with Stone Mountain, Georgia.

248 PAGES. 6X9. PAPERBACK. ILLUSTRATED. BIBLIOGRAPHY. $16.95. CODE: HCS

THE ENERGY GRID
Harmonic 695, The Pulse of the Universe
by Captain Bruce Cathie.

This is the breakthrough book that explores the incredible potential of the Energy Grid and the Earth's Unified Field all around us. Cathie's first book, *Harmonic 33*, was published in 1968 when he was a commercial pilot in New Zealand. Since then, Captain Bruce Cathie has been the premier investigator into the amazing potential of the infinite energy that surrounds our planet every microsecond. Cathie investigates the Harmonics of Light and how the Energy Grid is created. In this amazing book are chapters on UFO Propulsion, Nikola Tesla, Unified Equations, the Mysterious Aerials, Pythagoras & the Grid, Nuclear Detonation and the Grid, Maps of the Ancients, an Australian Stonehenge examined, more.

255 PAGES. 6X9 PAPERBACK. ILLUSTRATED. $15.95. CODE: TEG

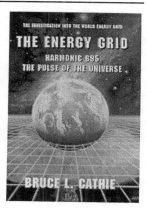

THE BRIDGE TO INFINITY
Harmonic 371244
by Captain Bruce Cathie

Cathie has popularized the concept that the earth is crisscrossed by an electromagnetic grid system that can be used for anti-gravity, free energy, levitation and more. The book includes a new analysis of the harmonic nature of reality, acoustic levitation, pyramid power, harmonic receiver towers and UFO propulsion. It concludes that today's scientists have at their command a fantastic store of knowledge with which to advance the welfare of the human race.

204 PAGES. 6X9 PAPERBACK. ILLUSTRATED. $14.95. CODE: BTF

One Adventure Place
P.O. Box 74
Kempton, Illinois 60946
United States of America
Tel.: 815-253-6390 • Fax: 815-253-6300
Email: auphq@frontiernet.net
http://www.adventuresunlimited.co.nz

ORDERING INSTRUCTIONS

✓ Remit by USD$ Check, Money Order or Credit Card

✓ Visa, Master Card, Discover & AmEx Accepted

✓ Prices May Change Without Notice

✓ 10% Discount for 3 or more Items

SHIPPING CHARGES

United States

✓ Postal Book Rate { $2.50 First Item
50¢ Each Additional Item

✓ Priority Mail { $3.50 First Item
$2.00 Each Additional Item

✓ UPS { $5.00 First Item
$1.50 Each Additional Item

NOTE: UPS Delivery Available to Mainland USA Only

Canada

✓ Postal Book Rate { $3.00 First Item
$1.00 Each Additional Item

✓ Postal Air Mail { $5.00 First Item
$2.00 Each Additional Item

✓ Personal Checks or Bank Drafts MUST BE

USD$ and Drawn on a US Bank

✓ Canadian Postal Money Orders OK

✓ Payment MUST BE USD$

All Other Countries

✓ Surface Delivery { $6.00 First Item
$2.00 Each Additional Item

✓ Postal Air Mail { $12.00 First Item
$8.00 Each Additional Item

✓ Payment MUST BE USD$

✓ Checks and Money Orders MUST BE USD$
and Drawn on a US Bank or branch.

✓ Add $5.00 for Air Mail Subscription to
Future *Adventures Unlimited* Catalogs

SPECIAL NOTES

✓ RETAILERS: Standard Discounts Available

✓ BACKORDERS: We Backorder all Out-of-

Stock Items Unless Otherwise Requested

✓ PRO FORMA INVOICES: Available on Request

✓ VIDEOS: NTSC Mode Only. Replacement only.

✓ For PAL mode videos contact our other offices:

European Office:
Adventures Unlimited, PO Box 372,
Dronten, 8250 AJ, The Netherlands
South Pacific Office
Adventures Unlimited Pacifica
221 Symonds Street, Box 8199
Auckland, New Zealand

Please check: ☑

☐ This is my first order   ☐ I have ordered before   ☐ This is a new address

Name	
Address	
City	

State/Province		Postal Code
Country		

Phone day	Evening	
Fax		

Item Code	Item Description	Price	Qty	Total

Please check: ☑

☐ Postal-Surface

☐ Postal-Air Mail
(Priority in USA)

☐ UPS
(Mainland USA only)

Subtotal ➡	
Less Discount-10% for 3 or more items ➡	
Balance ➡	
Illinois Residents 6.25% Sales Tax ➡	
Previous Credit ➡	
Shipping ➡	
Total (check/MO in USD$ only) ➡	

☐ Visa/MasterCard/Discover/Amex

Card Number

Expiration Date

10% Discount When You Order 3 or More Items!

Comments & Suggestions	Share Our Catalog with a Friend